EUROPE:
HIERARCHY AND REVOLT

the text of this book is printed
on 100% recycled paper

HISTORY OF EUROPE
edited by J. H. Plumb

———◆———

*in preparation

George Holmes

EUROPE: HIERARCHY AND REVOLT
1320-1450

HARPER TORCHBOOKS
Harper & Row, Publishers
New York, Hagerstown, San Francisco, London

This book was originally published in 1975 by William Collins Sons and Co Ltd, London, in the *Fontana History of Europe* series, edited by J. H. Plumb. It is here reprinted by arrangement.

First HARPER TORCHBOOK edition published 1976.

LIBRARY OF CONGRESS CATALOG CARD NUMBER: 75–43489

STANDARD BOOK NUMBER: 06–131908–2

76 77 78 79 80 10 9 8 7 6 5 4 3 2 1

For my children,
Susan, Catherine and Nicholas

CONTENTS

Contents

INTRODUCTION

This book contains an account of European history approximately between the dates 1320 and 1450. It begins at a time when 'medieval' institutions were at the height of their development. In 1320 we are near the summit of the medieval expansion of population. One of the most powerful of medieval popes, John XXII, ruled from Avignon over the European church. Armies of knightly cavalry, if not unchallenged (Flemish townsmen won a famous victory over one of them at Courtrai in 1302), were certainly dominant. Great cathedrals like Rheims and Ely were being built. When the book ends in 1450 many characteristic medieval forms of life – the papal control of the European Church, Gothic art, chivalric warfare, for example – will be in decay. Movements that we associate with the 'Renaissance' and the 'Reformation', like Italian neo-classical architecture, the rise of printing, voyages of exploration in the Atlantic and the Hussite rebellion against the Church, are in full swing. Very roughly, this book is about the transition from 'medieval' to 'Renaissance' Europe. Such descriptions of periods are, of course, highly impressionistic, but as long as they are not taken too seriously, they usefully convey something about the character of civilization.

Within the period the choice of topics is bound to be very selective. The aim will be to approach Europe from two main angles. Firstly, to describe in outline the political story, the main events in the relations between the larger political powers. This cannot be done in a single narrative because the kings and princes of medieval Europe did not belong to a single diplomatic 'concert' like the European powers in 1914. The continent has to be broken up into areas each of which, though they overlap, has a large degree of autonomy. The politics of the Iberian peninsula for example involved a different collection of powers from the politics of north-west

Europe, though they were connected; the King of France was involved in both, the Count of Flanders was not. The second main aim will be to describe very broadly some of the changes in social structure and ideas. This is also difficult to do on a European scale. To make the subject manageable, it is obviously wise to concentrate on the areas where the best known and most obviously interesting manifestations of civilization were produced, that is Italy and north-west Europe. But the most interesting part of European history is not the separate political record of its various states or the social condition of individual societies but the interaction between politics, society and ideas throughout the continent. Perhaps the best way to introduce the reader to the period is to explain something in very general terms about fourteenth-century Europe as it appears from this point of view.

Latin Christendom in the early fourteenth century covered roughly present-day Europe without the Balkans. It was unmistakably a single civilization. An educated man could travel from Sicily to Scotland talking with his equals in Latin, visiting houses of the same religious orders, which unquestioningly accepted the authority of the Pope at Rome, meeting lawyers who practised the same ecclesiastical law and recognized degrees awarded by their colleagues in remote universities licensed by the same pope. In many countries he would find laymen practising the same civil law inherited from the Roman Empire and noblemen who had been brought up in similar codes of military behaviour and had heard local versions of the French chivalric romances. This recognizable unity was not the result of political unity: on the contrary, western Europe was extremely disunited. The title of Roman Emperor existed but its holder was usually, by this time, a German princeling whose political pretensions were of little interest to the majority of Europeans. Since the primitive empire of Charlemagne in the ninth century, Europe had escaped the atrophy of world government. The normal political condition of much of the continent was a fragmentation of authority bordering on anarchy. Its political history was a mass of undignified petty conflicts from which it is difficult to disentangle the more significant threads of events and which will often have to be simplified in the pages of this book in a manner which can easily be misleading. What distinguished Latin Christendom was a uniformity of culture. It depended chiefly on the church. The general recognition of the authority of the pope was the most obvious factor in the unity of 'Europe'. It had led to a diffusion of similar types of monasteries and church organization, not only of buildings, but also of ways of thought. The uniformity of culture had also been promoted by the expansive energies of the nobles and knights of northern France and the merchants of the Italian cities, who had carried their customs over large parts of the Latin world.

In 1300 western Europe was probably already by far the richest part of the world if wealth was measured by head of the population. Most of the wealth was concentrated in a band running across the continent from south-east England to northern Italy, including northern France, the Netherlands and the Rhineland. Within that region intensive agricultural production had led to dense population, large surpluses, advanced industries and towns. As a result – and this is one of the most important features of the civilization – European society contained great diversities of economic and social structure. Between the isolated peasant communities of the Alps, the rich aristocratic estates of the Ile de France and the industrial towns like Arras and Ypres, there were great contrasts of social structure within quite small spatial distances. In particular, urban civilization with all that it implies in industry, commerce and popular government, though distributed very unevenly, was widespread and highly developed.

The combination of political fragmentation and social diversity was crucial. Of course, the dominant outlook of Europeans was the framework of values established by nobles and churchmen presiding over landed estates. For want of better words, it could be described as 'feudal' or 'hierarchical'. But where political authority was so broken up it was possible for communities of other kinds to assert their autonomy, not only their political autonomy but their ways of life and their ideas as well. We shall be observing in this book the interaction not only between political powers but also between com-

munities of different kinds. European history is increasingly
made up of the interaction between divergent ways of life and
thought.

At the beginning of the fourteenth century, the diversity of
Europe was only beginning to emerge. The Flemish cities
were asserting their independence against the French king. A
tiny nucleus of independent peasant communities which were
eventually to form the Swiss confederation had appeared. The
first sophisticated writers of the Italian city world were at
work in Florence and Padua. These manifestations were
tentative. The European world was very much dominated by
the Pope, the King of France and other monarchs, its intellectual life by the University of Paris, its art by the style of
the Gothic church, which had spread over Europe from
northern France. As it turned out, the social history of the
next hundred years strongly favoured the greater diversification of society. It favoured the urban and peasant communities at the expense of the seigniorial classes. The strength
of the tendency could not have been suspected in 1320. It
was promoted by powerful economic factors among the most
important of which are certainly to be counted the Black
Death, which hit Europe in 1348-9, and the general contraction
of population which reduced the wealth and power of landowners. The results of economic changes became plain in the
condition of Europe in the first half of the fifteenth century
when the townsmen and countrymen asserted themselves.

It was during that period – about 1410-50 – that the Italian
cities gave birth to an ideology of republican government in
the writings of Leonardo Bruni and Leon Battista Alberti,
the Flemish cities produced the realistic art associated with
Jan van Eyck and his followers, the Bohemian Hussites
carried out a national Reformation in the course of which the
millennarian communism of Tabor became a political force, and
the city of Venice became a major European power. At that
period the centrifugal forces in European society were very
marked; large parts of Europe looked as though they were
completely breaking out of the framework of monarchy and
church that had been built up in the Middle Ages. At times the
papacy seemed to be on the brink of irreparable division

between rival popes and under attack from the national churches. Some of the monarchies seemed to be permanently enfeebled.

About the middle of the century the tide turned. The conditions for monarchy began to improve. Powerful princes, some of whom restored their kingdoms to strength – like Louis XI of France, Charles the Bold, Ferdinand and Isabella of Spain – are characteristic figures of the latter part of the fifteenth century. But these developments stretch beyond the period covered by this book which will be principally concerned with the crisis of the medieval world in the long period of population fall, and paradoxically of cultural efflorescence, which stretches from the 1340s to the middle of the next century. The movements of that period are interesting in themselves but their causes and their significance become apparent only in a European context. Neither the humanists nor the communists are comprehensible unless they are seen against the background of institutions and ideas against which they were rebelling. They appeared when and where they did because of the stresses in older ways of life and their ideas were incorporated into the European stock.

CHAPTER I

THE POLITICS OF WESTERN EUROPE IN THE FOURTEENTH CENTURY

i *The Netherlands*

The political and social fragmentation of Europe appears nowhere more clearly than in the Netherlands. Most of north-west Europe was, of course, predominantly agrarian, a world of fields and pastures in which wealth and power depended on the produce of the countryside. It was in the southern Netherlands, however, that the first steps were taken towards an industrial and urban civilization. This first industrial revolution in European history happened long before the point at which this book begins. In the early fourteenth century the belt of land which corresponds with the western part of modern Belgium (Flanders and Brabant) and the north-west corner of France (Artois) contained a number of towns whose inhabitants lived on a highly developed woollen cloth industry. Bruges, Ghent, and Ypres in Flanders, Brussels and Malines in Brabant, and Douai and Arras in France were some of the most important. There are thought to have been at least 4000 weavers alone, apart from other allied trades, in the city of Ghent in the mid-fourteenth century. Industry on this scale had led to the existence of substantial capitalists. A famous example was Jean Boine Broke, a draper of Douai in southern Flanders in the late thirteenth century. It is known from the records that he imported wool, employed workers in all stages of the clothmaking process, owned a dye house and sold the finished products. The cloth towns, nearly all purely industrial centres which had not grown up like many European cities as episcopal sees, developed on a large scale the characteristic physiognomy of the modern city: commercial wealth contrasting with the relative poverty of the numerous artisans and paid workers for whom the city bell rang out the beginning and end of the working day. The governor of Artois gave permission in 1355 for the erection of a belfry at Aire-sur-la-Lys in these terms which reflect both the social stratification and the development of an industrial sense of time: 'because the said town is governed by the craft of drapery and other crafts which require many workers by the day going and coming to work at certain hours, and also the mayor and magistrates and some of their burgesses going to and from the town hall to give justice according to custom several days each week, it is necessary to have bells in the belfry to be rung at the hours'.

The products of the industry of the Netherlandish cities, in particular fine cloths, were carried all over Europe. Their wealth depended on an extensive export trade and also on large-scale import of raw wool, especially from England. In spite of this, they did not, as one might have expected, nurture a native class of international merchants. In the strongest contrast to the commercial communities of the Italian cities Netherlandish industry was commercially passive. The cloths were carried to the more distant markets by foreigners, by Italians, Frenchmen and German Hansards. The Flemings did not develop the techniques of international company management and exchange which were so prominent in the Italian world. Therefore, they did not have an impact on Europe as a whole like that of the Italians. Bruges, which became the chief commercial city of northern Europe because it combined a large cloth industry with access to a port, was a commercial centre for foreign merchants rather than for the natives: the fame of the dykes to keep out the sea 'between Wissant and Bruges' had reached the ears of Dante in Florence and supplied him with a simile for one of the circles of his *Inferno* (xv, 4–6), no doubt because he had heard them described by Florentine traders who had been there. Within their own homeland, however, the Netherlanders created an early industrial civilization comparable in its social implications with that of Renaissance Italy, though also different in some important respects.

The government of these cities was in the hands of aldermen (*échevins*) elected from the wealthier burgesses, usually sharing their powers with a bailiff representing the Count or Duke.

Unlike the cities of northern Italy, the Netherlandish towns had not escaped from the seigniorial and princely world into total independence. The southern Netherlands were an area of political fragmentation, of small states, comparable with those of western Germany in scale, but still of princely states not city states: the counties of Flanders and Hainault, the duchy of Brabant and the bishopric of Liège, a striking case, like Cologne and Mainz in Germany, of a bishopric which had become a principality and not just an ecclesiastical division. Flanders was within the feudal and to some extent the political orbit of the King of France, of whom the count was a vassal, the other states theoretically within that of the less effective German King. Like the other princes of Europe in the thir-teenth century those of the Netherlands had consolidated their jurisdiction over the nobility and towns of their terri-tories: they had courts, taxes, administrators. But the dis-proportionate size and wealth of the towns of this region meant that the politics of each state, particularly Flanders, were characterized by an uneasy tension between princely authority and urban independence.

As in other parts of western Europe the fourteenth century was the crucial period for the development of parliamentary institutions. By this we mean systems of limitation and consultation imposed upon the prince not merely by the great feudatories as in earlier medieval society, but by wider sections of the population, like the knights of the shires and burgesses in the English parliament. The power of these parliaments was derived essentially from the princes' need for taxation, for which they had to obtain consent from elected representa-tives of the tax-payers, but it extended to other aspects of political life. One of the most famous documents thrown up by these institutions, a kind of Magna Carta of the post-feudal, parliamentary age, was the *Joyeuse Entrée* (Joyful Entry) of Brabant. This was extracted from Joan of Brabant, heiress to the Duchy, when she took it over with a foreign husband, Wenceslas of Luxemburg in 1356. It represented very clearly the concern of the politically important classes in Brabant to maintain the integrity of their liberties in the dangerous circumstances of the accession of an alien prince. It stipulated that the Duchy was not to be divided, that only Brabanters were to be appointed to hold government offices and that the prince was not to undertake war or coin money without the consent of 'the land in common', by which was meant in practice the prelates, nobility and towns, the 'three estates' as they came to be called in the fifteenth century. The *Joyeuse Entrée* was a characteristic expression of the political consciousness of a state with a traditional identity, the common political 'nationalism' of the fourteenth century. The situation in Brabant was fairly typical of north-west Europe. In Flanders the more common balance of classes was distorted by the preponderance of the three great towns of Bruges, Ghent and Ypres, which as the *Drie Steden* (Three Towns) or the 'Three Members of Flanders' came to be the essential counterbalance and rivals to the power of the Count.

In the Flemish towns were present, on a large scale and in a highly developed form, phenomena which are to be found on a smaller scale in many other medieval towns: firstly, the social conflict within urban society between the property-owning patriciate and the working artisans and employees, secondly, the conflict between town and prince. Elsewhere these conflicts were small and local or intermittent. In Flanders the towns were so large and carried such weight within the structure of the county that they dominated the political life of the state. Furthermore, Flanders and its industry were strategically so placed that its urban social conflicts created disturbances of general political importance in north-west Europe. The towns were really too big for the seigniorial country which enclosed them. From 1280 to 1302 there was a series of conflicts caused partly by the social divisions within the towns and partly by the ambition of the King of France to establish his feudal suzerainty more effectively over his rather weak neighbour, the Count of Flanders. The lower classes in the towns remained loyal to the Count; the patricians, the *Leliaerts* as they came to be called because of their devotion to the *fleur-de-lys*, appealed to King Philip IV of France (1285–1314), hoping no doubt to achieve a still greater republican independence for their cities within a larger princely structure. This period ended in 1302 with the surprising defeat of the French army by the textile workers of Bruges, Ghent and Ypres at the Battle of Courtrai. This battle had the effect of strengthening the comital power as against the King of France and preserving the independence of Flanders. In the early fourteenth century, therefore, Flanders was a country in which an urban industrial society with appropriate social and political structures was acquiring predominance.

The internal politics of fourteenth century Flanders, impinged at critical moments, as in the events leading to the Battle of Courtrai, on the general politics of western Europe, and will be mentioned as part of that wider story. This is the appropriate point to notice their significance for the internal structure of the county. The general revolt of Flanders in 1322–8 (see below, p. 31) led temporarily to the deposition of the Count, Louis de Nevers, and the effective establishment of control of the county by Bruges, Ghent and Ypres. The upheavals were touched off by the Count's action in granting rights of justice along the river Zwin to a relation. The Zwin was Bruges' crucial lifeline to the sea; such a threat was intolerable. The general economic interest of the big towns, in fact, encouraged in them an ambition to extend their authority over the surrounding countryside both in order to secure their lines of communication and to control the competitive cloth industry in the country areas and the smaller towns, which threatened producers in the city. The years of ineffective comital power between 1322 and 1328 saw some consolidation of this authority, especially by Ghent. Though the French restored the Count in 1328, Flanders was veering towards a situation in which the county was split up between its three main towns. The same process went even further in the years 1338 to 1347, when English intervention at the beginning of the Hundred Years War undermined the Count's power again (see below, p. 36). The régime which was established by the weaver, James van Artevelde, at Ghent in January 1338, led once again to the domination of the county by the three towns. The three towns formally divided the county between themselves in July 1343. For several years Flanders was effectively a state ruled by republican towns.

It is tempting to speculate how different the history of

Europe would have been if this remote precursor of modern republicanism had survived. It did not survive because the tradition of comital power – which passed after the death of Louis de Nevers to a much more able count, Louis de Male (1346–84) – and the influence of the French crown were too strong. But the conditions which caused it were also removed in time by more deep-rooted changes within Flanders. In the second half of the century the political position of the city oligarchies was undermined by the decline of the city cloth industry so that Flemish politics were more influenced by rivalries between competing towns and by rivalries between interests within the declining industry, such as between weavers and fullers. James van Artevelde of Ghent, the most famous exponent of urban liberties, was a thorough patrician but his position was weakened and finally wrecked by the conflict between the economic groups within the cities. In general, the fourteenth century was a period of democratization of city constitutions in which the patrician class lost power. Externally also the city cloth industry lost its unique status. Too many other cloth industries in other parts of Europe, such as England and Languedoc, flourished and stole its markets. The textile towns of Flanders provided the first example in modern Europe of the difficulties of an ageing industrial area which had lost the easy predominance built on the exploitation of one overwhelmingly successful product and had to go through the agonies of decline and diversification. By the later fourteenth century, the basic woollen cloth industry was very much in decline, particularly at Ypres. The process by which Arras for example, became famous for its tapestries rather than its cloth was in the long run the only way for the other towns of the same area to preserve their prosperity. The power of the captains of industry was also weakened. Within the Netherlands an increasing proportion of cloth was produced in the countryside rather than the towns. These trends will have to be related later to the general economic history of Europe (see below, p. 120). It is enough here to say that in the later years of the century, and especially after the last major revolt of the towns against the Count in 1379–82 (see below, p. 130) wealth and power were more evenly spread between town and country. But, though it became increasingly difficult to imagine that Flanders could be dominated by the cities, the Netherlands as a whole remained, in the Burgundian period and after, an area in which urban society was exceptionally important.

ii *The Kingdom of France*

In contrast to the Netherlands, France was the outstanding example of a great centralized kingdom. Broadly speaking, the French monarchy was throughout the later Middle Ages the wealthiest and most powerful institution in Europe. This statement must be qualified because there were quite long periods, notably in the 1350s and the 1420s, when the monarchy was rendered impotent by political division and by English invasion. Such periods of political decline and confusion were inescapable in a country ruled by a monarchical system of government presiding over a higher nobility which was still massively powerful. So much depended on the accidents of birth which threw up efficient or ineffective kings and quarrelsome or co-operative dukes. The play of political fortune should not divert our attention too much from the underlying structure which gave such immense wealth and power to the French kings. These periods apart, the territories of the French kings in the Languedoil (France north of the Loire from Normandy to Champagne) and the Languedoc (France between Gascony and the river Rhone), contained larger stretches of richly productive country than those of any other European prince and they were, therefore, the most powerful.

South of the Netherlands the feudal suzerainty of the King of France was accepted nearly everywhere west of the Meuse and the Rhone with the addition of the Dauphiné and Provence to the east. But it was a suzerainty which varied greatly in its effectiveness from one part of the country to another. Brittany was, for practical purposes, an independent duchy, as Flanders was an independent county, and remained so through this period. Their rulers recognized the overlordship of the King of France, but governed their states with little regard for him. Gascony, controlled by the King of England, was in a similar position. Apart from these two areas, the greater part of France was royal domain but the uniformity of the king's control was broken by large tracts in the hands of feudatories. These areas varied from time to time as a result of grants of lands and privileges made by the kings and of the extinction of noble families which restored their lands to the king's disposition, but at all times they were very substantial. They included, for example, the duchy of Burgundy and the duchy of Bourbon in eastern France and the domains of the counts of Armagnac and Foix in the south-west. The kings were accustomed to grant large fiefs to their sons, who sometimes established families which held them for generations. In the mid-fourteenth century, John II created large 'appanages' for his sons, the Dukes of Berry and Anjou, which lasted a long time. The great French feudatories held blocks of territory with much more substantial powers than their equals in England, who nearly always had very scattered estates clearly subordinated to the embracing royal administration. Their powers of jurisdiction and taxation gave them almost regal authority. Also the royal domain had been built up in the twelfth and thirteenth centuries by piecemeal absorption so that provinces such as Normandy or Languedoc had a strong sense of separate identity in addition to their loyalty to the king at Paris. France must, therefore, be imagined as a land with a complicated political geography, not a single undifferentiated unit.

The king's practical power over the country depended on two things: his judicial authority administered in his courts and his power to levy taxes to pay for his household and army. The summit of judicial power was the *parlement* at Paris, a central court with power to hear appeals from the provinces and to deal with cases touching the king. The royal domain was split up into areas controlled by *baillis* (bailiffs) or *sénéchaux* (stewards) who were the local representatives of the king, responsible for his lands in their area and for local justice. They were a semi-professional civil service, often with some

kind of legal training, and they gave the kings real administrative power in quite remote parts of the country.

Apart from the profits of justice and rents which he levied
on his domain and which constituted his ancient 'ordinary'
revenue, the king had developed claims to various kinds of
'extraordinary' taxes by which he could tap the wealth of his
more prosperous subjects in general. The king had the right to
call out his vassals to perform feudal military service and did
so frequently down to the early fifteenth century, but like all
other European princes, he was unable to make war without
spending large sums of money on wages and it was for this
purpose chiefly that he needed taxes. The fourteenth century
kings had three main kinds of taxes: direct hearth taxes,
levied on households (*fouages*), the salt tax (*gabelle*) and *aides*
(indirect taxes on commercial transactions). There were also
periods when considerable sums were made out of recoinage,
which amounted to a commercial tax. The summit of royal
financial administration was the *Chambre des Comptes* (Chamber
of Accounts) at Paris but other officials and bodies proliferated
to deal with various aspects of finances: the *Trésor* (Treasury)
for the ordinary revenues of the royal domain, the *Cour des
Aides*, the *Généraux des Finances* and the local *Élus* (elected
men) collected and assessed periodic taxation.

One part of the normal pattern of government in the first
half of the fourteenth century in France as in other parts of
Europe was that critical military situations led periodically to
extraordinary efforts to raise men and money: through the
general obligation to military service (*arrière-ban*) commuted
into various forms of taxation, summonses to the nobility,
direct and indirect taxation, to pay for mercenary companies.
Much of this mobilization involved negotiations with communities. These complex manoeuvres produced armies which
were for the times, very large indeed, probably the largest
armies which had been seen in medieval Europe. At the
height of mobilization in the summer of 1340, just before the
Treaty of Esplechin ended the first outbreak of the Hundred
Years War, it has been estimated (not on the basis of chroniclers' fantasies, but from reliable accounts kept by the royal
clerks) that Philip VI had about 19,000 men in Languedoc, of

whom over 5000 were cavalry, and 25,000, mostly horse, on the frontier of Flanders where war was mainly being conducted with the English: 44,000 men in all.

In comparison with England and some of the other more unified kingdoms of Europe, the development of parliamentary assemblies in France was extremely untidy. Inevitably, to raise taxes the king had to consult with the nobility, the rural middle classes, the clergy and the towns. The mixture of centralization and disunity which was characteristic of the political structure of France meant that it was a difficult matter of judgement whether to negotiate separately with tax payers according to class and area, or to assemble them in one meeting like an English parliament. A document composed in 1339 when Philip VI had to defend his kingdom against Edward III's invasion said '. . . the King may raise money . . . by asking his people, great, middling and small, and the clergy, and he has good reason for doing so, which will be told them. And the way to ask them is this: the King should summon them to Paris before him on a certain day, as has been done before. But if this way does not have his approval, then he should talk first to those of the town of Paris and of the *Vicomté* of Paris and those of the *bailliages* of Senlis, of Vermandois and of Amiens . . .' and so on through the whole of the royal domain. Every kind of local general assembly can be found in the early part of the fourteenth century. The attempt to bring representatives from the far south to Paris was abandoned in the middle of the century and Estates General when they were summoned met for Languedoil and Languedoc separately. In other areas, local parliamentary assemblies expressed a strong sense of provincial separateness, for instance estates of Artois and Normandy met frequently in the later fourteenth century. During the early part of the Hundred Years War in the reign of Philip VI, who was not a very commanding personality, it looked as though the command of local estates (such as those of Vermandois or Normandy) over taxation and the capacity of general estates to criticize the king were both growing. Philip was severely criticized by the estates of Languedoil and Languedoc in 1346 and 1347 for the ineffectiveness of his rule. The geographical fragmentation of political life meant that one did not find in fourteenth century France the continual, if intermittent, dialogue between the king and a national parliament which developed in England at that time. Nevertheless, there were periods, notably the critical times after Poitiers and at the end of Charles V's reign when general political discontent centred on the meetings of the Estates of Languedoil. During the period of military disaster and civil war between 1346 and 1358, there was a marked tendency for French politics to centre on fairly frequent meetings of the estates of Languedoil, and a more 'parliamentary' political structure appeared to be emerging.

That period was followed, however, by a reversal of tendencies. After the political and economic disasters of the reigns of Philip VI and John II, came a great king, Charles V (1364–80), who not only reconquered most of the French territory which had been lost but also strengthened the constitutional position of the monarchy. Dependence on the critical attitudes of general assemblies gave place to a stronger central control by the monarchy. Up to this period, taxes had generally been levied after obtaining some sort of consent on the grounds of military necessity. Charles V, in contrast, collected the main taxes, direct (*tailles* replacing *fouages*) and indirect (*aides*), without consent for most of his reign and was able to maintain a standing army of 6000 men, which was expanded at times of crisis, a very remarkable achievement by medieval standards.

This French state was a creation of the thirteenth century. It was a somewhat paradoxical combination of strength and weaknesses. There was – for the times – a highly centralized bureaucracy, responsible to Paris but also a strong sense of the continuance of the older political units which it contained, immense potential wealth but a rickety system of mobilizing it for the king's use. The kings of the fourteenth century preserved the monarchy intact through various genealogical and political misfortunes and at the death of Charles V in 1380, it was probably more powerful than ever before.

iii *The Hundred Years War: the first phase to 1385*

Most of the neighbours of the King of France were obviously lesser rulers like the Count of Flanders. He had one major rival, the King of England, who was capable of raising men and money on a comparable scale. England was a centralized kingdom with a very efficient taxation system. Though not as rich a country as France it could produce armies which could match theirs. Its warlike nobility preferred on the whole to look eastwards towards the rich pastures of France rather than towards Scotland and Ireland which offered much less attractive opportunities for fighting. English kings and nobles had an easy foothold for operations in France because the king was also Duke of Gascony. Rivalry between the kings of England and France was the dominant theme in the politics of north-west Europe. In the period from 1337 to 1453 there were a number of wars between the kings of England and France which are commonly remembered as a single series of conflicts: the Hundred Years War. There were elements of continuity in war aims which to some extent justify this description though there were also great differences in the character of the various outbreaks of the war. For over a century western France was a theatre of intermittent war between invading English armies and defending Frenchmen. This is one of the most prominent political features of the later Middle Ages.

The most powerful of the medieval kings of France, Philip IV the Fair, whose authoritarian command over his kingdom and ambitious exercise of power appropriately resembled that of his contemporary Edward I of England, died in 1314. After his death the Capetian dynasty, which had ruled from Paris in unbroken male succession since the tenth century, failed to produce a line of male heirs. Philip IV was succeeded in turn by his three sons, Louis X (1314–16), Philip V (1316–22), and Charles IV (1322–8), all of whom were short-lived and left no sons. They were succeeded by a cousin, Philip VI (1328–50), who introduced the Valois line of kings which was to extend

to the end of the sixteenth century. The succession was not
entirely undisputed. One possible alternative claimant was
Joan, the daughter of Louis X. Her claim was set aside and she
became Queen of Navarre but it was to be revived by her son
many years later. More important was Philip IV's daughter
Isabella who was unhappily married to Edward II of England.
Her son Edward III, who succeeded to the English throne
after a rebellion engineered partly by Isabella herself in 1327
which ended in the murder of Edward II, was a possible
claimant to the crown of France if descent through a female
should be admitted. The claim was put forward only tentatively
in 1328 because the English government in the aftermath of a
particularly nasty rebellion was shaky and Edward III in
effect acknowledged Philip VI by travelling to Amiens in 1329
and doing homage to him for the possessions which he held of
him in France. In 1331 when the English government was
again caught at a weak moment after the coup d'état which
ended Edward III's minority, Edward even admitted that his
homage was 'liege' homage, implying the duty to give military
help to the King of France. But the doubt about the legitimacy
of the rule of the French kings, created by this uncertain
succession, was a legal issue of the kind which medieval
politicians could easily revive for use as a *casus belli* or for
propaganda purposes. It was to be a major factor in the
diplomacy of north-west Europe for over a hundred years and a
major theme throughout the so-called Hundred Years War
between England and France.

Another major theme of future politics which appeared
more clearly at this period, though it was in fact already very
old, was the English king's possession of Gascony. English
kings had been holders of territory in south-west France since
the twelfth century. There had been constant disputes, firstly
about the geographical extent of the English territory and,
secondly about the nature of the English king's relationship
as Duke of Gascony with the King of France who claimed
suzerainty over this area. The legal arrangement as it existed in
the early fourteenth century dated from the Treaty of Paris
concluded in 1259 which established the right of the King of
England to certain territories in south-west France provided

that he held them by liege homage from the King of France. This was an arrangement fraught with problems which are very characteristic of the transition from overlapping feudal jurisdictions to unified states with a simpler sovereignty over blocks of territory which was taking place in Europe from the thirteenth century onwards – an extremely slow, untidy and incomplete transition, but nevertheless a distinct and general feature of Europe during this period. It was hard for the King of England to accept the position of vassal of a rival king for part of his territory, required in theory to pay homage in person and to give military support to his liege lord. It was also hard for the King of France to accept the exclusion of his jurisdiction from a part of his kingdom. As the fourteenth century advanced the acceptance of the idea of 'sovereignty', derived from Roman Law and very difficult to reconcile with feudal ideas, became more general. French kings naturally wanted to control Gascony and legal disputes provided plenty of opportunities to assert claims. Inland from Bordeaux was a no-man's land between English and French jurisdictions in which the rival administrations built opposing *bastides* and the nobility could change their allegiance to suit their convenience and the political climate. The administration at Paris constantly sought to encourage judicial appeals from Gascony to the *parlement* of Paris, appeals which implied a recognition of French lordship and which the English equally tried to prevent. The uneasy relationship blew up into a minor war between Charles IV of France and Edward II of England in 1323 because of a boundary dispute in the Agenais. Edward had not done homage to the new king who was no doubt touchy about it. Neither side pursued the matter very energetically, Edward because he was in an extremely insecure position at home, Charles no doubt to a lesser extent for the same reason. Charles did, however, invade and declare the Duchy of Gascony forfeit to the French crown. The War of Saint-Sardos induced Edward II to send his queen, Isabella, to France with her son to act as a mediator. This turned out to be an important stage in the rebellion against Edward. Isabella returned from her brother's country to overthrow her husband. She also made a peace agreement with Charles in 1327 in which she accepted a reduced Gascony without the Agenais, consisting now only of Bordeaux and a strip of the coast of south-west France. Gascony remained, however, a dangerous source of conflict. It was important to English kings because of the prestige which it gave and the opportunities for plunder in France. The commercial links between England and Bordeaux, which supplied most of the large English wine imports, were strong. The uncertainty of jurisdiction, and the tenuous links with both Westminster and Paris made it a marvellous field of operation for the local nobility.

A third source of conflict in the north-west European theatre was the relationship between France and Flanders. Over the Count of Flanders, as over the Duke of Gascony, the French king claimed a generally admitted suzerainty; but in this case he was concerned with an immensely wealthy state which had an autonomous economic and political life. The morsel was too large for France to swallow. Philip IV himself had received his most humiliating defeat from the Flemings at Courtrai in 1302. In an agreement with Count Robert of Béthune in 1320 Philip V accepted that he could not absorb the major part of Flanders into the royal domain. Count Louis de Nevers (1322–46) had closer ties with the French court. His accession started a period in which the reigning count was out of sympathy with the political attitudes of some of his most important towns, which were powerful enough to pursue an independent line. Louis had the support of many of the nobility and of Ghent. Bruges and Ypres were hostile. He was captured and forced by the people of Bruges to abdicate the county to their nominee, a relative and rival called Robert of Cassel. When he escaped he naturally turned to France for help. This political reversal coincided with a social rebellion in the countryside of western Flanders, one of the most substantial social revolutions of fourteenth-century Europe. It appears to have been a movement of the well-to-do peasantry against the local nobility, led by a peasant called Nicholas Zannekin and favoured by the cities of Bruges and Ypres. The social upheaval turned out to be deep-rooted and long-lived. It ended only when Philip VI of France led an army against the insurgents in 1328. The

French army met the Flemish popular forces at the battle of Cassel and beat them decisively. The burgomaster of Bruges was hanged at Paris. Louis de Nevers was thus restored to authority in Flanders under French influence. For its own reasons of political instability based on internal social and economic divisions, however, Flanders remained a volatile compound.

The frontiers between English and French territory in Gascony were never precisely settled by the detailed juridical negotiations that continued through the 1330s until Gascony provided the immediate occasion for the outbreak of the conflicts of the Hundred Years War in 1337. The development of Anglo-French hostility was stimulated mainly by other issues: by French help for the independent Scotland which Edward III was trying to subdue and by Robert of Artois. Robert was a brother-in-law of Philip VI who had quarrelled with him and taken refuge at Edward III's court and was thought to be persuading him to claim Philip's throne. These causes of enmity produced a deterioration of Anglo-French relations from the rather amicable attitudes of the beginning of the two reigns. From 1331 to 1336 the possibility of a crusade patronized by the Pope was a distraction but both Philip VI, who used crusading money to prepare for war with England, and Pope Benedict XII, who did not want a crusade unless the western kings were united behind it, were half-hearted and from 1336 the project was dead. In 1337 Philip ordered the seizure of Gascony and Edward claimed the French crown.

The intermittent enmity of England and France was to be a much more dominant factor in European politics in the succeeding century than it had been before. It seems difficult to avoid the conclusion that the main reason for this was the new English claim to the French throne which became a political obsession akin to the traditional German claim to Italy as part of the chimerical Holy Roman Empire. In a parallel way also the lush pastures of France became a hunting ground for the predatory English nobility from a more austere and northerly country, which they found rewarding and then irresistible. This did not happen however until after

Edward III had shown them the attractions of France. The two countries were not evenly matched. France was larger and richer and the resources of its kings always potentially greater. Except in Gascony or in reconquest of other territories the kings of France were generally of course defenders, mobilizing a sluggish military system. English success depended on French weakness. A united France had little to fear, but the tendency of France in the fourteenth and fifteenth centuries to fall apart politically offered splendid opportunities for invasion and there were some periods of appalling disorder.

Before plunging into the events of the Hundred Years War it will be worth pausing for a moment to enquire into the nature of fourteenth-century warfare and its place in life. The French kings of this period were capable of fielding very large armies. This should not mislead us into imagining the late medieval army as an organization subordinated to the purposes of the state like a modern army. For many of the *noblesse* of France, as of all other European countries at this period, the practice of warfare was not merely a profession or an art but a way of life and the chief means to the attainment of respect and glory. To understand medieval society it is important to grasp that war was both a more normal and a more individualistic activity than it is in modern states, an activity in which the fighting man expected to aim at his own advancement and personal fulfilment just as much as to advance the cause of his prince and commander. A Burgundian gentleman (himself killed at the battle of Poitiers) who wrote a treatise on the subject in the mid-fourteenth century divided 'feats of arms' into a number of types grouped into various kinds of fighting: jousts between individuals, tournaments between bodies of men, local warfare in defence of a man's own property or that of his lord, crusading adventures, service in mercenary companies in Italy. This classification smacks of the romances of chivalry but it was by no means anachronistic in the fourteenth century. Many French lords had engaged in all these types of fighting. Fighting for the king was one kind of warfare. These individualistic assumptions are exemplified in the customs relating to ransom: soldiers who captured gentlemen from the other side negotiated with them for ransoms; the commander took a percentage of the ransom money but essentially it was a personal matter between the prisoner and his captor. The politics and warfare of 'states' were therefore entangled with the personal careers of individual soldiers. In 1351 English misdeeds in Brittany inspired a French knight to challenge one of the English commanders to a fight in which each of them was to be accompanied by only thirty companions. The 'Battle of the Thirty English and Thirty Bretons' was fought with quite heavy casualties, including seven dead on the English side. When the Earl of Pembroke was captured by the Castilians at the naval battle of La Rochelle in 1372 he was imprisoned in Castile. Some time after this the great French commander Bertrand du Guesclin bought him from the King of Castile and arranged to free him in return for a considerable sum of money which was to be paid by his friends and relations in England. The Earl was by this time a very sick man and the bargain was that du Guesclin would get his ransom if he delivered his prisoner to the English at Calais alive by a certain date. Du Guesclin later claimed that the English sent out troops from Calais which deliberately hindered the last stages of the journey. At any rate the earl died a few miles away. It is difficult to know whether Du Guesclin took on the Earl's ransom as a financial proposition or out of sympathy for a sick nobleman. In any case considerations of this kind played just as large a part in war as the more abstract policies of kings. From the soldiers' point of view the main function of the monarchy was that it provided a rallying point and, through its power to mobilize taxation, the economic basis of armies. It is often difficult to know whose war a particular commander is fighting, the king's or his own.

Whatever the formal justifications for fighting between the kings of England and France there was a very large plundering element in most phases of the Hundred Years War which was partly the result of the sheer difficulty of keeping an army supplied with food and wages, partly a result of the individual rapacity of soldiers who hoped to make individual fortunes out of the war. Jean Froissart, the Hainaulter who wrote the famous chronicles describing the Anglo-French conflicts of the fourteenth century with a rather romantic interest primarily in the feats of arms, gives this realistic description of the English army marching through Normandy in 1346 during the campaign which culminated in the Battle of Crécy:

'You have heard before about the order of march of the English, how they rode in three battles, the marshals to the right and left and the King and the Prince of Wales his son in the middle. I told you that the King rode in short stages. Every day they set up camp between midday and terce. They found the countryside so fruitful and well supplied with foods of all kinds that they needed to make no purveyance except of wine and even found a reasonable amount of that. It was no wonder that the people of the country were afraid for they had never before seen anything of war or battle. So they fled before the English at the first hearing of them, leaving their houses and their granaries full, and had no means of saving or protecting themselves. The King and the Prince had about 3000 men at arms, 6000 archers and 10,000 foot soldiers with them apart from those with the marshals.

So the King rode on as I have described, burning and wasting the country without breaking up his order of march. He did not turn aside for the city of Coutances but went on towards the big town of Saint-Lo in Cotentin which at that time was very rich and given up to trade and was worth three times as much as Coutances. This town of Saint-Lo had a great cloth industry and a profusion of rich burgesses. there were eight or nine thousand men in the town, burgesses and craftsmen. When the King of England had come close enough he camped outside, not wishing to lodge in the town for fear of fire. So he sent his men ahead and the town was immediately taken with little trouble, run through and plundered throughout. No one could believe the great wealth which was taken there and the quantity of good cloths that were found there. They would have been sold cheap if there had been anyone to sell them to.'

Much of the fighting consisted of campaigns like the one

described in that passage in which the English invaders, like ninth-century Vikings, pillaged a richer country. At other times and in other areas the war was broken down into more localized and intermittent fighting.

The character of the Anglo-French war in its first phase in the years 1337–40 was dictated by Edward III's strategy which consisted in building up an alliance in the Low Countries and western Germany with which to attack France. Edward's allies included his father-in-law, the Count of Hainault, Holland and Zeeland and other Netherlandish rulers. He also won over the Duke of Brabant so that his following in the Netherlands except for Flanders was fairly complete. He even won the support of Lewis of Bavaria, the German Emperor, with whom he made an impressive alliance at a personal meeting at Coblenz in 1338. The Count of Flanders, Louis de Nevers, was too attached to France but here Edward adopted an appropriate policy of dividing the Count from his subjects. In 1336 an embargo was placed on the export of English wool to Flanders, partly in the hope of detaching the Flemings from France by economic pressure. In combination with the widespread resentment against French control in the Flemish towns and English intervention this eventually had a considerable effect. A movement in the towns threw up one of the most famous Flemish popular leaders of the Middle Ages, James van Artevelde, who became Captain of Ghent at the beginning of 1338 and leader of the other cloth towns. Louis de Nevers failed to suppress the alternative government in his own country and left it in command when he fled to France in February 1339.

The French response to these manoeuvres was quite active at sea and there were raids on the English coast, but it was slow on land. Philip had to go through the elaborate procedures of squeezing money and military service out of many separate provinces. The estates of Normandy for example held out against paying any subsidy. In the end Philip's financial success was impressive. He took the initiative in 1340–2 by ordaining the levying of a tax on commercial transactions, a *taille* and a *gabelle*. Stonewalling was in fact all that was necessary to counter Edward's brilliant but insubstantial achievement. Edward crossed the Channel in 1338 and set up his headquarters in Brabant to invade France. He made a close alliance with Artevelde and in February 1340 he was able to assume the title of King of France at an assembly at Ghent with very widespread Flemish support. The spectre of a union of England and the Low Countries, based on their complementary economies and natural hostility to the French crown, rose up more clearly than at any other time in the Middle Ages. In the same year the French fleet, including ships from Castile and Genoa, which was assembled off the Flemish coast at Sluys, was heavily defeated by the English – the worst French loss in this phase of the war – and Edward advanced on land to attempt the siege of Tournai. By this time he had simply run out of steam. The allies were not helping him with armies and his money was exhausted. France was too big a country to be tackled in this way. The two kings made the truce of Esplechin which ended the first phase of the war and also ended the impracticable strategy of a coalition of England, the Netherlands and the Rhineland against France.

The Anglo-Flemish alliance was never revived with the same intimacy after 1340 although in a more modest form it was sometimes important later in the century. For this there are two reasons. Firstly Edward had not the resources to revive his Netherlandish alliance policy, secondly Artevelde failed in the long run in maintaining his supremacy in Ghent and Flanders because of rivalries within the various sections of the cloth industry. He was assailed by threats from all sides: from the Count, from the enemies of Ghent's supremacy in Flanders and from the enemies of the weavers within Ghent. He was increasingly thrown back on the English alliance without adequate support from his own countrymen. He died in a revolt of cloth workers at Ghent in 1345. The following year Louis de Nevers was killed in battle against the English at Crécy to be succeeded by Count Louis de Male who was more independent in his policy. The great days of Flemish republicanism as a factor in international politics were over.

From 1340 onwards for more than twenty years the Anglo-French war depended not so much on international alliances as on divisions of various kinds within France itself. The next episode was provoked by a dispute about the succession to the Duchy of Brittany. King Philip of France favoured the claim of his nephew Charles de Blois but the duchy was also claimed by a cousin, John de Montfort, who, having seized it, went to England in 1341 and offered Edward III recognition as King of France in return for English support in Brittany. Edward III welcomed the opportunity for direct intervention in France and quickly agreed to support John. Philip took possession of Brittany in the name of Charles de Blois. Edward III invaded Brittany in 1342. The conflict was indecisive and it was ended by a truce at Malestroit in 1343 which left Brittany in effect divided between the two parties. Edward III continued to support the Montfort cause for the rest of his life. John de Montfort died in 1345 to be succeeded by a young son who was brought up at the English court and maintained the claim for over half a century with intermittent English support. For a whole generation Brittany was divided and a prey to English troops. Though a poor and remote part of France and not closely attached to the crown, it became strategically important and was certainly one of the areas which suffered most from the disorders of the mid-century.

Another English invasion in 1345 was assisted by another man with a grudge against the French king, Geoffrey de Harcourt, claimant to the great Norman castle of St Sauveur-le-Vicomte near Cherbourg. Harcourt was supposed to have persuaded Edward to take an army into Normandy. This invasion turned into the Crécy campaign. The original intention may have been to contact another English army which was operating in Gascony in 1345–6 and had advanced far north into Poitou. In fact, Edward, after landing in the Cherbourg peninsula, advanced eastwards to Caen, which he sacked, and then to the Seine threatening Rouen, the capital of Normandy, and possibly Paris itself. Philip VI acted rather indecisively, allowing Edward to trick him and cross the Seine. A considerable French army chased the English northwards and met them at Crécy. Against all expectations the French army was very heavily defeated. Edward then continued his march to Calais which he took after a long siege curiously unhindered by the King of France. Calais, as a seaport on the border of Flanders, made an ideal continental base for English wool exporters and was to remain in English possession for two centuries.

In 1348 the Black Death swept across France. In 1350 Philip VI died. His successor, John II (1350–64), a self-indulgent, impetuous devotee of the chivalrous life who left the government to favoured officials of low birth while he concerned himself with the festivities of the Order of the Star, which he founded, was not competent to be the ruler of a great kingdom. The combination of social and political misfortune brought on by these two events, in the face of an ascendant English military power, produced a decade of extraordinary political confusion in much of northern and western France.

From a political point of view perhaps the most serious element in this situation was a split within the French nobility which led to civil war and therefore made the French monarchy a fairly easy prey. The king's opponent was Charles the Bad, King of Navarre, grandson of Philip IV's eldest son Louis X through a female and therefore, like Edward III, a possible claimant to the French throne. In addition to his kingdom in the Pyrenees he held lands in Normandy but believed that the Valois kings had tricked him of other lands due to him by inheritance. In 1354 he murdered a favourite of King John on the grounds that the victim had been given the county of Angoulême which properly belonged to his mother. John feared an alliance of Charles the Bad with the English and therefore reacted weakly by giving him the Cotentin. Charles the Bad continued to intrigue with the English, promising to recognize Edward III's claim to the throne. John climbed down again but relations between the two kings continued to be extremely hostile and the French nobility were divided in sympathy. John took the decisive step of seizing and imprisoning Charles the Bad at a banquet at Rouen in April 1356, only five months before the crisis of the Battle of Poitiers. The important duchy of Normandy therefore rose against the king at a time of extreme danger from the English.

The fateful battle of Poitiers followed some years of rather slack military activity. It was part of a campaign waged by

Edward III's son the Black Prince from the base at Bordeaux
in 1356. He was returning from a rather venturesome march
up into the Loire valley when he was caught by King John's
army and probably unwillingly forced to give battle near
Poitiers. King John was captured and carried off to London.
The French kingdom was now in a state of unprecedented
political collapse, both prostrate before English arms and
headless. King John left as his deputy his son, the inexperienced and, at first, not very successful Dauphin Charles
later King Charles V. Charles the Bad was supported by a
number of nobles. In these circumstances disaster was compounded by disaster. A common pattern of events within the
late medieval political structure was that in a period of ineffective royal leadership divisions within the nobility encouraged an aggressive attitude by the tax-paying middle
classes. What now happened in France was an extreme case
of this pattern. In the circumstances of labour shortage
following the Black Death, and discontent with the ineffectiveness of John II's government, the Estates of Languedoil had
already been difficult to manage. At their meeting in 1355
they had insisted that the money for the taxes which they
granted should be collected and allotted to troops by their
officers, not the king's. The meeting of the Estates which
followed Poitiers in 1356 exploited the predicament of the
king. The leadership of the parliamentary critics of the crown
was taken by a Parisian merchant called Étienne Marcel and
Robert le Coq Bishop of Laon a supporter of Charles the Bad.
They demanded drastic reductions in taxation, a purification
of the allegedly wasteful administration and a continual
parliamentary council to see that reforms were carried out.
The reformers were sympathetic with Charles the Bad and
there was a natural alliance between them and his party.
The Parisian merchants were behind the reformers. The
next meeting of the Estates in 1357 promoted a reforming
Grande Ordonnance which again was to introduce government
by council, and provide for regular meetings of the Estates
and control by them over peace and war and coinage. The
Dauphin's government was paralysed by this combined
opposition of pro-Navarrese nobility, estates and insurgent

Parisian bourgeoisie. At the end of 1357 Charles the Bad was released from captivity. He and his supporters controlled Normandy and threatened to control Paris. The Dauphin was reduced early in 1358 to leaving Paris and trying to assemble a more sympathetic meeting of Estates away from the capital at Compiègne. The final disaster was the peasants' revolt to the north of Paris in the region of Beauvais and Soissons which broke out in the same year, the *Jacquerie*. This eventually divided the opposition to the crown. Marcel and his Parisians tried to ally with the peasant rebels but Charles the Bad did not. The revolt collapsed, Marcel was assassinated in Paris and the monarchy's nightmare, or at least the worst phase of it, came to an end. After this the royal administration proceeded to negotiate seriously with the English for peace and also to attempt, eventually with success, to overcome the internal Navarrese threat. Political order was at a low ebb with bands of *routiers* living off various parts of the French countryside.

The widespread breakdown of royal authority in western France in the 1350s and 1360s produced a period of remarkable disorder and insecurity in which townsmen and peasants suffered severely from depredations by unattached bands of soldiers. The situation after 1360 was described thus by Froissart:

'There were many men of other nations who were great captains and great pillagers and who had no wish at all to depart so easily: Germans, Brabanters, Flemings, Hainaulters, Bretons, Gascons and bad Frenchmen who had been impoverished by the wars – and wanted to make good their losses at the expense of the Kingdom of France. Such men persevered in their wickedness and did much harm to the kingdom. Those who had learnt to pillage and who knew that it would not be profitable for them to return to their own countries or dared not return because of the crimes of which they would be accused gathered together and chose new captains, electing the worst men to command them, and then rode out. Thus they gathered first in Champagne and Burgundy and made up great troops and great companies, calling themselves the "Late Comers" on the grounds that they had not yet pillaged much in the kingdom of France. So they came and took suddenly the Castle of Joinville in Champagne and great wealth inside it which had been gathered from all the country around. And they held the castle for a while and wasted all the land of Champagne and the bishoprics of Verdun, Toul and Langres. When they had pillaged enough they passed on but they sold the castle of Joinville to the people of the land for 20,000 francs. Then they entered Burgundy and came to disport themselves there and rest and refresh themselves waiting for one another; and there they committed many evils and foul deeds because they had come to an agreement with certain knights and squires of the country who led and guided them. So they stayed a long time between Besancon, Dijon and Beaune and robbed all that country.'

Even powerful lords protected themselves with difficulty. In 1364, for instance, the ducal castle at Argilly near Beaune in Burgundy was occupied by a band of *routiers*.

At this point the Dauphin Charles emerged as the real leader of the country. In 1359 he and the Estates General at Paris rejected a humiliating treaty with England which King John in captivity was apparently willing to accept. Edward III responded by invading again in the autumn of 1359. His route north of Paris into Burgundy and back south of Paris to Normandy was impressive but as the French army offered no resistance and kept out of the way the English won no victory. Talks at Brétigny, near Chartres, in the spring of 1360 established the outlines of a treaty and later that year John II was released at Calais. Edward III was to hold an enormously enlarged Gascony stretching from the Pyrenees almost to the Loire. King John was to pay a huge ransom. These provisions were carried out. In the face of a good deal of resistance from the population the English took over substantial areas of France. The complementary agreements by which Edward III was to renounce his claim to the throne of France and King John was to renounce sovereignty over Gascony, which might conceivably have had the effect of establishing the division of

France permanently, were dropped on both sides so that the legal basis for a resumption of the conflict remained.

King John died in 1364 in England where he had returned to captivity because of the difficulty of paying his ransom. The Dauphin Charles, who now became Charles V (1364–80), though an enigmatic compound of physical weakness and political strength (he was no soldier and the military honours in this reign went to his famous Constable Bertrand Du Guesclin), has generally been regarded as one of the great French kings. He insisted on the highest respect for royal majesty, emphasizing for example the power to heal scrofula which was conferred on him by his coronation, and perhaps did more than any other French king of this period to encourage the ideological elevation of the monarchy. In the world of deeds he succeeded in raising the monarchy from the depths to a position of internal and international power. The next phase of conflict extended from the serious resumption of the war in 1369 to 1385 after Charles V's death. The achievements of the monarchy in that period were very considerable. Not only were the lost areas of France reconquered but the long battle for Flanders was won by its decisive absorption into the Valois orbit. This second achievement was prepared before 1369. The last of the independent Counts of Flanders, Louis de Male, had no son. His only daughter and heiress Margaret was, after 1361, a young widow. She united in her person the inheritance of the County of Flanders from her father and the Duchy of Burgundy from her husband. Her hand was sought by the triumphant Edward III for one of his sons. This plan, which would have had the effect of creating an English state in the Netherlands, was prevented by the King of France with the connivance of the Pope, perhaps the most obvious service which the Avignon papacy performed for the French crown. Urban V declared the marriage to be within the prohibited degrees of relationship and therefore illegal. This left the field clear for French diplomacy to persuade Louis de Male to agree to a French marriage and by 1369 the marriage of Margaret to Charles V's brother Philip the Bold was agreed upon. Louis still had some years to live and Flanders had to be actually taken over. The diplomatic victory however was to lead to the creation of Valois Burgundy, a Netherlandish inheritance ruled by a French prince for the best part of a century, an important alteration in the political structure of north-west Europe.

After the death of John II in 1364 Charles had taken the offensive against the remaining Navarrese strongholds with the assistance of du Guesclin who emerged in this campaign as an important leader. The Navarrese were defeated at the Battle of Cocherel and systematically mopped up. Charles the Bad accepted a settlement and did not henceforward play a major part in French politics. In Brittany, on the other hand, du Guesclin suffered a reverse at the Battle of Auray in 1364 when John de Montfort and the English defeated him. At the Treaty of Guérande in 1365 Charles V accepted John de Montfort as duke.

By the end of the 1360s Charles V had made considerable progress in strengthening his internal position and providing a financial basis for his armies. He had established a sufficient power over the provinces of the Languedoil to be able to levy the main taxes, the *aides*, the *gabelle* and the *taille* fairly continuously without the frustrating business of resort to the Estates. The constitutional crisis of the 1350s had been left well in the background and France now had an effective monarchy. This was the essential pre-condition for the effort to reverse the Treaty of Brétigny. The opportunity for action was offered, as often in the past, by a dispute about sovereignty over Gascony. Edward III had established his eldest son, the Black Prince, as Duke of Aquitaine at Bordeaux, ruling over a sub-state which gave him the status of one of the circle of European princes. A dispute arose between the Black Prince and two great Gascon magnates, the lords of Armagnac and Albret, about the payment of a tax. They appealed to Charles V as overlord. This case revived the whole question of the status of Gascony which had been left uncertain in 1361. Charles decided in 1368 to allow the appeal to the Paris *parlement*, encouraged a number of others from the same area and announced publicly that he accepted them. He summoned the Black Prince to appear in Paris and when he did not appear he declared the Duchy confiscated.

Between 1369 and 1374 most of the enlarged Gascony of Brétigny was reconquered. This was done not by a few dramatic blows but by a laborious piecemeal effort, in which towns and castles were won over in succession by diplomacy or force. But it was a very decisive effort. Since Charles V himself did not venture onto the battlefield, the leadership of French forces was mainly in the hands of his brother, Louis Duke of Anjou and Du Guesclin who was made Constable in 1370. In the years 1369–73 Poitou was recovered by the pressure of Du Guesclin and Anjou. During this phase of the war France benefited considerably from an alliance with Henry of Trastamara, King of Castile, who provided a superior fleet which was sometimes very effective in the Bay of Biscay and the Channel. One of its best exploits was the naval victory of La Rochelle in 1372 in which an English force sent to bolster the defence of Poitou was destroyed before it got to land. Apart from defence in Gascony the English responded with some ambitious raids into northern France of the mobile, destructive kind which Edward III had undertaken in 1359. The most remarkable of them was John of Gaunt's expedition in 1373. Landing in Calais he marched by a circuitous route around the east of Paris by Rheims and Troyes and the Auvergne to Bordeaux. An enterprise such as this – destructive, resulting in no conquest of territory, scarcely indeed making contact with the French royal forces – showed the limitations of royal power even under Charles V. It also illustrates the primitive side of the war, the indulgence in large scale foraging and plunder for its own sake, which was still a considerable part of all late medieval warfare. In 1373 however the French achieved their aim of preventing John of Gaunt from linking up with the English forces still in Brittany and Normandy and thus hindering the apparently inexorable reconquest of France which would eventually make it secure from such enterprises. By 1375 French pressure was making it difficult for the English to hold on to a few points in Gascony and sustain John de Montfort in the patches of Brittany remaining under his control.

Meanwhile under the auspices of a serious minded Pope, Gregory XI, who hoped to unite western Europe in a crusade, peace negotiations between the two sides were being carried on in neutral territory at Bruges and were prosecuted in earnest in 1375-7 when Bruges at times housed a full-scale peace conference attended by the Duke of Lancaster and the Duke of Burgundy and Cardinals acting as mediators. These talks continually broke down on the two intractable issues of the claim to the French throne and, even more, the status of Gascony. The negotiators could produce truce but no peace. French arms were now definitely in the ascendant. England held only Calais and a Gascony reduced to the limited proportions of half a century earlier, before the English conquests. A new French navy inspired by the example of Castile dominated the Channel and raided the English coast in 1377. But the monarchy still had considerable problems to trouble it. The question of Brittany had still not been settled. Brittany had been reconquered but Charles V acknowledged the Montfort Duke who had been most of his life an English protégé and ally. In 1378 Charles decided to confiscate the Duchy on the grounds of Montfort's lèse-majesté. But the Bretons turned out to be as unenthusiastic as the Gascons and the Flemings about incorporation in the royal domain. John de Montfort re-established control over much of Brittany. Another daring English expedition into Picardy and the Loire Valley in 1380 supported him. He had to be accepted by the French crown in 1381. Brittany remained an almost independent duchy loosely attached to the king. Charles the Bad of Navarre, whose hostility to the Valois had smouldered throughout the intervening years also became a threat again in 1378.

At the end of Charles V's life opposition to the pressure of royal taxation broke out again. There were minor rebellions in 1379 which persuaded Charles to abolish the *taille*. The reign of King Charles VI, who was a boy when he ascended the throne in 1380, therefore started in an atmosphere of popular unrest. There were outbreaks of violence at Paris and elsewhere in the north which led to a general removal of Charles V's more or less continuous taxes and in 1382 to the anti-tax rebellion of the 'Maillotins,' (see below, p. 132). The renewed weakness at the political centre of France came at an awkward moment because the affairs of Flanders were moving towards a crisis. In 1380 began a new revolt at Ghent, the last stirring of communal independence before the County was absorbed in Burgundy. Its links with earlier movements was symbolized by the election of Philip van Artevelde, son of James, as the leader. Louis de Male lost control of the County. He turned for help to his son-in-law Philip the Bold, who was very willing to intervene in order to ensure the safe succession of his own future property and to apply the military power of the French crown to that end. In 1382 he invaded Flanders and defeated Artevelde's army at Roosebeke. Artevelde and his natural allies, the merchants of London, tried to revive the old Anglo-Flemish axis with some success. An English expedition was dispatched to Flanders in 1383 in the guise of a 'crusade' led by the Bishop of Norwich: Flanders like England supported the cause of the Roman Pope against the Avignon Pope in the recently opened Great Schism. It was a failure. When Louis de Male died in 1384 Philip the Bold was able fairly easily to take over the county and to make his peace with it at Tournai in 1385.

At the time of Charles V's death in 1380 the first long phase of the Hundred Years War was already drawing to a close. After the failure of the Bishop of Norwich's crusade fighting petered out. Charles V had succeeded in reversing the catastrophies of the two previous reigns and restoring the French monarchy to the position it had held before, as well as incorporating Flanders more firmly in the French sphere of influence. The English did not accept the situation. Their king retained his claim to the French throne and the position of Gascony as well as of Calais and Brittany remained anomalous. But for the next quarter of a century there was little large-scale fighting.

iv *Germany and the Empire to 1378*

From the valley of the Rhine eastwards across the hills of central Europe and into the great plains of the east was another region of Europe with a complex political life of its own. This part of Europe was to a large extent dominated by the German-speaking peoples. Not only had they populated that part of Europe which we today think of as 'Germany,' during the great period of population expansion and colonization from the eleventh to the fourteenth centuries they had penetrated in great numbers into the areas of eastern Europe settled mainly by Slav peoples, exerting a profound influence at all levels on agricultural settlement, on commerce and towns and on the political institutions. German peasant settlers in the Slav areas introduced a freer system of tenant right which was generally known as 'German right'. Eastern European towns had constitutions on the model of German towns. Bohemia and Poland were colonized by the establishment of houses of Cistercian monks sent out from German monasteries. Areas such as Brandenburg and Austria had been fully Germanized. In Bohemia and Moravia the influence of German people and German ways of life was a leaven introduced into a still predominantly Slav population.

The area of German predominance or influence may conveniently be divided into two regions in which different types of political organization, in part reflecting a very different social basis, predominated. What would now be described as western Germany – the Rhineland, Swabia, Franconia, Hesse – was a region of highly developed agriculture and of many towns, one of the richer parts of Europe. It was also a region of extreme political fragmentation. In all this it resembled the French- and Flemish-speaking Low Countries to which it was adjacent. The typical political unit of that area was the very small state such as the county of Nassau or the 'County Palatine' which spanned the middle Rhine between Speyer and Mainz, or Cologne which was a small territorial state ruled over by the Archbishop, enclosing an independent city. The failure of any major political power to establish a widespread authority in western Germany earlier in the Middle Ages had resulted in the development of a bewildering complexity of small independent states and overlapping jurisdictions. The state of affairs was summed up in a comment made by a Heidelberg professor in 1408: 'Every nobleman, however modest his standing, is king in his own territory;

every city exercises royal power within its own walls.' The remark was broadly true of the same area a century earlier.

To the east the political geography was very different for here there were large states controlled by princely rulers whose constitutional character is in some ways more similar to that of England, France and Iberia. This was the area where the German merged into the Slav world. There were the wholly German Duchies of Bavaria, and Austria and the 'Mark' of Brandenburg. Bohemia was a largely Slav kingdom with a Slav nobility, ruled until 1305 by a Slav monarchy, but for most of the fourteenth century by German princes and much influenced by Germany and German politics. Prussia was one of the strangest political structures in medieval Europe. It had been conquered during the thirteenth century by the knights of the Teutonic Order who subdued the previously pagan Slav inhabitants and established themselves as an oligarchy presided over by the Grand Master and supported by German noble and peasant immigrants. Most of the rest of east-central Europe was occupied by the huge but loosely centralized kingdoms of Poland and Hungary.

From the thirteenth century onwards it is proper to regard Germany as divided into a number of political units – except in some parts of Swabia and Franconia where particularism had gone so far that it is difficult even to distinguish political units as opposed to lordships – each of which was practically independent of external authority. The usual name for such a unit was in German *Land*. Regarded as political structures, the proper parallel to England is not Germany but Bavaria or Austria or the small Rhineland state of Jülich-Berg – they have the same kind of jurisdictional independence. As in England the basis of the king's authority was his jurisdiction, his control of the powers of higher justice, so in the Empire the man with the right to try the highest kind of legal cases generally became the prince. But the *Land* also involved a sense of political community in its population. Most of the nobility of this part of Europe were conscious of belonging to one land or another – one area in which a particular set of laws and customs were accepted – even though geographical areas of total jurisdiction exercised by princes would not be easy to define with sharp lines in the manner of a modern political map. The German political theorist Althusius gave a definition of a *Land* about 1600 which would apply perfectly well in the fourteenth century: 'a province is that which contains many country districts, towns, castles and villages associated and bound together under the communion and jurisdiction of one law'. Within each German *Land* there had commonly taken place by the fourteenth century a constitutional development which was in the barest essentials similar to the evolution of large western states like England and France. In most of them, that is to say, princes had developed systems of general taxation and assemblies of 'estates' – nobles, gentry and towns – had grown up with powers derived from the practice of granting taxes. This is true not only of big states like Austria but also of small ones like Jülich-Berg.

Germany also contained a large number of semi-independent towns and cities which unlike the boroughs of France and England had not been incorporated into the larger areas of princely jurisdiction. They ranged from tiny places to great cities with an international commercial importance such as Cologne and Strasburg, both of which were independent of the states controlled by their archbishops. The more independent of these were known as 'imperial cities' because they acknowledged no superior jurisdiction between them and the emperor. They were an important factor in political life and they grew more important as this period advanced.

Germany included the areas of the most extreme political fragmentation in Europe. Paradoxically, the Germans acknowledged as in some sense their overlord a ruler whose power was theoretically grander and more embracing than that of any other layman: the Holy Roman Emperor. There is no office in which the gap between theory and reality has been greater, but there were different levels of theory and reality which must be distinguished. At the most abstract level the Holy Roman Emperor had claims to be considered a universal ruler, the temporal counterpart to the Pope as a political head of all Christians. That conception was by no means entirely dead. It was still possible for Dante to use it. At a lower level

there was a large area of Europe in which the overlordship of
the Holy Roman Emperor was in some more or less vague way
accepted, to the extent that it might be prudent for a ruler to
have a political title confirmed by him. This area included
Italy as far south as Rome, the whole of modern Germany
and Switzerland, most of the Low Countries (but not Flanders), Prussia, Silesia, Bohemia and Austria. Descending still
further towards the realities of everyday power, one can
discern some specific and generally accepted rights which the
Emperor had in Germany but not in Italy. There were some
financial dues payable to him, particularly from so-called
'imperial' towns. There were a few courts and jurisdictions,
mostly in south-west Germany. There was the power to
summon a *Reichstag*, a meeting of the princes and towns of
the empire at which disputes might be settled, perhaps money
sought to pay for an army. There was also the general right of
feudal overlordship which gave the emperor some influence –
which could be politically useful – over the disposition of
states and estates, especially if male heirs failed. These were
not negligible rights; they could be important additions to the
powers which the holder of the imperial office derived from
possession of his own territories.

The title of Holy Roman Emperor could be obtained only
by going to Rome and receiving the crown there from the
Pope. This generally accepted custom still helped to perpetuate in the fourteenth century that conception of a division
of the world between mighty spiritual and temporal powers
which descended from the days of Constantine and Charlemagne. And still in the fourteenth century the conception
exerted its influence as an incentive and justification for
intervention in Italy by German princes. Until he had made
the journey to Rome the potential emperor was only 'King of
the Romans'. This meant in effect King of Germany. As a
political office the German monarchy involved little more than
the presidency of a very loose confederation of largely independent states. It also had the disadvantage that it was an
elective monarchy. The electors were four Rhineland powers
(the archbishops of Mainz, Cologne and Trier and the Count
Palatine) and three eastern rulers (the Elector of Saxony, the

Markgraf of Brandenburg and the King of Bohemia). The electoral principle naturally made the position of the king or emperor very insecure. He could not easily ensure the succession in his own family. He might disagree with the electors to the point that he was faced with deposition and a rival king, or divisions among the electors might produce two candidates. Later on, in the fifteenth century, the imperial crown became virtually the property of two houses, first the Luxemburgs and, after their extinction, the Habsburgs. In the fourteenth century, however, its descent was still always in doubt; the electors' power of choice was real and they tended to be frightened of over-successful kings so that a balance of power system operated in imperial elections.

At the other extreme from the imperial grandeur of the German monarchy the empire also contained a small political unit which can be described without excessive distortion as a peasant state. This was the confederation of the cantons of Uri, Schwyz and Unterwalden, the nucleus of modern Switzerland. The Swiss confederation dated from the thirteenth century. It was in a region where political authority was generally weak. The cantons themselves were an area of scattered agriculture where manorial authority was also weak and there were a large number of substantially independent peasants. The Habsburg family were the most important nobility in that area at the end of the thirteenth century and as their power grew the confederation became increasingly a league for defence against them. In 1315 Leopold of Habsburg attacked them with a proper feudal army. He was defeated by the peasant army of the confederation at Morgarten, an event of symbolic importance in the social history of Europe comparable with the defeat of Philip IV by the Flemish townsmen at Courtrai. In 1332 the confederation was joined by the first town, Lucerne, a Habsburg town seeking a refuge against its lord. The next town to join in 1351 was more remarkable, Zürich an imperial city and the largest industrial centre in the area, brought into the confederation by an internal faction opposed to another faction which was supported by the Habsburgs. In 1353 Berne, also an imperial city, found it convenient to make a less intimate alliance with the cantons.

After the middle of the fourteenth century therefore the Swiss confederation embraced quite a substantial area organized according to the interests of peasants and townsmen, not lords, facing the growing powers which controlled the lands around, the Habsburgs, Burgundy, Savoy and Milan.

Another confederation which developed during the four-teenth century was the Hanse. The Hanse was primarily an organization of the north German coastal towns, Bremen, Lübeck, Wismar, Danzig and others. These towns were concerned not only with German trade properly speaking, but also with the long-distance trade between western Europe and the Baltic: the movement of cloth, salt and wine from the west, grain and forest products from the east, fish from the North Sea and Scandinavia. Their activities stretched from Novgorod in the east and Bergen in the north to Bruges where they maintained an important and privileged community of 'the common merchants from the Roman empire of Germany'. Their tendency to act together was very much strengthened by their conflict in the second half of the fourteenth century with the kings of Denmark over commercial privileges. Under the stimulus of this danger – Denmark controlled the traffic in and out of the Baltic and also important herring fisheries – the Hanse towns established a confederation for war at a meeting at Cologne in 1367. They defeated the King of Den-mark and in 1369 imposed upon him the treaty of Stralsund by which they acquired wide freedom and even control of castles in his country.

The political structure of the Empire in general however was a framework within which, as in the rest of Europe, noble and royal families played out their competitive struggles for power. The tangled story of fourteenth-century German politics is made somewhat easier to follow if it is regarded as centring primarily around the conflicting ambitions of three major families: the houses of Luxemburg (originally rulers of the Duchy of Luxemburg, for most of the fourteenth century kings of Bohemia as well), Habsburg (originally counts of Habsburg in Switzerland, now dukes of Austria and rulers of other south-eastern lands) and Wittelsbach, a family whose members included the dukes of Bavaria and counts palatine of the Rhine but which was chronically weak in political power because the whole inheritance was never united in the hands of one person. Kings of both the Luxemburg and Habsburg families had used the royal authority after their election to add great eastern territories to their smaller western states. This interaction between territorial family aims and royal powers – the use of imperial authority to build up the territory of the family – is a continual and peculiar feature of German history resulting from the elective kingship. During the period from 1320 to 1378 which is the subject of this chapter the political history of Germany was dominated by two very different but masterful and, within the limits of the political structure, successful kings: Lewis the Bavarian (1314–47) and Charles IV (1347–78).

In 1314 two rival candidates were elected by two groups of electors, Lewis the Bavarian (the Wittelsbach Duke of Upper Bavaria) and Frederick of Habsburg. After some years of uncertainty Lewis was decisively vindicated in 1322 when he defeated Frederick, with a great slaughter of Austrian knights, at the battle of Mühldorf in Bavaria, one of the major battles of medieval German history and the last on such a scale to be fought before the days of firearms. Mühldorf gave him a secure position in Germany and made possible a period of intervention in Italy (1327–30) which inflamed his violent and lifelong conflict with the Papacy and with its opposing interests in Italy. Pope John XXII, who had favoured the candidature of Frederick of Habsburg, deposed and excommunicated Lewis in 1324 – the style, 'Lewis the Bavarian', by which he is commonly known originated in papal references to him without his titles. Thus began a series of political, procedural and doctrinal conflicts, not only with John XXII but also with his successors Benedict XII and Clement VI which ceased only with Lewis's death. Lewis gave asylum at his court to the important ideological opponents of the papacy: Marsilius of Padua, William of Ockham and Michael of Cesena the general of the Franciscan Order. The Pope condemned him as a heretic in 1327. The main ground of these conflicts was neither the ideological issue nor Lewis's position as king in Germany; it was the conflict of papal and

imperial pretensions in Italy (see pp. 96-98) where Lewis
spent three years from 1327 to 1330; but they had important
implications for the history of Germany too. After Mühldorf
Lewis's chief opponents in Germany were not the Habsburgs,
who came to terms with him and played comparatively little
part in imperial politics in the next generation, but the
Luxemburgs who, feeling threatened in their position in
East Germany, tended to seek support from the King of
France and the Pope. An alignment of the Pope with France
and the Luxemburg family developed and reached its height
in the period 1337-41, the first years of the Hundred Years War.
Lewis became an ally of England and invested Edward III
with the powers of an Imperial Vicar while Pope Benedict XII
and the Luxemburg King John of Bohemia on the whole
supported Philip VI. John of Bohemia was the famous blind
king who fell in the French army at Crécy in 1346. Papal
support for him was exemplified in 1344 by the erection of
Prague into an archbishopric with a province, independent of
the great German church of Mainz to which it had previously
been subordinated.

Throughout this period Lewis was remarkably successful
in holding his position in Germany against his complex array
of internal and external opponents. The attempts of Benedict
XII to stir the German electors into choosing an anti-king
provoked them to issue a statement at Rhens in 1338 which
rejected all papal rights in the election of a German king and
enabled Lewis at a Reichstag at Frankfurt shortly after this to
assert the entire dependence of the Empire on the German
electors. Apart from the imperial question Lewis was equally
concerned to build up the territorial possessions of his own
family in Germany. A piece of luck gave him the Mark of
Brandenburg. Its ruling family died out in 1320 and, claiming
that as a fief of the Empire it reverted to him, he was able to
grant it to his son. But, in addition to the imperial conflict
with the papacy, German politics in the next generation were
partially dominated by a long drawn-out dispute over the
succession to the territories of Tirol and Carinthia whose
previous ruling family died out in the male line in 1335. After
various vicissitudes Lewis was able to secure the marriage of

the heiress for his son in 1342. By the 1340s therefore Lewis the Bavarian did appear to have increased the family power of the Wittelsbachs very substantially by adding Brandenburg and Tirol to Bavaria and thus to have made them the most powerful family in central Europe.

This success however had already brought the balance of power principle into operation and the Rhenish electors had begun to swing over to sympathy with Lewis's enemies, the Avignon pope and the Luxemburg family. Lewis had particularly aroused hostile opinion by his action in another succession question. Count William of Hainault and Holland died in 1345 leaving no male heir but three sisters. One of them was married to Lewis (another was Philippa of Hainault, wife of Edward III of England) and Lewis used his imperial power to seize both counties for his wife without considering the claims of the other co-heiresses. In the atmosphere of resentment caused by Lewis's success the French and papal cultivation of the Luxemburg family at last bore fruit: the electors chose Charles of Bohemia as anti-king in 1346, the year in which his father John was killed fighting with the French at Crécy. In 1347 Lewis was killed in a bear hunt and Charles became acknowledged King of both Bohemia and Germany.

Charles IV appears in retrospect to have been a ruler with a much clearer sense of political possibilities than Lewis the Bavarian and his reign (1347–78) saw some important changes in the direction of central European politics resulting from his initiatives. In the first place Charles abandoned Italy as a serious sphere of political ambition for German rulers. It had played quite a considerable part in the life of Lewis. Charles made two visits to Italy but they were both short and had severely limited objectives. The first in 1354–5 took less than a year and was little more than a journey for the ceremonies of coronation as King of Italy at Milan and Emperor at Rome, made possible by a lucky conjunction of diplomatic understanding with Pope Innocent VI. On a second journey of about the same length in 1368–9, when he actually met Urban V in Rome, he sold imperial rights in Tuscany to Florence and Siena and established quite clearly the inability of German rulers to act as more than grandiose hirelings in Italy.

In central Europe however Charles established a new pattern of power which was to be influential in the future. His most famous action was the issuing of the Golden Bull in 1356. This famous and over-rated document did little more than freeze the practice of imperial elections in the form which they had already acquired. It named the seven electors. It excluded the Papacy from any right to influence imperial elections. The territories to which the electoral functions were attached (Bohemia, Brandenburg, the Palatinate, Saxony, Cologne, Mainz and Trier) were declared to be impartible and their rulers to have within them all the royal rights of high justice and taxation. The last provision was a recognition of the complete independence of the princes which had become a fact of German politics not only in the electoral states but in others as well. In practice the clear definition of the electoral procedure was to facilitate the hereditary transmission of the crown through the Luxemburg and then the Habsburg families. Charles himself succeeded in achieving something that had eluded his predecessors for over a century: he persuaded the electors to choose his son as king in 1376 two years before he died. King Wenceslas had therefore already been crowned at the traditional place, Aachen before he succeeded in 1378.

The great importance of Charles IV in the long run was the result of his policy in strengthening the territorial position of his own house – his *Hausmachtpolitik* ('policy of dynastic power') in the language of German historians, rather than his imperial policy. The chief Luxemburg lands were Luxemburg in the west and Bohemia in the east. Charles failed eventually to enlarge the western territories – he temporarily established a big Netherlandish block consisting of Luxemburg and Brabant, but these lands were lost to the family in the fifteenth century. He succeeded, however, in building a great eastern block around Bohemia by the addition of Niederlausitz and Brandenburg, acquired from the declining Wittelsbach family, and various other pieces. He allowed Tirol to go to the Habsburgs in 1364, but made an inheritance treaty according to which in the event of failure of heirs in either the Luxemburg or the Habsburg family, all the territories of both parties were to go to the family which survived. Charles did this, of course, in the expectation that his descendants would benefit. As it turned out, it was to be the Habsburgs who profited from the failure of the Luxemburg family. This is less important than the fact that Charles ensured by his policy that imperial politics should be dominated for the next century by rulers whose power depended on family territories concentrated in the east; by the Luxemburgs until 1437, thereafter by the Habsburgs.

Charles's ambitions extended also further into eastern Europe. The kingdoms of Poland and Hungary were ruled in the mid-fourteenth century by two successful kings, Casimir the Great, the last of the native Piast dynasty in Poland (1330–70) and Lewis the Great (1342–82), the last of the Angevin rulers of Hungary. Both Casimir and Lewis, who was his nephew and succeeded him, died without male heirs. In expectation of these deaths, Charles IV made indefatigable attempts to secure the succession in these kingdoms for his own family. The succession, in fact, went in both cases to daughters of Lewis of Hungary. In Poland one heiress married a Jagiellon and thus established a new native dynasty. In Hungary, however, the other heiress was married to Charles's second son, Sigismund. So, four years after Charles's death and as a result of his diplomacy, this kingdom also was absorbed into the territories of the Luxemburg family.

v *Iberia*

By the fourteenth century, most of Iberia had been reconquered from Islam. Of the Mohammedan Empire, which had once covered the whole peninsula, there remained only the small state of the King of Granada, feudatory and tributary of the King of Castile. That, however, survived almost to the end of the fifteenth century, keeping alive the crusading spirit of the Castilian nobility. The kingdom of Portugal, one of the most enduring features of the political map of Europe, had roughly its present frontiers. In the western Pyrenees was the small kingdom of Navarre. The rest was divided between two kings, who were major European powers, the kings of Castile and Aragon. In the fourteenth century there was no suggestion of the union between them which was to come after 1469. They were quite independent, had quite separate political interests and were in some ways, strongly contrasted kingdoms. They must be described separately.

Castile was one of the largest kingdoms in fourteenth century Europe and one of the most backward – if we take the urban and industrial life of Italy and the Netherlands to represent the future. The preceding centuries of reconquest had encouraged the development of a high nobility with very extensive landed estates, often acquired by grants out of Moorish territory in the course of the Christian movement from north to south. Like other European nobilities, they wanted to preserve their family properties and avoid being subdued by an over-powerful monarchy and there was, at that period, not much to prevent them from achieving this aim. The crusading reconquest had also led to the establishment of the peculiarly Spanish military orders of Calatrava, Santiago and Alcantara, fighting men with a Christian mission. The Spanish orders did not, like the Teutonic knights in Prussia, actually become rulers but they did acquire very great economic and political powers which, at this time, really had no parallel in the rest of Europe.

The most remarkable feature of the Castilian economy was the enormous development of sheep farming to provide wool for the textile industries of Flanders and Italy. The climatic conditions of the country favoured very large scale transhumance, seasonal movement of flocks from north to south. This traffic was already organized on a national scale, under royal protection, by the *Mesta*. In the prominence of this raw material production in its economy, Castile resembled medieval England which was also a relatively backward area but, while in late fourteenth century England wool production was being cut back and replaced by more profitable agriculture and industry, in Castile it seems to have become increasingly prominent.

Another similarity between medieval England and Castile is the development of a unified parliamentary system. The Castilian *Cortes* consisted of the three estates of nobility, clergy and towns. The decisive English distinction between peers and knights was not paralleled but Castilian towns were much more likely to include gentry among their leading inhabitants. It was on the Castilian towns, as on the English commons, that the burden of taxation fell, in the form of the *montazgo*, imposed on municipalities, and the *alcabala*, or sales tax. The towns sent *procuradores* to the *Cortes*, who like the members of the English Commons, voted taxes and presented grievances. Towns were an important feature of the Castilian political scene and sometimes increased their influence by joining in leagues – *hermandades* – which were to some extent a counter-balance to magnate power. They are less remarkable as centres of industrial or mercantile growth. Indeed, another manifestation of economic backwardness which Castile exhibited, was the prominence of Jews or *conversos* (converted Jews) as money lenders, financial agents for the religious orders and tax-farmers for the crown. The continued importance of the Jews in Castilian financial life is at least one of the reasons why anti-Jewish atrocities, notably the great pogrom of 1391 which started in Seville, are so much more prominent here than elsewhere in Europe in the late Middle Ages.

Another aspect of Castilian life, however, foreshadowed the maritime future. This was the prominence of Castilian shipping. Castile touched the sea at three points: on the shores of the Bay of Biscay, at Seville and at Cartagena. Castilian sailors were, therefore, in contact with the methods of ship construction used both in the Mediterranean and in the Atlantic. This is an important factor in the discovery of the New World. It is also important in fourteenth century politics, because Castile introduced galleys, constructed on the Italian pattern and originally under the supervision of Genoese experts, into the naval warfare of north-west Europe, where they became a new and decisive factor in the late fourteenth century. The seaports of the north coast were well-developed and involved in a trade with Flanders in wool, iron and wine.

From southern ports there were links with north Africa and Seville was an important centre of Genoese merchants.

The reign of Alfonso XI, who succeeded as a child in 1312 and lived until 1349, saw the last effort of the Moors, the King of Granada in alliance with the Emir of Morocco, to recover their position in Spain. They took Gibraltar in 1333. The main effort came a few years later and ended with the decisive Castilian defeat of the Moors at Rio Salado in 1340. Algeciras was taken with the help of Crusaders from other parts of Europe in 1344. Though Alfonso XI died in 1349 at a siege of Gibraltar, which was not recovered for another century, this was virtually the end of Moorish aggression in Castile.

For the next forty years, Castilian politics were dominated by a dynastic succession dispute for which Alfonso XI was partly to blame. He had been married to a Portuguese princess and by her had a legitimate heir, Peter the Cruel, who succeeded in 1349. He also left a son by a famous and powerful mistress, Leonor de Guzman: Henry of Trastamara. Alfonso had been a successful king with a high conception of the royal office and an effective controller of the power of the nobility, an employer of Roman lawyers to strengthen the judicial position of the crown. In 1348 he had proclaimed that *Las Siete Partidas*, the lawbook compiled for his predecessor, Alfonso the Wise a century earlier, should have the force of law. *Las Siete Partidas* were to a large extent an attempt to establish the role of the King of Castile as a paternalistic ruler with powers based on Roman and Canon Law. They were to have a great future in the development of the theory of Spanish monarchy. They were unfriendly to an independent-minded magnate class some of whom saw their opportunity in the next reign.

Peter the Cruel, like his father, neglected his wife (a French princess, Blanche of Bourbon) for a mistress (Maria de Padilla). This insulting behaviour which culminated in the death of Blanche in 1361, possibly poisoned by the king, inclined the French court to the support of his opponents. Henry of Trastamara, an exceptionally ambitious and ruthless man, was glad to use any help which would enable him to supplant his half-brother as king and found such support both among the nobility of Castile and abroad. He led a magnate revolt against Peter in 1354, which failed, and fled to France. Thereafter he was supported by Aragon and by France. The alignment of the Hundred Years War dictated that England should take the opposite side and support Peter the Cruel. For a time the internal political division in Castile became an important side issue in the Hundred Years War. Peter was dethroned in 1366 by an invasion from Aragon in which, in spite of the alliance, English mercenaries (unemployed during the lull in fighting in France) played a prominent part. Peter fled to Gascony where he was sheltered by the Black Prince and from there he returned to Castile with an English army, which defeated Henry of Trastamara at Najera in 1367. Two years later, Henry of Trastamara recovered control with the help of the French commander du Guesclin and Peter the Cruel was killed.

As a result of this long civil war, the house of Trastamara ruled Castile until the unification of the kingdoms by Ferdinand and Isabella a century later. But the dynastic issue continued for some time to have a European importance because of its connection with the Anglo-French war. Not only did the Black Prince and his brother, John of Gaunt, continue to hope that they might repeat the glorious invasion of 1367, John of Gaunt married one of Peter the Cruel's heiress daughters and became himself the anti-Trastamaran claimant to the throne of Castile. The division within Castile, therefore, became ever more closely identified with the Hundred Years War between England and France. Hence the great activity of the Spanish galley fleet in the English Channel and in raids on the English coast around 1380, a faint presage of the Armada. When the Anglo-French conflict in France died down, English energies again found an outlet for a time in Iberia. After the death of Henry of Trastamara in 1379, his son, John I (1379–90) married the heiress to the throne of Portugal, hoping to join the two kingdoms. But when the union seemed imminent on the death of the Portuguese king in 1383, the Portuguese nobility refused to accept the idea and raised to the throne a bastard of the royal family, John of

Aviz. Portugal then provided a foothold for renewed English intervention in Iberia which led to the defeat of a Castilian army at Aljubarrota in 1385. This encouraged John of Gaunt to take an army to Galicia. There was no real hope of de-throning the Trastamaran dynasty. In 1387 he was bought off with a large sum of money and the marriage of his daughter to John I's son. The dynastic conflict was ended.

In the eastern part of Iberia the kings of Aragon ruled, in fact, over three kingdoms which were united only by the crown: Catalonia, Aragon and Valencia. Catalonia from which their family had originally come was united by similari-ties of language and society (the fourteenth-century kings spoke Catalan) with southern France, rather than Iberia, but its most striking peculiarity, and in a sense the most remarkable feature of the whole kingdom of Aragon, was the city of Barcelona. Barcelona was to decline dramatically in the fif-teenth century, so that its medieval greatness is often forgotten. In the fourteenth century it was a commercial metropolis on the scale and sharing the characteristics of the major Italian cities. Its commercial importance was backed by a major textile industry. It was a centre of banking. The ramifications of its commerce extended throughout the Mediterranean including Egypt and Byzantium. Colonies of Catalan merchants in the Islamic ports enjoyed local jurisdictions presided over by consuls sent from the homeland and the code of commercial and maritime law drawn up for them, the *Llibre del Consolat de Mar*, was widely observed by traders of other nationalities as an international standard. In conformity with its great econ-omic importance, the city had developed a unique constitution. It was, in effect, governed by a small council of magistrates who had exceptionally independent powers, including the right to negotiate with other states. Catalonia therefore was a kingdom dominated by one great city whose characteristics put it in the same class, both economically and politically, as the cities of Italy or Flanders, rather than with the poor seigniorial world of the rest of Iberia. It is also partly because of the outward looking eye of Barcelona that the political vision of the Aragonese kings was directed towards the Mediterranean, even to the distant Levant, as well as to Iberia.

Barcelona was the centre of a political as well as a commercial empire in the Mediterranean.

In contrast with Catalonia, Aragon itself was a land-locked kingdom, dominated by an exceptionally powerful and independent-minded nobility. The formula which the nobles of Aragon were supposed to use in acknowledging a new king ('We who are as good as you swear to you who are no better than we to accept you as our king, provided you observe all our liberties and laws, but if not, not') has now been exposed as a later invention of constitutional theorists; nevertheless, it conveys something of the flavour of relations between the kings and nobles in the early fourteenth century. In 1283 the nobility had joined in a Union to defend their privileges against the king and then compelled him to grant a *Privilegio General*, which, as well as confirming existing rights, permitted them to serve any other lord but forbade him to include foreigners in the royal council. Aragon had a Cortes (as did Catalonia and Valencia, separately). This met every other year in the early fourteenth century and contained the nobility (in two houses, upper and lower), burgesses and clergy. In between sessions, a small committee, the *Diputacion del Reyno*, remained in existence to ensure that the decisions of the parliament were observed. Aragon also had a unique judicial office, the Justice, an independent judge, who acted as a kind of supreme court. Altogether the institutional development of the thirteenth century had saddled the king with a legacy of limitations and obligations which might be crippling.

While these constitutional fetters had been imposed in Aragon itself, the Aragonese kings had acquired claims to rule in various distant parts of the Mediterranean, all of which were important at one time or another in the fourteenth century: Sicily, Sardinia and Corsica, Majorca and Greece. Sicily had been, since 1302, in the hands of a separate branch of the Aragonese royal house, but was to return to the main line in the fifteenth century. In compensation, the Papacy had granted the king of Aragon a claim to Sardinia, which was conquered in 1324 but contested by Genoa. The desire to enforce his claim led Peter IV of Aragon (1336–87) to take

part in a Mediterranean naval war between Venice and Genoa
in the years 1351-5. Catalan ships fought with Venetian
against the Genoese in the Bosporus. It was not until the
early fifteenth century that Aragon subdued the wild island.
Still more remote, and in fact rather marginal, was the
Aragonese interest in Greece. This stemmed from the activity
of the 'Catalan Company', an adventurous group of soldiers
of fortune, who operated in the Levant in the early years of
the century. They established a Duchy of Athens, which their
descendants placed under the protection of Peter IV in 1380
and which survived until near the end of the century.

Much more serious, however, was the Aragonese interest
in the kingdom of Majorca. This kingdom included not only
the Balearic Islands and some lands in the Pyrenees (held
of the King of Aragon) but also Montpellier (held of the King
of France). Peter III coveted these territories. The last of the
independent kings of Majorca, James II, was foolish enough to
isolate himself by quarrelling with his other overlord, the
King of France. In 1343-4 all his territories in the islands and
the Pyrenees were taken over by Peter, who thereafter ruled
them in spite of the efforts of the Majorcan king and his son
to interest other European powers in the recovery of them. In
the later fourteenth century, therefore, the King of Aragon
ruled over an empire which has been described with some
appropriateness as a medieval thalassocracy consisting of his
three Iberian kingdoms, the Balearics, Sardinia, with an
interest in Sicily and Greece, not to speak of wide commercial
activities of his Catalan subjects.

The conquest of Majorca was closely followed by a remarkable internal political crisis in Aragon. In 1346 Peter IV,
having no son, decided that he could not tolerate the descent
of his kingdom to his brother, James, the Count of Urgel,
and nominated his daughter, Constance, as his heir. This
inspired furious resistance from the Count of Urgel and from
the more independent-minded of the nobility of Aragon,
who revived in an extreme form the policy of the Union under
the leadership of the count. Valencia imitated this reaction,
the nobility there founding a Union modelled on the Aragonese. In the midst of the crisis, the queen died immediately

after bearing a male child, which also died. The personal bitterness was intensified. In 1347 the king was forced to meet the Cortes of Aragon at Saragossa, the capital of that kingdom, in a ceremony which is one of the classic expressions of magnate political power in the later Middle Ages. The king was forced to reaffirm the powers of the Cortes including their right to nominate the heir, if he had no son. Peter IV bowed and withdrew to Catalonia where he had more supporters. Shortly after this, the Count of Urgel died – it was suspected that he had been poisoned – and an open rebellion was started by the Union of Valencia. Peter went to Valencia and was again forced to make concessions to the nobility in the early part of 1348. At this point, when the king was a prisoner in the Palace at Valencia, it looked as though the future of the monarch was black. It was saved by the shifting factions, characteristic in Aragon as elsewhere of magnate politics. The extremist leaders of the revolt in Aragon besieged a royalist garrison at Epila near Saragossa. They were defeated with heavy losses in July 1348 and the force of the revolt was broken. Peter returned to Saragossa to revoke his concessions and then was able to put down the Valencians, executing the ringleaders.

While the rival factions were fighting over their ephemeral divisions, a far more important storm broke on them. The Black Death entered Catalonia early in 1348, bringing with it mortality on an unprecedented scale which was to have far greater repercussions than civil war. The long-term political implications of the social changes connected with the plague are material for a separate chapter. The Aragonese crisis of 1346–8 is a suitable end to a survey of the politics of the European kingdoms in the fourteenth century. The political manners of Spain were, perhaps, more violent than those of other parts of Europe, but the crisis of 1346–8 exemplified very well the common elements of the political scene in the feudal monarchies of Europe: the constant succession of dynastic ambitions, the conflicts between kings and endlessly changing groups of jealous nobility, struggling for power and wealth above the heads of the indifferent mass of the population.

CHAPTER II

ITALY, THE PAPACY AND EUROPE

i *Italian Commerce*

In northern and western Europe, though it included such great cities as Barcelona, Bruges and Cologne, urban life in the Middle Ages was in general a secondary phenomenon and cities were overawed by kings. In northern Italy alone urban civilization could be said to have escaped from the political domination of kings and to have reached such a high level of sophistication and independence that it exhibited ways of life and values significantly different from those accepted in the rest of Europe. In the early fourteenth century, for the first time since Greece was swallowed in Alexander's empire, a galaxy of city states had emerged with their own peculiar problems and intellectual and aesthetic tendencies. The Italian cities and the political life of the peninsula in which they were immersed form part of the subject matter of this chapter. The rest is concerned with the popes as heads of the western Church. It may seem strange to see Italy coupled in the title with the Papacy which for most of the fourteenth century had its seat at Avignon in France. There are two reasons for treating them together. Firstly, even when it was at Avignon and largely French in personnel, the papal court remained inseparably linked with Rome and its temporal concerns with the politics of the Papal state. Secondly, the pan-European activities of the popes were inextricably bound up with the commercial expansion of Italian business: they had grown together. It is easier to understand them in conjunction than apart. We begin with the economic basis of Italian city life.

By the fourteenth century the merchants of the Italian cities had established themselves in a relationship with other parts of Europe which was in some respects similar to the relationship of commercial imperialism which has existed between economically advanced European countries and primitive societies elsewhere in more recent times. One might even say that these economic relationships of the modern world existed in embryo within late medieval Europe. Here, for example, is a description of a commercial situation in the early fourteenth century as it was seen by the Florentine chronicler Giovanni Villani. It relates to the activities of Florentine merchants in England during Edward III's war with France in 1338 and after.

'During this war between the kings of France and England the merchants of the King of England were those of the Bardi and Peruzzi companies of Florence. Through their hands went all his revenues and wools and other things and they supplied from them all his expenses, wages and other needs. The expenses and other needs of the king so exceeded the rents and receipts that when he returned from this campaign, taking into account loans, purveyances and repayments made to them by the king, the Bardi found themselves to be his creditors in more than 180,000 marks sterling. And the Peruzzi more than 135,000 marks sterling which, since a mark was worth more than $4\frac{1}{2}$ gold florins, makes a total of 1,365,000 gold florins – as much as a kingdom is worth. This sum included many purveyances made to them by the king in the past but, however that may be, their great folly was that through greed for profit, or to recover what they had foolishly lent, they put all their wealth and that of others in the hands of one lord. And note that the greater part of this money came from investment or deposit from many citizens and foreigners. So that there was a great danger to them and to our city as you may see. Being unable to repay to their creditors in England, in Florence and elsewhere, they lost their credit and failed to pay and especially the Peruzzi, though they did not come to an end because of their great power and possessions in Florence and in the *contado* and their influence in the commune. But because of the defalcation and because of the expenses of the commune in Lombardy, the power and state of the merchants of Florence was reduced, and that of the whole commune and the merchant community. Every trade suffered from it, because with the failure of these two pillars, which by their former power had divided with their great enterprises a great part of the commerce of all Christians and almost nourished the whole world, every other merchant was suspected and lost credit. . . . And to add to the bad state of these companies the King of France seized their partners and goods in Paris and throughout his realm and those of other Florentines; and because of the great sum of money which the commune had taken by forced loans from the citizens and spent in the campaigns of Lombardy and Lucca, because then of the repercussions of the loss of credit, other lesser companies of Florence soon afterwards failed.'

The Bardi and Peruzzi mentioned by Villani were as he said among the greatest commercial companies of the period. They imported wool from England to Florence, they farmed the English customs and they handled the transfer of money to the papal court. They were also deeply involved in lending to King Robert of Naples who, like Edward III, was an ambitious, extravagant ruler of a kingdom with limited native commercial institutions. Their overextended operations were vulnerable to changes in the fortunes of the European powers. At one end of the chain, they were so deeply involved in lending money to the King of England that his failure to repay was ruinous; at the other end they had borrowed so much money in Florence to finance their operations that their failure shook the city and made it difficult for the commune to maintain its military expenditure. The failure of the Bardi and Peruzzi was a crisis of quite exceptional dimensions, but it illustrates the normal commercial network centring on the north Italian cities which involved the whole world of Europe and the Mediterranean. What was the nature and basis of the economic pre-eminence of these cities?

In the first place the Italian cities were notable centres of manufacture which gave them products to sell superior to or cheaper than those of other parts of Europe. The best known of these industries, which will serve as an example, is the cloth industry of Florence. Florence had seven major guilds in

which the entrepreneurs of the city's leading trades were
organized. Two of these were concerned with cloth: the
Calimala guild whose members imported unfinished cloth
from other parts and sold it, sometimes finishing it in their
workshops and the *Lana* ('wool') guild whose members imported raw wool and made it into cloth. By the fourteenth
century these industries were highly organized and produced
on a large scale. According to Villani, the chronicler quoted
before, the members of the *Lana* guild in the 1330s had over
200 workshops which supported 30,000 people. These numbers may be exaggerated but it is certainly true that Florence
at this period was a considerable industrial city with some of
the characteristics associated with modern industry. There
was a large wage-earning proletariat which was to play a
prominent part in the social revolution of 1378, called the
revolt of the *Ciompi* – wool carders – after a large and inferior
section of textile labour force (see below, p. 129). The characteristic industrial devotion to punctuality is shown by the fact
that the guild provided a bell to summon employees to work.
The industry was highly specialized, different quarters of the
city concentrating on weaving the wool from different parts
of Europe. The concentrated industrial population was
entirely dependent on imported grain and vulnerable to the
shortages and famines which periodically affected a society
with only a primitive agriculture, especially a large city like
Florence situated in an area which was unsuitable for grain
production; so food supply was a prime concern of government
policy. In the famine of 1328–9 the commune organized the
import of grain from Sicily and eventually took over the baking
trade to ensure cheap bread. The products of manufacturing
industry were of course largely exported as the raw materials,
such as English wool, were imported and created commercial
links over long distances. Other Italian cities also had characteristic trades. Lucca which had a great silk industry imported
large quantities of raw silk from Asia and exported some of the
finished goods to the West. Milan was famous for its arms
industry.

The most remarkable aspect of Italian economic expansion,
however, was not industry – at least one other area of Europe,

Flanders, could show a highly capitalized textile industry –
but trade. The Italians traded in other people's products at
least as much as their own. It was the extent and proliferation
of their trading activities rather than the development of
native industry that was really remarkable and unique.

There is first of all the geographical extent. There were
Italian trading communities in every city from London to
Alexandria. Marco Polo who described China for Westerners
at the end of the thirteenth century was one of a family of
Venetian merchants. In the time which we are describing,
the first half of the fourteenth century, journeys by Italian
merchants across Asia from the Black Sea to China were
commonplace. The Orient was much less mysterious than it
became later as the rise of the Ottoman Empire established a
barrier to the east of the Mediterranean. Muslim North Africa
was equally a sphere of Italian commerce and important as a
source of gold. The extremities of Italian commercial activity
were linked in part by the regular trade routes that they had
set up. It was in 1277 that merchants of Genoa – the most
enterprising of the Italians in the far west and also responsible
for an abortive attempt to reach Asia around Africa nearly two
centuries before the Portuguese succeeded (see below, p. 234)
– established regular trading links with north-west Europe by
sea, through the Straits of Gibraltar and across the Bay of
Biscay. Transport by sea was cheaper than the inefficient use of
carts and pack animals along bad roads, so the sea routes gave
the Genoese an advantage. Venice followed suit. In the early
fourteenth century both cities had networks of regular routes
stretching from the Black Sea to Bruges, the commercial
centre of the north-west. Genoa's mercantile marine was more
individualistic. Venice provided its trading nobility with a
state controlled shipping service of galleys built in the Arsenal
– the world's largest shipbuilding industry – travelling in
carefully organized convoys and hired out to merchants who
wanted goods carried in them.

One of the essential features which distinguished the
Italian merchants from others was the development of the
large firm with representatives who could maintain contacts
from a number of different centres. The Florentine com-

panies were commonly partnerships described by the name of the major shareholder, for example 'the company of Dardano degli Acciaiuoli and companions'. A branch in another city might be managed by a partner or by a 'factor' who had no stake in the business. A wealthy merchant might be involved in a number of partnerships and have a number of factors in various cities. The Bardi for instance had over 100 employees at this level. Their geographical spread might be considerable. In the 1360s the Alberti company had branches at London, Bruges, Paris, Avignon, Barcelona, Venice, Genoa, Bologna, Perugia, Rome, Naples and Barletta.

The commercial forms developed in the three major trading cities, Florence, Venice and Genoa, differed. Florence had no port and therefore no fleet of galleys but the very elaborate world-wide Italian firms like the Bardi or Alberti were a Florentine speciality. The characteristic Venetian, settled in Venice or at Constantinople or Bruges made his money out of a large number of import or export deals in a variety of goods. It was the Venetian merchant who corresponded most closely to the popular idea of Italian commerce, taking the cloth, tin and iron of western Europe to the eastern Mediterranean, bringing sugar, pepper and silk to Europe from the Levant and the Orient. Venetian interests were always centred where they had begun, in the eastern Mediterranean. Trade with north-west Europe was a later and subsidiary development. By the fourteenth century their interest in the eastern Mediterranean had led the Venetians to acquire a substantial land empire including the islands of Negroponte and Crete and many lesser places on the route between Venice and the Black Sea. The Corner family who were the wealthiest in Venice in the late fourteenth century were also the owners of sugar plantations in Cyprus and figured prominently in the politics of the Levant. Peter of Lusignan, King of Cyprus, stayed in Federico Corner's house when he came to Europe looking for allies against the Turks in 1361 and borrowed money from him. In material terms Venice was the greatest commercial success story of the Middle Ages – a city without much industry which came to bestride the Mediterranean world and to control an empire through mere trading enterprise. In the fourteenth century she was in the ascendant but the greatest periods of success and power were to come later. Genoa was a rival however, comparable in many ways. Like Venice she was a city of the sea, cut off by the Apennines and relatively little interested in the hinterland. Like Venice she had built up a commercial empire in the eastern Mediterranean. If Venice had sugar plantations in Cyprus, Genoa controlled the alum mines of Phocaea and alum was a vital raw material for the textile industries of Europe. Genoa played a larger part in the trade of the Mediterranean coast. Their rivalry in the eastern Mediterranean, jostling for favours from the Byzantine emperors, bickering about settlements on the Aegean islands, strangely reminiscent of the rivalries of imperialist powers in the early twentieth century, produced bitter wars in the later fourteenth century.

Apart from trade in real commodities itself, Italian merchants had created a variety of financial devices which facilitated trade: marine insurance (which appears clearly in fourteenth-century Genoa), arrangements for sharing profits with partners or depositors, accounting systems (double-entry bookkeeping also appears in early fourteenth-century Genoa), letters of exchange payable in distant cities in foreign currencies, loans. Because of the extent of their interests and the sophistication of their methods, Italian merchant communities scattered about Europe and the Mediterranean constituted a commercial network which to a large extent dominated European trade. The popes and the merchants of Paris and Bruges had to use the commercial and financial services of Italians even outside Italy, for sending money from Bruges to Venice for example. The communities of Italians – Florentines, Lucchese, Genoese and others – which one would find in the main centres of European finance outside Italy, at Avignon, Barcelona and Bruges, were the leaders in the trade of the continent.

The general predominance of the Italians in European trade was at its height in the early fourteenth century. At that time it was one of the most conspicuous forces making for unity in Latin Christendom. For Italy itself of course the most obvious result was the development of her cities into centres with an exceptionally wealthy and advanced population, including merchants who had very large sums of ready money at their command. This applies not only to the 'big four' who tended increasingly to dominate Italy north of Rome – Milan, Venice, Genoa and Florence – but also to a number of much smaller communes. Asti, Piacenza, Bologna, Lucca, Pistoia, Siena were also towns whose merchants were to be found widely scattered over the European world. At home they constituted a bourgeoisie living in independent communes.

ii *The City-State*

A contemporary description of a crisis in the city of Siena in 1317 gives a good introduction to the political character of the Italian commune:

'At the time of the *podestà* called Messer Monte de' Subi da Fermo and of the Nine *Signori* a plot was discovered which involved the butchers and the notaries and the Forteguerra and Tolomei and their followers – the leaders were Ser Pino d'Asciano and Ser Antonio d'Asciano and other notaries . . . Cione di Vitaluccio a butcher . . . among the knights Gabrielo di Speranza de' Forteguerra, and the heads of the Tolomei family were Messer Deio de' Tolomei and also Messer Sozo de' Tolomei [was involved]. The plot was revealed on 26 October. The men at arms and knights and foot soldiers being ready came to the doors of the family houses and began to shout "death to the Nine *Signori*". They began to come on to the main square and to the foot of the palace and wanted to set fire to the door. In the palace the Nine *Signori* had got ready many men with catapults and other arms and came out with shields and chased them to the doors of the houses and many of them were killed by darts from the commune's big catapults. And immediately the bell was rung to call to arms and many people came on to the square so that there were dead on all sides; the butchers and notaries and the Forteguerra and Tolomei and their followers were put to flight and among others four butchers were caught and handed over to the *podestà* and many others fled and were proclaimed rebels. Some of them, seeing that the plot was discovered, did not go on to the main square as they had promised and on the advice of Messer Deio de' Tolomei stayed on the Piazza Santo Cristoforo. Still, after peace was restored the Nine *Signori* wrote down all those who had been leaders of the plot and their followers and told the *podestà* that all the ones captured should have their heads cut off and those who were not be proclaimed rebels. One, who was a friend of the Tolomei family knew what had been decided and immediately informed Messer Sozo and Messer Deio. Hearing how things were, Messer Deio decided to make off and told his friends and followers and together with Messer Sozo went and had no more to do with the affair. The *podestà* next Sunday put up the banner and had the condemnation read out and executed these four butchers and then proclaimed rebels all those who had been the cause of this plot and their followers. But if the conspirators had been in agreement and had come on to the square all at once, the Nine *Signori* would have been in danger of losing their power.'

This brief and unimportant episode contains in essence much of the character of town politics in fourteenth-century Italy. The norm of Italian politics was instability, strife unchecked by firmly established authorities. During the twelfth and thirteenth centuries much of Italy north of Rome had come to be dominated by communes, that is independent towns, large or small, freed of royal or noble authority, managing their own affairs. The element of lordship was not destroyed; there were a great many lords controlling country estates, sometimes towns. Many noble families remained for example in the Apennines often uneasy neighbours in close proximity to independent towns. This made for continual strife between commune and commune or between communes and the surrounding countryside. Inside the communes the instability was also striking. Town life in Italy, to a greater extent than in northern Europe, was dominated by extended family clans and by constant ambitious strife between them. The image of the Montagues and Capulets stands not for a romantic myth but for a harsh and pervasive reality of Italian life. Important families with a continuity of interest extending over generations (like the Medici at Florence, the Fieschi and Adorno at Genoa, Corner, Barbaro and Contarini at Venice) were a dominant feature of city life in Italy which has no real parallel in northern cities. The Forteguerra and Tolomei in Siena were examples of this type. There were also of course conflicts of interest between classes and between professional groups organized in guilds. The strength of family interests in particular made it extremely difficult to devise a system of republican government which would maintain peace within the commune.

The Sienese crisis shows us some of the elements of this situation. The Forteguerra and the Tolomei were powerful families which were difficult to reduce to obedience to the general will of the Sienese people. Their wealth and also their control over dependants and servants made it easy for them to upset the peace of the city. The Nine *Signori* constituted a government of magistrates set up by the broad ruling class of mercantile families within the city. This constitution lasted from 1287 to 1355 and could therefore be counted highly successful as communal governments went in medieval Italy. During that period it contained internal upheavals and prevented external disasters, but the success as the extract shows was precarious. Like many other Italian cities Siena had attempted at an early stage to defuse the conflicts within the city by entrusting powerful but temporary official positions to foreigners who would be independent in the face of the local feuds. The *podestà* who appears in the Sienese story was a kind of city minister of justice brought from outside. Siena also had a foreign *capitano* to command its armed forces. By devices of this kind an uncertain tranquillity was maintained, often for long periods.

The importance of individual families and their feuds can be reckoned a universal feature of the communes. It was partly for this reason that the exile of political enemies, a rather unusual phenomenon in northern Europe, was common in Italy: it was often the best way of restoring peace in a town. *The Divine Comedy* was written by a political exile under sentence of death if he was captured. Overt class conflict was also a common characteristic of city life. Northern chroniclers of the time do not often see politics as conflicts between groups held together by class interests; Italian city chroniclers often do so. Not only were there the corporate interests of professional and trading groups, like the butchers and notaries at Siena in 1317, there was also the conflict between the more and the less wealthy. The distinction between *magnati* (great men) and *popolo* (people) was a commonplace of urban literature. This was not like the modern distinction between employers and proletariat because nobody thought that servants and employees had any political rights, but it was a social distinction. Social conflict of this kind was much more apparent in the early fourteenth century, when economic expansion, population pressure and immigration from the country were normal phenomena, than in the fifteenth century when demographic and social pressures had been relaxed and city oligarchies enjoyed an easier superiority. The early fourteenth century was therefore a period of political turbulence and constitutional experiment.

The towns had strengths as well as weaknesses. Many of them, especially the larger, controlled substantial areas of the country outside the town walls. They did not extend the benefits of political enfranchisement to these subject areas. The republicanism of the city state existed only within the city. The role of the population of the *contado*, that is the subject countryside, was to obey and pay the taxes imposed upon them, which were often an important source of material strength to the dominant city. Next to the republican form of government, which frequently permitted a genuine government by committee and fairly widespread consent, the most striking feature of the Italian communes to a modern eye is the sophistication of their finances. The dependence on hired mercenaries for warfare in the fourteenth century meant that communes had to raise large sums of money or perish. Since the cities contained relatively large trading communities with

money to hand, town governments could advance beyond the
primitive finances of northern kings. Some of them relied
partly on voluntary or forced loans on which regular interest
was paid. In the two greatest republican communes, Venice
and Florence, public finance was increasingly dominated by a
state debt built up from the proceeds of forced loans, with
interest-bearing credits which could be bought and sold. The
debts of the Florentine government were consolidated in
1345 into a single *Monte* and the wealth of individual citizens
thereafter commonly consisted partly of shares in this state
debt. Thus the property owners of the commune became in a
sense a financial as well as a political corporation.

In 1337–40 Ambrogio Lorenzetti painted a famous fresco
portraying an allegory of good and bad government in the
council room of the palace at Siena. This was a pictorial
defence by a republican régime of its own virtues and precepts.
The central figure was probably intended to represent the
'Common Good', an exhortation to the citizens to set aside
their private ambitions and feuds for the sake of the city.
This was the hope of all communal governments but very
often the inherent instability of city society was too much for
them. The pictorial image which the magistrature of the Nine
used to represent the common good looks remarkably like an
enthroned king. Siena in fact managed to retain a republican
constitution but in most of the towns of Italy the solution to
internal strife, voluntary or involuntary, turned out to be a
lord of some kind. By 1320 the relatively brief interlude of
communal governments was, for most of Italy, drawing to a
close.

The decline of communal republicanism happened in
various ways. One cause of it was the marked tendency for the
larger powers to consolidate territory around them so that the
number of political units was reduced. Thus in the fourteenth
century Florence absorbed Prato, Volterra and Arezzo which
had all been independent communes. On the other hand the
establishment of a despotism in an individual town might
come about either through the assumption of control by a local
lord or through the elevation of some outstandingly powerful
or wealthy citizen. In the early fourteenth century there were

already important dynasties such as the Visconti at Milan, the Della Scala at Verona, the Este at Ferrara, some of which were to survive for a long time, and many tyrants of smaller towns.

In some places however republican constitutions remained. Siena was obstinately republican throughout the Renaissance, Bologna intermittently. Above all there were three major cities – Venice, Florence and (intermittently) Genoa – which retained the republican ways of political life. Size and wealth were undoubtedly factors in the survival of republicanism. It was much more difficult for one man or family to overtop the others in a large commercial city than in a small town. A big city was also much less likely to be conquered by a neighbouring lord, as Lodi, Como and Bergamo for example were absorbed into the Milanese state of the Visconti. The distinction between communes and despotisms should not be exaggerated: no despot could dispense entirely with the communal element in his state and the establishment of a despotism did not of course alter the basic fact that they were urban communities. However, because of their size and their economic and cultural prominence the fact that three big cities did remain republican is of great importance for the history of institutions and, perhaps even more, of ideas in Renaissance Italy.

In later centuries Venice was to become famous in Italy and in Europe as the state with a constitution which mysteriously ensured stability and the absence of revolution. The legend of the changeless efficiency of the Venetian constitution had not yet grown up but the elements of the system which were to persist through the Renaissance period were already in existence. Political power in Venice was limited to certain families whose legitimate male descendants were the only members of the Great Council. The families had been fixed by the so called 'Closing' of the Council in 1297. Other citizens could and did hold many administrative offices but were excluded from the political hierarchy. The Great Council elected a Senate of 300 which actually governed policy. In 1310 one of the few internal upheavals in Venetian history, a conspiracy by three nobles from leading families, Tiepolo, Querini and Badoer, led to the invention of another body which was to be important. This was the Council of Ten, set up as an emergency committee but later perpetuated as a small executive cabinet, which together with other small committees and ministers carried out the real work of government. At the summit of the constitution was the Doge, a patrician elected for life to fill the role of a constitutional monarch. This was the constitution which presided over Venice's extraordinary growth in the course of the fourteenth and fifteenth centuries into the unique position of a city republic which was also a major European power. In this respect the history of Venice was a striking contrast to that of its great commercial twin and rival Genoa. Genoa's trading strength, no less brilliant and indeed perhaps rather more spectacular in the early fourteenth century was accompanied by extreme political instability. Genoese politics were traditionally dominated by some very great families of patrician merchants – Doria, Fieschi, Grimaldi and others – whose feuds filled its political history like those of the magnates of a headless kingdom. Genoa never achieved political peace for any great length of time. During the fourteenth century it suffered the popular tyranny of Simone Boccanegra who was elevated to a personal dogeship on the Venetian model (1339–44). The institution of the doge survived but after Boccanegra it too became the prey of the old families of *nobili*. From the mid-fourteenth century Genoa also, though never losing its republican constitution, fell intermittently into the political control of Milan and accepted the Visconti sometimes as external *Signori*.

Florence, the city which was eventually to produce the most remarkable literary expressions of republican ideology, falls in political experience somewhere between the cases of Venice and Genoa. In 1320 she already had a very long republican experience including many upheavals. Dante, not long before this, contrasted the (as he imagined) fixed constitutions of ancient Athens and Sparta with the constant alterations of the Florentine body politic which he said constantly changed position like a fevered invalid. 'What you spin in October does not last to mid-November. How often in the time you remember have you changed laws, coinage, office and customs.' (*Purgatorio*, vi, 143-8). In fact the broad outlines of the Florentine polity were fairly constant. At the head of the state was a group of seven men: six *priori*, chosen to represent the wards of the city from among the guild members, and a 'Standardbearer of Justice'. These men held office for only two months. During that time they lived in the palace and acted as heads of state, initiating laws and conducting diplomatic negotiations. They could not be re-elected for some time, so there was a constant turnover of personnel. The priors could not legislate; laws had to be submitted to various councils which included in all several hundred citizens. They had judicial and executive officers – a *podestà* and *capitano* like the Sienese – who were always foreigners. The constitution, though it had developed piecemeal, was clearly designed as far as possible to prevent individuals or groups from getting control of the state by enforcing frequent changes of office. It did not of course destroy the influence of the rich but it did limit it. Certain families which had been well known for their knightly and proprietorial background, the *magnati*, were excluded from some political functions. At the other end of the scale most of the population of Florence was excluded also – one had to be a self-employed guild member to qualify for the political rights – but the number of genuinely enfranchised citizens probably ran to several thousand.

Between 1313 and 1322 the republican constitution was partially abrogated in favour of a limited *Signoria* exercised by King Robert of Naples who had the power to nominate the city's *podestà*. The reasons for this sacrifice of independence were common ones in the Italian world. The deal with King Robert had been made in 1313 towards the end of the great expedition of the German Emperor Henry VII to Italy (1310–13) which had greatly strengthened the Ghibelline (or pro-imperial) party against the Guelfs (or anti-imperialists). Under the severe strain of this situation the commune could not keep peace among its own citizens and it could not protect itself against the Ghibellines of Tuscany under the leadership of the rival city of Pisa. Henry VII died in 1313 but he left as a legacy a strengthened Ghibelline party in Italy which persisted for some years. In 1320 the chief representative of this

alliance in Tuscany was Castruccio Castracani, tyrant of
Lucca, whose power was still alarming enough for the
Florentines to value the protection and capacity for leadership
of a great *seigneur*. It was not until 1322 that Florence released
herself from King Robert and reverted to an unmixed republican constitution. In 1325 however Florence suffered a
severe military setback when Castruccio defeated the Tuscan
Guelfs at Altopascio. The Florentines reacted by placing
themselves under the lordship of Duke Charles of Calabria,
a son of King Robert, and surrendering autonomy much more
completely. Charles could appoint all the city's main officials
as long as he maintained a mounted army at the commune's
expense. This régime lasted until Charles's death in 1328 soon
after the death of the enemy Castruccio. Florence again
reverted to a communal government strengthened by the
introduction of an element of election by lot (the names of
magistrates were drawn at random from bags which contained
all those eligible) which in medieval Italy as in ancient Greece
was respected as a device which discouraged the concentration
of political power. Fourteen years later in 1342 the conquest of
Lucca by Pisa created a threat which inspired Florence again
to choose a lord, this time a Frenchman, Walter of Brienne
called Duke of Athens, who was a soldier and courtier at the
Angevin court at Naples. Engaged first as a mercenary commander he was given judicial authority for life apparently in
an attempt to restore confidence in the general panic which
followed from the disastrous collapse of the Bardi and Peruzzi
companies (see above, p. 68). His *signoria* lasted less than a
year. Republicanism was restored in 1343.

1343 was the end of experiments with lordships. After this
Florence remained a republican commune until the slow erosion
of republican institutions was begun by the Medici nearly a
century later. The reasons for the end of the experiments were
largely related to the external balance of power. At the beginning of the fourteenth century it was difficult for a city, even a
big one like Florence, to do without protection. The power of
monarchical, Angevin Naples was attractive to an embattled
city, bad at managing its military affairs. The days of the
citizens defending themselves, a communal army such as the

young Dante had served in, were over. In the early fourteenth century cities had to pay for squadrons of expert knights. In the later fourteenth century however a further stage had been reached. By that time no lord, German or French, carried enough weight in that part of Italy to be worth taking up. It was a result of the relative decline of seigniorial power. Florence, being a very big and wealthy city could afford independence, she could do better by using her money to buy mercenaries who remained in a strictly subordinate position.

The years from 1343 to 1382 have generally been regarded as the period in which Florentine republicanism was most broadly based. In reaction against the failure of the great merchants to control affairs before 1343 the extent of eligibility for office of members of the 'lesser' guilds, as opposed to the 'major' guilds was increased. Broadly speaking the 'major' guilds were those which included the merchants on a larger scale, such as cloth merchants; the 'lesser' guilds were the organizations of shopkeepers and artisans. During the period 1343–82 the constitution on the whole favoured the smaller men. The point cannot be pressed very far. Great merchants and proprietors still had a disproportionate share of power. It was impossible for a city state to be more than a narrow oligarchy tempered by a wider oligarchy. At one point, in 1378, the city was totally disrupted by the revolution of the *Ciompi* (below, p. 129) which temporarily broke the normal organization of power. But the interruption was very short-lived. In 1382 the power of the seven major guilds was reinforced and the old republican – oligarchical course of city politics was to continue for at least another half century.

iii *The Avignon Papacy*

In 1320 the papal court had been established for eleven years at Avignon on the banks of the Rhone in southern France where it was to remain until Gregory XI took it back to Rome in 1377. The papacy at the beginning of this period was therefore a court in exile. The popes were absent for an unprecedently long stretch of time, a whole life-span, from their proper place: the see of St Peter at Rome. Many people both at the time and since have regarded this as a deplorable aberration and the residence of the papal court at Avignon was looked on by many contemporaries as a 'Babylonish captivity'. The court at Avignon was no doubt corrupt like all courts, certainly all papal courts in the Middle Ages, but not exceptionally so, and the moral disapproval which the Avignon papacy incurred has diverted attention from important historical circumstances. As far as real power was concerned, the Avignon period saw not a collapse but in many ways the culmination of the medieval papacy and the greatest extension of its influence.

There are two ways in which this judgement can be defended: one geographical, the other institutional. The development of the medieval papacy involved the extension of acceptance of its authority over nearly the whole continent of Europe. South-east Europe and the eastern Mediterranean had been closed by the refusal of the eastern churches to accept papal leadership in the eleventh century but since then the popes had progressively asserted their control over the churches of north-western Europe. The strengthening of the links with France was part of this process – the Kingdom of France was the centre of European culture and the king was usually the most powerful prince of the West. The settlement of the papal court at Avignon took place in 1305 partly because French political intervention disrupted central Italy and created divisions within the College of Cardinals and partly because the new pope at that time was the archbishop of Bordeaux. It was in some respects however a very natural culmination of the development of the medieval papacy. North-west Europe was much more accessible from Avignon than from Rome. When Petrarch condemned the residence of the popes at Avignon a French writer replied with some justice: 'The case for Avignon is established by the very situation of the place, which is more equidistant from the modern boundaries of the Catholic Church and whence our lord the pope may forever administer to the Christian faithful his spiritual medicine with more ease and equity.' Even the last of the Avignon popes, Gregory XI, who did eventually manage to return to Rome, several times put off his move because he found Avignon a more convenient place from which to mediate between the kings of France and England. For the papacy as it was at this time – essentially a western European, not a purely Italian or a Mediterranean institution – Avignon was almost an ideal residence.

It was during the Avignon period also that the papacy reached the height of the medieval growth of its administrative control over the western church. This is something rather different from spiritual prestige. None of the Avignon popes was a man of great prophetic authority or a great religious reformer. The papal court and its personnel were regarded by contemporaries with moderate or even exaggerated cynicism. The institutional power of the papacy however had never been so great. In the halls, offices and courtrooms of the Palace at Avignon – rebuilt with greater splendour by Clement VI (1342–52) who claimed that his predecessors 'did not know how to be popes' – decisions were taken every day which affected the lives of clerics and laymen all over Europe. The European churches had gradually come to accept that the papal court was the ultimate court of appeal in many cases, that the pope had a right to a say in a very large proportion of the appointments of clergy and that he had a right to certain kinds of financial support.

The pope was quite unlike other great powers: a spiritual authority with enormous temporal power, the ruler of an Italian state who drew most of his resources from outside Italy. Let us look first at his authority in the church as a whole. It can be largely traced to two things: (1) control over appointments to benefices and (2) financial rights to various kinds of dues and taxation.

The foundation of papal control over the personnel of the church as a whole was the doctrine that appointment to certain classes of benefices was 'reserved' to the Curia. These classes included for example benefices whose previous holders had died while they were at the Curia, benefices whose previous holders were deposed or deprived or which had become vacant through the holder being transferred to another benefice by a papal 'collation'. The multiplication of special and general reservations had proceeded far before the Avignon period and went on during it to the point where all appointment of bishops and priors of monasteries and a large proportion of ordinary parish rectories were reserved to the papacy. The original power to appoint these clergy might be in the hands of the monks of a monastery, the chapter of a cathedral, the local lord as patron of a village church, but however strongly they backed him the aspirant to one of these benefices had to go through the elaborate procedure of obtaining a 'provision' at the papal court before his election was valid. This system curtailed the independence of local authorities and was used by popes to some extent in the interest of sustaining their own court and bureaucracy by providing sinecures for their cardinals and officials and also in the interest of scholarship. Sinecures were provided for scholars working in universities and universities regularly sent up lists of graduates as candidates for benefices whom it was hoped the papacy would support in preference to less educated priests. Of course it was open to abuse, of which the most obvious kind was the collection of sinecures by cardinals. At the highest levels the administrative system became involved with politics. For example in 1366 Edward III of England was anxious to promote his favourite clerk, William of Wykeham, to the bishopric of Winchester. He secured his election but the papal provision had to be obtained so an embassy was sent to Avignon. It was a failure. Pope Urban V was not particularly well disposed either to Wykeham or to Edward III, whom the Pope suspected because he was negotiating a marriage alliance with an enemy of the papacy in Italy, Galeazzo Visconti, Duke of Milan. Next the king asked the Duke of Bourbon to use his influence with the pope; again no success. Finally the king sent another direct mission to the Curia with letters not only to the pope but to all the cardinals individually and offers to some of them of valuable benefices which Wykeham would vacate if he were appointed. This time it worked. The interesting thing is that the necessity of obtaining papal approval was sufficiently well established for Urban V to be able to use it as a weapon in diplomatic relations even with a great king near the height of his power. If that was so it is easy to imagine the awe with which it was regarded by lesser men even though in most cases the papal provisions they needed were matters of routine requiring only trouble and expense.

The papal court was largely supported by the funds derived from various conventional dues which were payable by churchmen all over Europe. The most important of these were essentially payments made by men newly appointed to benefices. New bishops and abbots paid 'services' which were often sums approaching a year's income from a see; for a great diocese it might be 10,000 florins. Lesser clergy who were provided to benefices were supposed to pay the first year's revenue to the pope. There was thus a fairly close connection between the extension of papal control over appointments and the papal income from the church. Payments of this kind were a good source of revenue because the individuals obliged to pay them were anxious to obtain the papal approval which gave them legal security. But in addition to occasional individual payments popes also claimed the right to tax beneficed clergy, in much the same way as kings taxed their subjects, by demanding a fraction of the assessed income from their benefices. The papacy had long ago established lists of assessments of benefices throughout Europe so it was a relatively simple matter to present the clergy of a province by means of a letter to their archbishop with a demand for money and to apportion the burden among them. To enforce the demand was a different matter. Popes were met with obstinate refusal not only by the clergy but, even more effectively, by local princes who did not like the spectacle of gold flowing out of their countries to Avignon. In spite of enormous obstacles however, papal rights of taxation were theoretically accepted and were often an important source of income.

The popes at Avignon had the most elaborate court in Europe, a palace with the bureaucratic appurtenances of royal government to serve operations on a European instead of merely a national scale. The Chancery contained the writers of bulls and letters. The Apostolic Chamber was the financial office receiving the payments and keeping the accounts. The many legal disputes about rights to benefices were decided by a court called the Rota. Dispensations and moral censures were entrusted to the Penitentiary. These institutions required hundreds of officials who, together with the hordes of cardinals' servants, merchants, bankers, lawyers and visiting litigants and dignitaries gave Avignon its peculiar flavour as a cosmopolitan capital city, the smell and bustle of which drove Petrarch to look for peace and quiet in the countryside at Mont Ventoux.

But the pope was a lord with two natures; a spiritual head in Europe, a temporal prince in Italy. Though for most of the time from 1305 to 1377 the popes were at Avignon, for a great deal of that time their political attention was concentrated on their temporal possessions in Italy, the band of territory which stretched diagonally across the peninsula with its northern and southern extremities at Bologna and Terracina. The papal state was a temporal kingdom but a kingdom of an exception- ally troublesome and intractable kind. It was conventionally divided into the provinces of Romagna, the March of Ancona, the Duchy of Spoleto, the Patrimony of St Peter and Campagna and Marittima but these provinces give no indication of the complicated and fragmented sovereignties out of which the papal state was built. The papal lordship consisted of a col- lection of particular lordships and jurisdictions over com- munities, communes and lords which had never been effectively cemented into a general sense of belonging to a political community such as that which gave coherence to the political life of, say, England, Flanders or Bohemia. The pope's subjects included powerful and semi-independent lords and cities with developed communal institutions such as the Malatesta lords of Rimini and the commune of Perugia. The boundaries of his lordship were very much disputed, especially in the north where Bologna, the largest city of the state, was held, when it was held at all, in uneasy and fitful subjection. He was vulner- able to external dangers from two directions in particular. Firstly from the German aspirants to the title of Roman Emperor who wanted coronation at Rome and had traditional imperial claims to loyalties in Italy which could be used by enemies of the pope. These had worn thin by 1320 but they still played some part in the politics of the next two decades. Secondly from the great expanding power of the north, the duchy of Milan, which was beginning to cast its eyes outside

Lombardy in the direction of Romagna and was to become a dangerous rival.

The jurisdictional claims which constituted the pope's authority in the papal state had been built up over centuries. In spite of their absence from Italy the Avignon popes were certainly not less tenacious in holding on to them than their predecessors had been and a remarkable effort of reconquest and reconstruction was undertaken in the years following 1353 when the enterprise was entrusted by Innocent VI to the Castilian churchman and soldier Cardinal Gil Albornoz Archbishop of Toledo. The Avignon period saw therefore no diminution of papal control in central Italy and no fading of the prominence of the papal state as an object of policy though much of the direction of the administration was in the hands of foreigners – Albornoz was a Spaniard, many of the most important administrators were Frenchmen. In the eyes of Italians papal rule came to have increasingly the appearance of an alien domination exercised indecently by barbarians over the descendants of the Romans.

The maintenance of papal political interests in Italy required continual and extremely costly military effort which the papal state itself was totally unable to support. Only the ecclesiastical resources of north-western Europe could enable the popes to maintain their position in Italy. It has been estimated that the annual income of Pope Gregory XI (1370–8) 'varied between 200,000 and 300,000 gold cameral florins annually of which not more than a quarter came from the Papal State'. The nature of the papacy as a political institution hinged on this basic material relationship. Most of its money came from the 'collectories' into which Europe was divided for convenience: one for England, one for Germany, one for Portugal, several in France. Maintaining this European ecclesiastical empire was of course a constant problem which taxed the relatively efficient French bureaucracy of the Avignon popes. The effort put into it is indicated for example by the experiences of one of the officials, a priest named Bertrand du Mazel, whose career has been reconstructed. Urban V sent him to Germany as collector of the papal tenth in 1366. After battles with the local clergy and imprisonment he got back to Avignon without much money. In 1368 he was sent on a mission to the four collectories of the Iberian peninsula where he struggled hard to get together some of the arrears due from Portugal, backed up by a threat of interdict and the actual excommunication of the Archbishop of Braga. In 1371 his assignment was the collection of a subsidy in Sicily while he again met violence and danger. In 1376 after a decade of tough jobs he was rewarded with the position of Treasurer of War in Italy, to receive and disburse the money which collectors like himself squeezed out of other parts of Europe.

Though the papal bureaucracy, even in Italy, was increasingly French, the management and indeed the whole centralized organization of the church's finances was dependent upon the Italian banker. The transfer of papal moneys to Avignon and Italy, the prompt lending of money to pay for military expeditions when the papal treasury was empty, the financing of payments and visits to Avignon by postulants and litigants – all these functions were indispensably performed by Italian bankers. Only they had the network of representatives necessary for financial dealings on a European scale and only they had the reserves of cash at Avignon and in Italy to finance papal operations. They were inextricably involved in papal government and indeed the two sets of institutions – the papal control of the church and the Italian financial network – had grown up together since the twelfth century in mutual interdependence. The leading part in this business was taken by Tuscan firms, especially Florentine, which for most of the Avignon period were honoured and influential members of the papal court. A Florentine aspirant to a benefice in 1364 was advised to get letters of recommendation to the papal court from the Archbishop of Genoa, the general of the Franciscan Order and a member of the Alberti banking family. The connection between commerce and papal business is indicated by this piece of advice offered somewhat later in an Italian merchant's handbook: 'At Genoa money is dear in September, January and April because of the departure of the ships . . . at Rome, where the pope is, the price of money varies according to the number of benefices vacant and the movements of the pope who raises the price of money wherever he is . . . at

Montpellier there are three fairs which cause a great dearness of money.'

The papal court of the Avignon period, though cosmopolitan, was predominantly southern French in character. Of 134 cardinals created by the Avignon popes well over half came from the Limousin, Quercy, Gascony, Narbonnais and other districts of the Midi. John XXII wrote to Charles IV of France on one occasion saying that he found the king's letters difficult to follow because he had forgotten the *langue d'oil* during long use of the *langue d'oc*. Nevertheless it was undoubtedly with the French court at Paris that the papacy had the closest ties and common interests. How did the popes manage the difficult and complex feat of managing at the same time their interests in Italy, their connections with France and their position in the western church as a whole?

John XXII (1316–34) enjoyed the longest of the Avignon pontificates and was perhaps the toughest politician. He was a canon lawyer from Cahors and had been bishop of Avignon. He set the pattern for his successors. In retrospect one can see that John XXII was faced by three threats to his conception of the papal position. One was the enthusiasm of the Spirituals in the Franciscan Order who wanted to tie their order – a very important element in the church as a whole – to the ideal of apostolic poverty. John effectively suppressed this movement – that episode is described in a later chapter (below, p. 152). The second was the pretension of the ambitious German King Lewis the Bavarian (see above, p. 54) who wanted to be accepted as Roman Emperor. The third was the threat of the expansive power of Milan under Matteo Visconti. John's crucial objective was to defend the northern part of the papal state against the intervention of Visconti and Lewis and it was to this aim that he devoted the main political effort of his pontificate. The command in Italy was entrusted to another churchman from southern France, Cardinal Bertrand du Poujet, in 1319 and under his leadership papal armies were almost continually fighting until John XXII's death. The result was not very successful. Lewis the Bavarian did get to Rome and stage a coronation in 1328. When John XXII died, Bologna and the Romagna were out of his control. This, however, was the pattern of Avignon policy clearly manifested: an unyielding insistence on the traditional hierarchical authority of the papacy (John and his great administrative assistant Gasbert de Laval the Chamberlain, greatly extended control over benefices) determination to control the papal state, friendship with the court of France, resistance to the powers of Milan and the empire.

His successor Benedict XII (1334–42) from Foix in south-west France was a Cistercian monk and a theologian who had much less interest in temporal politics and much more in promoting a crusade and trying to prevent the great war between France and England which started during his pontificate. But although he played down the papal aims in Italy and the expansion of the papal court he did not reverse tendencies and his successor was in contrast the grandest of the Avignon popes. This was Clement VI (1342–52). His original name was Pierre Roger, he came from the neighbourhood of Limoges and he was a Benedictine monk and a canon lawyer. Before he became pope he had reached an outstanding administrative position in the service of the French crown: he had been Archbishop of Rouen and Chancellor of France. It fell to him as it happened to crush the attempt of Cola di Rienzo to refound a Roman republic: the natural reaction of a seigniorial lord to a movement which embodied Italian dreams of millennial revival and of classical reawakening but which was politically feeble and must have seemed contemptible to him. Clement was relatively inactive in Italy. He proclaimed a jubilee which attracted crowds of pilgrims to Rome in 1350, but he did not go there himself. He allowed Bologna to remain under the control of the Visconti. Clement conceived his role as pope after the pattern of the kings and lords of the northern courts where he was at home. He bought the city of Avignon from Queen Joanna of Naples and developed the palace. He would have liked to promote a crusade to help the Christians of the East; other Western powers were in practice indifferent to such plans. Though the Black Death, which was eventually to have profound effects on the position of the papacy by undermining the high population level on which its income ultimately depended, occurred during his pontificate, he was the supreme example of the pope as a great *seigneur*. Like other great *seigneurs* he succeeded in founding a dynasty. The next pope but two (Gregory XI) was his nephew.

Innocent VI (1352–62) was a Limousin canon lawyer. The most remarkable fact about his pontificate is that he set in motion the successful reconquest of the papal state by Albornoz. With his successor Urban V (1362–70) the impulse to leave Avignon and return to Rome – which had always been a declared policy though not very seriously pursued – acquired a new urgency. Urban was not only a monk, he seems to have had more of the idealist in his character than his politically prudent predecessors. He took the crusading idea very seriously and seems to have thought that he could persuade the King of France and Bernabò Visconti, who was given Bologna as a pledge, to lead an expedition against the infidel. He was mistaken. But the return to Rome was within his power. He went there in 1367 and though he did not move the papal administration, stayed himself for two years. The renewal of war between France and England in 1369 brought him back to Avignon from where he hoped to be able to act as a mediator, to reunite Europe again for the purpose of the Crusade; but he was dead within a few months. In his place the cardinals elected as Gregory XI (1370–8) Pierre Roger de Beaufort, nephew of Clement VI, whose career symbolized the nepotism of Avignon. He had been a canon at the age of eleven and a cardinal at nineteen. The early years of his pontificate were dominated by a bitter war with Milan of the traditional kind but he turned out to be a man of inflexible, self-sacrificing idealism who subordinated everything to the dream of a crusade and in the end to the return to Rome which was to be politically disastrous for the papacy.

It is difficult to enter sympathetically into the amalgam of princely power and spiritual authority which made up the world of the Avignon popes. Gregory XI's will protected the inherited property of his family from papal claims, but pledged the revenues of the papacy from Germany, England and Iberia for the establishment of a college of monks at the church where he wished to be buried. But although the seigniorial family sense was very strong there is equally no doubt that Gregory had a grandiose idea of his mission as the leader and inspirer of Christian kings. The two components were present in varying degrees in all the Avignon popes. Avignon was an artificial capital where they were exceptionally cut off from the springs of piety – much more so than at Rome – and this accentuated the remote bureaucratic formalism of their rule. As long as it lasted, however, the union of the see of St Peter with the seigniorial church of the dioceses of north-west Europe made the most impressive hierarchical imperialism that Europe has ever seen. Later ecclesiastical authorities have been pale copies of it.

iv *Italian Politics to 1378*

Italy then as now was a geographical area containing cultures at vastly different levels. The differences within small distances – from the cosmopolitan sophistication of a Tuscan city to the solitude of the Apennines a few miles away – could be great. There was also the broad distinction between north and south. Italy south of Rome was a backward country, a different world from the centres of the north but politically it was a relatively stable kingdom. The Kingdom of Naples was ruled at the beginning of this period by King Robert the Wise (1309–43) a member of a French dynasty descended from a Count of Anjou who had conquered Naples at the invitation of the pope in the thirteenth century. The kings of Naples also claimed to rule Sicily but this was in fact held by a prince of the house of Aragon, King Frederick II. They did however rule as counts in Provence and King Robert had the lordship of various north Italian cities. Naples, with its well developed royal administration was for Italians still the *Regno*, 'The Kingdom,' the most impressive power in the peninsula. But it was in some respects a fragile political structure. The power of the nobility was great. Commerce and public finance were controlled by the great Florentine merchant houses who had established an almost colonial domination.

A glance at the political map of Italy north of Naples shows that it contained two powers larger than the others but each of rather uncertain dimensions and potentialities. The pope ruled over the papal state, a very large area but very insecurely held together. In the valley of the Po Matteo Visconti (1295-1322) held a lordship which included not only the great city of Milan but also some of the surrounding cities and increasingly dominated the plain of Lombardy. Unlike the papal state this was a compact and aggressive power. The pope and the tyrant of Milan were the most powerful forces in northern Italy. But neither of them could hope to dominate it. They were not the only major powers which had an interest in the area. The German King Lewis of Bavaria (see above, p. 54) claimed imperial rights in Italy and the power to exercise these rights by appointing imperial vicars, one of whom was the tyrant of Milan. These claims were bitterly opposed by the pope who responded to the Imperial-Milanese threat by calling on the traditional papal ally Naples. He set up King Robert as a rival vicar to those appointed by Lewis. The main powers to be reckoned with in northern Italy around 1320 were then the pope, the King of Germany, the tyrant of Milan and the King of Naples. Except for Milan all of these powers were partially or entirely external to the region. Most of the area of northern Italy was made up of states which were relatively weak politically. Some of them – notably Florence, Venice and Genoa were strikingly advanced and of great European importance from an economic and social point of view. Within the predominantly seigniorial world of the early fourteenth century, however, commercial pre-eminence did not yet confer great political power on them. They did not command great armies of knights and archers and though their governments were of course capable of producing large sums of money they could not rival the command over conventional armies which could be exercised by a king of Naples or still more by a king of France. It is at first sight paradoxical that the financial resources of the Bardi and Peruzzi, two private Florentine companies, could exercise a decisive influence in the policy of the King of England while, about the same time, the commune of Florence placed itself under the government of a rather obscure French soldier of fortune, Walter of Brienne, (see above, p. 82). The paradox however does represent the real position of the commercial cities. Though their wealth made them attractive prey they were still small fry in the world of royal and seigniorial rivalries. Northern Italy was therefore largely a political vacuum, a field in which the rivalries of great powers were played out. Petrarch, reflecting on Italian politics with humanist nostalgia in the middle of the century said, 'nature gave us as defences the Alps, the sea, the passes of the mountains closed as a gift of God. With the keys of avarice and pride we have opened them to the Cimbri, the Huns, the Pannonians, the Gauls, the Teutons and the Spaniards'. Divisions and rivalry between small political units made Italy continually a prey to invaders from the north. The Italian states were traditionally divided into two groups, the 'Guelfs', supporters of the papacy, and the 'Ghibellines', supporters of the emperor. This division which dated from the conflicts between popes and emperors for control of Italy in the twelfth and thirteenth centuries no longer necessarily corresponded to any real division of opinion about central matters of political thought or even about the political constitution of Italy. It owed its continuance to the fact that here as in any political situation the states tended to align themselves in two groups held together by certain continuities of political interest. The last revival of the traditional quarrel between pope and emperor as a real political issue, in the time of John XXII and Lewis the Bavarian, meant however that the Guelf-Ghibelline division took on a new lease of life for a generation and has to be included among the distinctive features of the period.

In 1320 Robert the Wise was the strongest power in Italy. In addition to his kingdom of Naples he commanded, as acknowledged leader of the Guelfs, the allegiance of a number of states in the north. He was titular lord of Florence and papal rector in Romagna. He had established himself by intervention as lord of Genoa. The Guelf alliance was faced by two substantial rulers who claimed the title of imperial vicar in Lombardy, Matteo Visconti of Milan and Can Grande della Scala the tyrant of Verona, so that Lombardy was effectively a Ghibelline area and anti-papal forces here posed a serious threat to the papal state. It was for this reason that John XXII sent Cardinal Bertrand du Poujet to Italy with French troops and money in 1320 and also conducted a campaign of heresy accusations against the Lombard Ghibellines. In 1322 Matteo Visconti died, to be succeeded by his son Galeazzo (1322–8). It looked as though du Poujet might be able to crush Milan.

After Lewis the Bavarian had established his claim to the throne of Germany by his victory at the battle of Mühldorf in 1322, he was able to turn his attention seriously to Italy and his imperial claims. The revival of serious German leadership by Lewis gave new .strength to the Lombard Ghibellines. He and John XXII were declared enemies, Lewis claiming imperial rights in Italy, John claiming that he had been elected king without papal acquiescence so that even his kingdom was illegitimately held. Italian politics were dominated for a while by a duel between them. In 1327–9 Lewis made his expedition to Italy. First he went to Milan where he was crowned King of Lombardy. Then he went on through Tuscany to Rome itself where he was crowned emperor by the city magistrates and he nominated an antipope. Robert of Naples sent galleys up the Tiber, forcing Lewis to leave Rome. He moved slowly back north to Germany. Lewis's expedition was the last occasion on which a German king in defiance of the opposition of the papacy, marched to Rome and had himself crowned emperor. One of the recurrent patterns of medieval politics, sustained by the chivalric ambitions of the German nobility and the lure of Italian wealth thus came to an end.

Lewis left the Italian scene somewhat changed. The position of Milan was temporarily weakened. The most powerful state in the north was for a time Verona ruled by Mastino della Scala (1329–51). To balance him a new and unexpected German fortune-seeker, King John of Bohemia, was invited into Italy in 1329. John of Bohemia stepped for a time, with papal approval, into the position of Guelf leader in Lombardy and was supported by du Poujet, but the opposition was too strong and he left Italy in 1333 thoroughly defeated by the Visconti and della Scala. The della Scala state based on Verona grew to enormous proportions in the years 1335–7 for Mastino became lord of Parma, Reggio and Lucca so that his dominion stretched across Italy almost from the Alps to the Mediterranean but the possibility that Verona might replace Milan as the dominant power of the north did not materialize. Guelfs and Ghibellines allied against him and by 1341 the Veronese state had been reduced to its old proportions. The conflicting ambitions of John XXII, Robert of Naples, and Lewis of Bavaria gave some unity to Italian politics in the 1320s and 1330s. After that time, though the names were often used, the Guelf-Ghibelline issue was dead. The death of Robert in 1343 removed the last major politician whose career could usefully be described in those terms.

In the general political history of Italy in the second half of the fourteenth century the outstanding feature is undoubtedly the continuance of the rise to ascendancy of Milan after the interlude produced by Lewis's intervention. The Visconti family continued to produce masterful and ambitious rulers. Azzone (1328–39) added Como, Lodi, Vercelli, Piacenza and Brescia, to the towns which had submitted to the Visconti, leaving his heirs a substantial confederation of cities in central Lombardy. Luchino (1339–49) extended control to much of eastern Lombardy. From 1444 to 1446 he carried on a war, involving most of the neighbouring lordships, for the city of Parma. In 1347 he turned his attention to the west and acquired Alessandria. His successor was his brother Giovanni (1349–54) who was also Archbishop of Milan and ruled both church and state effectively. His successes in the temporal world were spectacular. Archbishop Giovanni was the initiator of the Visconti policy of ruthless expansion beyond the confines of Lombardy which made Milan for a century the chief motive force in Italian politics as a whole. In 1349 a rising in Bologna against papal rule gave him the opportunity to step in and acquire the lordship of the city. He confirmed the powers of the city council with a proviso which sums up the characteristic relationship of the tyrant to the commune in fourteenth-century Italy 'saving always our commands in all things to be ordained by us'. The lordship of Bologna was a very different matter from the lordship of Brescia or Como; Archbishop Giovanni had now entered into the spheres of influence of other ma or powers. His attack on the papacy led to his excommunication but bribery on a vast scale at Avignon eventually secured the acceptance even by the papacy of the *fait accompli*. In 1351 and 1352 his armies were pressing further afield again towards Florence. In 1353 Genoa, terribly weakened by a war against Venice, was his next victim and he was made lord of that city. These extensions were not permanent but they show how dangerous Milanese power was becoming, even beyond Lombardy. His unexpected death in 1354 was a cause of relief to most other Italian powers.

Between 1354 and 1357, fall the campaigns conducted by Cardinal Albornoz to restore and extend papal power in the papal state. As a modern historian has said, 'Albornoz applied to the Papal State the mentality and skills which he had acquired in the direction of the Castilian *Reconquista*'. He moved northwards from Rome subduing the pope's unruly subjects in succession: the lord of Vico and the city of Orvieto, the Malatesta lords at Rimini, the lord of Cesena, and eventually in 1360 Bologna. He also made a little progress in the difficult business of moulding the papal state into a more unified structure by calling assemblies and by issuing the Aegidian Constitutions in which its laws were partially codified. Albornoz of course profited from the death of Archbishop Giovanni Visconti and was able to recover Bologna. But eventually he came into conflict with Giovanni's successor Bernabò and the papacy had to submit in 1364 to a peace by which the Milanese tyrant was paid a substantial sum of money. Albornoz did not cure the essential weakness of the papal state, its lack of unifying institutions. He did, however, establish a buffer against Milanese expansion. He also committed the popes to a long struggle with Milan hinging on the control of the great city of Bologna where their spheres of influence met.

The Visconti lands passed from Giovanni to two nephews, Galeazzo II and Bernabò, who divided the dominions between them and maintained ⌐e tradition of despotism and expansion. Galeazzo took the western half and decided early in his reign to incorporate Pavia, at that time still independent. He took it after a long siege in 1359 and thereafter made it his head-quarters. Bernabò, an extraordinary man whose cruelty and sensuality were legendary, took over the Archbishop's policy of expansion towards the papal state and Tuscany and there-fore also his conflict with the church. The earlier part of his reign coincided with the reconstruction of the papal state by Albornoz, the latter part saw the return of a pope to Italy. This conflict continued with brief intervals from the beginning of his reign until 1375. It culminated in a very bitter war from 1371 to 1375 fought against Bernabò by Gregory XI with the help of Padua, Genoa, Florence and Savoy in which the papacy successfully employed armies commanded by the English captain, John Hawkwood. The efforts of the popes contained Milanese expansion. In 1375, apart from the acquisition of Pavia, the Visconti had not significantly improved on the position attained by Archbishop Giovanni. The pope still precariously held his position at Bologna. Then came the great revolt of the papal state coinciding with Gregory's return to Rome and an alliance of Milan and Florence against the papacy (see below, p. 170).

Milan and the pope contended for the dominant position in northern Italy. Other powers had more peripheral or local interests. Genoa accepted for some years the lordship of Robert of Naples and for a short time that of Giovanni Visconti. These were intervals in the disturbed but generally republican politics of the city. Genoa was never a great power on the mainland, but in 1350 began a new epoch in Genoese-Venetian rivalry in the eastern Mediterranean which led to extensive fighting both there and in Italy. In the war which lasted from 1350 to 1355 each of the two cities won a serious naval battle, Venice at La Loiera off the coast of Sardinia, Genoa at Sapientza off the Peloponnese. Twenty years later in 1376 one of the most bitter wars of the century broke out between the two republics, the so-called War of Chioggia. The conflict arose over claims to the Island of Tenedos in the Aegean. Two rival claimants to the Byzantine throne had granted it to Venice and Genoa. The war of Chioggia derives its name from the fact that, in 1379, a Genoese force with great

daring established itself at Chioggia across the lagoon from
Venice. They were eventually defeated but the war dragged
on into 1381 when the two cities made peace at Turin, both
financially and morally exhausted by a war which is perhaps
the most remarkable clash of two rival commercial empires
in the Middle Ages.

In some ways the most extraordinary episode in Italian
politics in the mid-fourteenth century was the career of Cola
di Rienzo. Cola (short for Niccola) was a Roman notary of
humble origins who built up a world of fantasy based partly on
classical reminiscences of the ancient glory of Rome (supported
by study of the ancient inscriptions with which the city was
littered) and millennial hopes of a holy empire which he picked
up from religious enthusiasts. The real Rome was at this time
a miserable place, forsaken by the papal court and fought over
by the local nobility. Cola travelled to Avignon in 1343 in an
attempt to persuade the pope to recognize his Roman obligations and met Petrarch who sympathized with him. In 1347
he emerged at the head of a popular insurrection at Rome, set
himself up with popular approval as 'tribune' and for six
months ruled the city. His government was a strange, visionary
mixture of communal republicanism and ideas of extending
Rome's function to the leadership of all Italy or even the world.
At his height he called himself 'Candidatus Spiritus Sancti
miles Nicolaus Severus et Clemens liberator Urbis zelator
Italiae amator Orbis et Tribunus augustus.' The combination
was to have some influence in Italian thought, in which the
ideas of classical republicanism and Italian unity were to be
important, but Cola di Rienzo's régime was short-lived. A
papal legate secured his overthrow before the year was out and
Rome relapsed into its previous condition.

The death of Robert of Naples in 1343 ended an era in
Naples itself as well as in the pattern of international politics.
The succession was not secure. Robert's direct heir was a girl,
his granddaughter Joanna I. Her position was disputed from
two sides. Firstly, from the Hungarian branch of the Angevin
family, the head of which was now King Lewis the Great of
Hungary, a powerful prince. (Robert had attempted to neutralize
this danger in advance by betrothing Joanna to Lewis the

Great's brother, Andrew.) Secondly from another branch of
the Neapolitan Angevins, the house of Taranto. Joanna turned
out to be, in the early years of her reign at least, an extremely
unsuitable ruler for such a perilous political situation – remote
from political realities and interested chiefly in the amorous
intrigues with which she surrounded herself at court. A
considerable part was played by Pope Clement VI who,
although far distant at Avignon, had a keen interest in the
preservation of political stability at Naples, both because the
pope was the titular feudal overlord of the kingdom and
because of the importance of Neapolitan relations for the
papal state. A succession of papal legates attempted to manage
the politics of the kingdom. Two years after Joanna had succeeded to the throne, her Hungarian husband – a rough
fellow for whom she and her court had shown little sympathy –
was murdered in obscure circumstances, perhaps with the
connivance of Joanna or her relatives of the line of Taranto.
The kingdom was plunged into civil war. Eventually reconciliation was effected between Joanna's supporters and the
family of Taranto based on a marriage with one of them,
Lewis, which took place in 1347. A major part was played in
this settlement by one of the most remarkable figures in
fourteenth-century Italy, Niccolò Acciaiuoli, a member of a
great Florentine merchant family in whom the political effects
of Florentine commercial imperialism in the kingdom of
Naples reached its culmination. He had established a unique
position for himself in Naples as a confidant of the Angevin
family and played a central role in its politics.

The greatest danger however was Hungarian invasion by
Lewis the Great which actually materialized in 1347. Lewis
brought an army of Hungarians and Germans down the
peninsula. Joanna fled by sea to Marseilles and then Avignon –
which was indeed her own property until she sold it to the
pope to pay her current expenses. The invading king, burning
to revenge his brother, imprisoned and killed some of his
Neapolitan cousins. He could not establish a secure control
over the turbulent Neapolitan nobility. Joanna returned to her
kingdom. Her forces, organized by Niccolò Acciaiuoli, were
defeated by the Hungarians even though Lewis the Great

had gone and the war dragged on for years through another invasion in 1350. Not until 1352 was an effective settlement made both within the kingdom and with the Hungarian king. For the next decade Joanna reigned with Lewis of Taranto. The real ruler was Acciaiuoli. The decline of Neapolitan power continued but the internal history of the state was relatively peaceful from 1362 until Joanna's support of the Avignonese pope after the Great Schism of 1378 gave the opportunity for another Hungarian invasion. Joanna herself was murdered and the new conflict initiated another period of instability in Neapolitan politics with repercussions in Italian history as a whole.

In 1380 the native north Italian powers were fewer and larger than they had been in 1320. Verona had declined from its great days and was to be swallowed up in Milan in 1387. Milan, Venice and Florence were all bigger: the process of gradual absorption of the smaller communes in larger states had progressed. The only important newcomer was Savoy which Amadeus VI (1343–83), the 'Green Count' had greatly enlarged and made into one of the main powers in the Italian world, though never in this period a very aggressive one. The influence of foreign powers in the north Italian world was changing. German princes now played a negligible part: the visit of the Emperor Charles IV to Rome for his coronation in 1364 was unpretentious and rapid though he was a great king in central Europe. The attempt of another King of Germany, Rupert of the Palatinate, to intervene in Italy in 1401 was a fiasco. The French crown played little part in Italy in the late Avignon period, in contrast with the opening years of the century when Philip IV's emissaries sacked the pope's palace at Anagni. More powerful Italian states were emerging out of the political fragmentation of the peninsula.

One of the events which Italians have often regarded as symbolic of an epoch in their history took place in 1379 when an Italian force of mercenary soldiers led by Alberico da Barbiano fighting for the Roman Pope Urban VI defeated a Breton mercenary force fighting for the schismatic French Pope Clement VII at Marino. This event has been taken to symbolize the end of the dominance of foreign troops over

Italian politics. There is some truth in this idea, though the significance of the change is not clear. In the thirteenth and early fourteenth centuries the arbiters of Italian politics had very often been armies imported into the peninsula by French or German rulers. When foreign political intervention ceased to be so important there followed a period (about 1340–80) during which a very prominent part was played by independent companies of mercenary soldiers from Germany, France or England. The Italian cities could not by this time rely on armies of their own citizens. The pope did not have the kind of feudal hierarchy in the papal state which helped to provide armies for lay kings in other countries. An Italian state which needed an army, made an agreement, a *condotta*, with a mercenary captain. The captains and their employees were called *condottieri*. There were of course Italian condottieri but for about a generation the foreigners were on the whole more prominent. The most famous example is Sir John Hawkwood, an Essex knight whose company achieved legendary success in the 1370s and after, when they fought at various times and at high prices for the pope, Milan and Florence. Though he was the perpetrator of atrocities, Hawkwood was commemorated after his death by a fresco on the wall of the cathedral of Florence which had owed many victories to him. The age of the Companies in Italy was in part a side effect of the Hundred Years War and should perhaps be explained by the evolution of other European states, rather than the evolution of Italy. The generation following the Black Death and the collapse of France after the Battle of Poitiers was a period when the states of northern Europe were less capable of providing profitable employment for soldiers than they had been; the Italian cities were more attractive paymasters. The Companies were the last stage of political dominance of medieval seigniorial Europe over Italy. For a century to come Italians were to control their own politics more than they had in the past.

CHAPTER III

ECONOMIC AND SOCIAL FORCES

i *Population*

The first two chapters of this book have been largely devoted to describing the social and political structures of Europe in the years between 1320 and 1380: the industrial and commercial cities of Italy and the Netherlands, the papacy, the aristocracies and monarchies of northern and western Europe. These structures, the typical social forms of what is commonly called 'medieval' Europe were the product of a long period of uninterrupted material growth and expansion extending from the eleventh century to the early fourteenth century. Throughout this period there appears to have been generally a continuous expansion of population, an increase in the areas of land cultivated and an increase of commercial activity which tended to strengthen the social structures based upon the European economy. Noble estate owners, kings, commercial cities, bishops and popes all developed more elaborate and powerful institutions fed by the wealth which they extracted from an expanding economy. The great monarchs of the mid-fourteenth century, Pope John XXII, Edward III of England, the Emperor Charles IV, Charles V of France, were the beneficiaries of medieval expansion, manipulating state systems more intricate and effective than those of their predecessors; the cities of Bruges, Venice and Florence rested on a highly developed commercial system.

In the next century, extending from about 1350 to about 1450 most historians have discerned a fundamental break in the development of Europe. Expansion along the old lines of development ceased. A number of historians have described this period as an age of 'contraction' or 'depression'. The general phenomenon appears in a variety of widespread manifestations, some of them basic economic and social features – decline in population, decline in the volume of trade, contraction of areas under cultivation – and some more complex social changes such as decline in the authority of the nobility over their tenants, social revolutions by the lower classes, decline in the authority of the established church and of princes. This is the only period in the history of Europe, at least since the Dark Ages, for which historians would postulate a general and prolonged contraction. It therefore presents very unusual problems of interpretation and has a peculiar status in European history. It also contains features which are at first sight difficult to fit into a general picture of 'contraction', for instance, the beginnings of voyages of exploration in the Atlantic and the beginnings of what are usually called Renaissance thought and art in the Italian cities. Much of the rest of this book will be concerned with exploring the problems raised by the development of European society in a period of material contraction.

It is best to start from the most basic feature of society, population. Before plunging into this question it will be as well to make clear that medieval demography is a very insecure subject. This is a period long before the days of censuses. Absolute figures of population even for restricted areas at one time are rare. Most statements about medieval population, and especially about population trends are hypotheses based on the interpretation of indirect evidence such as the relationship between wages and prices or changes in rents. Nevertheless, the accumulation of evidence and interpretation is now considerable and there are some things which can be said about population with reasonable confidence.

The population of fourteenth-century Europe was struck by two major natural catastrophes. The first of these was the European Famine of 1315–17. Exceptionally bad weather produced a series of bad harvests from 1314 to 1316. The price of grain rose to unprecedented heights; food was extremely scarce. Over a great part of north-west Europe (there is evidence from France, the Netherlands, Germany, England and Scandinavia) mortality from famine was high. It has been estimated for example that more than ten per cent of the population of Ypres died within 6 months in 1316.

The second catastrophe was of quite a different kind and

was more general and more severe. At the end of 1347 the
Black Death carried by rats imported by ships from the Near
East reached Marseilles. It spread rapidly to the rest of
Europe, Italy, Spain, France and southern England in 1348,
Germany, the Netherlands, central Europe, in 1349. Some
parts of Europe did escape it, but not many. Estimates of the
death rate vary enormously but they are generally somewhere
between ten and fifty per cent of the population. Contemporary writings are full of expressions of horror at the disease
and of the deaths resulting from it; the most famous of course
is the prologue to Boccaccio's *Decameron* in which the story-
tellers flee from the city of Florence to a suburban villa to
escape infection. Modern investigators have collected much
evidence from documents such as lists of tenants which are
difficult to convert into percentages of the population but
certainly indicate a heavy mortality. Thereafter plague was
endemic in Europe for the rest of the period covered by this
book and for long after. No outbreak on anything like the scale
of the first one occurred but many towns and regions were
attacked by the disease at one time and another and suffered
severe loss of life.

The Great Famine and the Great Plague have been taken by
historians to signify two kinds of reasons why the population
of Europe fell in the late medieval period. Firstly the population rise of the eleventh to fourteenth centuries had produced
a very heavily populated countryside living precariously with
primitive methods of agriculture and therefore vulnerable to
famine. The high mortality and the high prices of food
produced by the harvest failures of 1315–17 indicate that the
population was dangerously near the margin of subsistence.
The land could not easily support such a population without
improved agricultural methods. As such advances in technique
did not appear there was a natural limit to population growth.
Secondly from the mid-fourteenth century, Europe was
subject to outbreaks of disease which tended to reduce population and prevent it from recovering its old levels.

There is much uncertainty about the relationship between
these factors and the actual levels of population. And there
may have been other factors, in particular social controls on

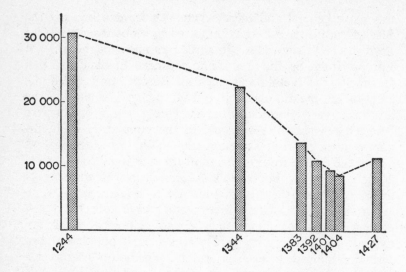

POPULATION OF THE COUNTRYSIDE OF PISTOIA
(after D. Herlihy, *Population, Plague and Social Change in Rural Pistoia,
1201-1430*, Economic History Review, Second Series, XVIII, 1965, 233)

population by changes in the age of marriage or restrictions on
family size which we do not know about. There is, however, a
good deal of independent evidence to suggest that in many
parts of Europe population continued to fall from the mid-
fourteenth century until some time in the first half of the
fifteenth century or even later. It has been calculated that the
population of the contado, the countryside around Pistoia,
near Florence, fell from over 30,000 in the mid-thirteenth
century to about 24,000 before the Black Death, under 10,000
in 1404 and about 12,000 in 1427; that the population of the
Ile-de-France was halved between 1348 and 1444; that the
population of Toulouse fell from 30,000 in 1335 to 8000 in
1430. Calculations of this kind, insecure because they usually
depend on tax assessments, rent rolls, lists of households and
not on censuses of all the people in one place, but nevertheless
impressive because they so often tell a similar story, exist for
many parts of Europe. In many parts of Europe also the combination of written and archaeological evidence proves the

existence of deserted villages, places which had been in-
habited earlier, but were abandoned some time in the fourteenth or fifteenth centuries. In substantial parts of Germany,
particularly the region between the Weser and the Elbe,
forty per cent of the medieval villages are said to have disappeared. Lost villages are also known to be very common for
example in parts of eastern England and southern Italy. The
evidence is not all uniform; there are places where population
appears to have risen. But it is difficult to avoid the conclusion
that in most parts of Europe there were many fewer people in
the first half of the fifteenth century than there had been a
century earlier.

ii *Landlords*

The most obvious effect of the long depression of population
in the century from 1350 to 1450 was to weaken and undermine
the social structures based on agriculture. In the medieval
world the large societies based entirely on industry and
commerce were comparatively few, apart from northern
Italy, the southern Netherlands and the Rhineland, only a
few scattered cities; towns of lesser size were numerous but
they were small enclaves in a largely agricultural world. Most
of Europe was dominated by landlords. The social prestige
and political power of both the lay nobility and the upper
ranks of the clergy were closely dependent upon the possession
of the profits of landowning. The activities of these upper
classes, fighting, politics, prayer, administration, frequently
had little to do with estate management but their social
position was ultimately dependent upon it. The nobility
presided over a very sharply hierarchical society including a
large segment of very poor people. The population of some
parts of rural Picardy in the late thirteenth century has been
analysed as follows: 12 per cent beggars or occasional wage
labourers, 33 per cent with very small plots of land eked out
by labour for others, 36 per cent with small plots barely
supporting livelihood, 16 per cent with larger farms up to
$7\frac{1}{2}$ acres, 3 per cent richer peasants and lords lay or clerical.

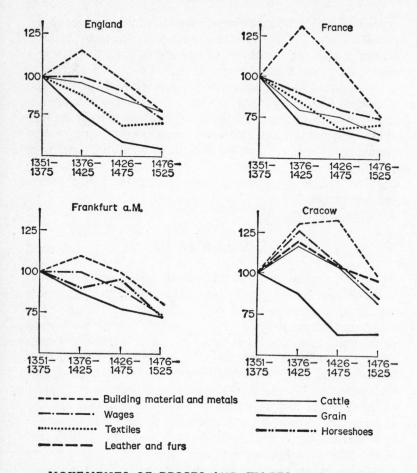

MOVEMENTS OF PRICES AND WAGES 1351–1525
(50-year averages, 1351–1375   100%, silver prices.)

(after W. Abel, *Agrarkrisen und Agrarkonjunktur*, Hamburg and Berlin, Verlag Paul Parey, 1966, p. 58)

Such analyses are of course extremely fallible. It is difficult to discover what contributed to the sustenance of a medieval peasant and 'subsistence' is a vague concept. There is much evidence however to suggest that landless and almost landless men were a large proportion of the population in many rich agricultural areas. In detail of course the social customs of the nobility and the forms of agricultural life varied widely from one part of Europe to another. Everywhere, however, their wealth was derived either from rents paid by their tenants or from the sale of agricultural produce from the 'demesne' estates which they managed directly. In most parts of Europe the possession of landed estates commonly carried with it jurisdiction over the tenants living upon them and some degree of unfreedom imposed upon some of the tenants who were serfs who could be bought and sold with the land. In most parts of northern and western Europe some form of estate corresponding to the English manor or the French *seigneurie*, combining possession of land with jurisdiction over tenants, was common and provided the material support alike for lay nobles, for monasteries and for bishops.

Broadly speaking the decline in population made land less valuable and manpower more valuable than it had been in the previous centuries of rising population. This affected landlords in two ways. In the first place it made it more difficult for them to retain control over their tenants. Much land, as the lists of rent-paying tenants and the remains of deserted villages show, actually went out of cultivation. Landlords therefore commonly suffered from a loss in the numbers of their tenants and also from difficulty in keeping up the level of rents and services of those who remained because of competition from other landlords and employers. Secondly they were affected by the movement of prices and wages. Medieval agriculture had been heavily orientated towards the production of cereals, the most economic way to feed a dense population. The contraction of demand and abandonment of poorer lands meant that the prices of cereals in the period 1350 to 1450 were commonly either stable or declining; price series for wheat and rye in a number of places in north and west Europe support this pattern. On the other hand prices for other less basic foods, beef, butter, wine were more likely to go up. While cereal prices stayed down, the wages of labourers tended to rise and were generally higher in the first half of the fifteenth century than they had been in the previous century. From the point of view of the landlord this meant simply that agriculture was less profitable than it had been, he obtained a smaller price for goods which cost more to produce. This phenomenon has been described as a 'price-scissors'. The landlord was caught between the two blades and suffered. The earnings of labourers and artisans were larger and more profitable than before. In at least one part of Europe, Iberia, a serious attempt was made to compensate for the native labour shortage by the importation of slaves from Africa and Asia. It has been estimated that there were over 20,000 slaves in Catalonia and Valencia in the early fifteenth century. Asiatic slaves were not uncommon also in rich households in Italy at this time, though they were not present in numbers large enough to affect the economy. For most of Europe however importation of alien manpower was not a practical possibility. The seigniorial classes had to resign themselves to a large scale shift of wealth and weakening of old authorities. Moreover, landlords frequently had to react by abandoning the increasingly unprofitable demesne agriculture which they had previously practised and letting out their lands to tenants.

In 1452 three men describing themselves as 'laboureurs' took over a house and lands belonging to the abbey of St Denis at Tremblay near Paris on a six year lease. They promised to make certain annual payments of grain and 'to work and reclaim all the said lands, to cut down the willows and other bad trees on the land', and to keep the building in order. But they added that 'if by fortune of war, pestilence or stormy weather the takers of the lease cannot work or harvest then they are not bound to pay. . . .' It will be noticed that apart from the universal problem of the weather the two potential catastrophes mentioned are war and pestilence. Northern France had by this time seen a great deal of fighting in the campaigns of the Hundred Years War and there is no doubt that in some places the destruction caused by war was the reason for depopulation and abandonment of agriculture. There has been much debate about the relative parts played by warfare and demographic decline in producing the symptoms of decay in the late medieval countryside. However, apart from the Hundred Years War which did lead to a series of military orgies in many parts of France, it is very doubtful whether the later Middle Ages witnessed a greater quantity of destructive warfare than earlier centuries. The English countryside, which was almost entirely free of internal war in the period 1330 to 1450, experienced similar economic and social movements. Europe as a whole by the mid-fifteenth century was dotted with decayed, unworked, overgrown lands like the lordship of the abbey of St Denis, produced not by local administrative or political difficulties but by a fundamental demographic movement which affected the whole continent.

The ultimate effects of the prolonged seigniorial crisis varied greatly from one part of Europe to another. In northwest Europe (western Germany, northern France, Netherlands, England) it appears to have produced already by 1450 a change in the social balance in which wealth and power had shifted somewhat down the social scale. Well-to-do peasants, who benefited from the decline of rents and the letting of demesne land, and rural craftsmen were the beneficiaries. Serfdom was disappearing. In northern Italy the rural lordship or manor characteristic of northern Europe had already ceased to exist by the fourteenth century, but lordships of a different kind based on *mezzadria* (share-cropping) or money rents and owned by city merchants, churchmen and nobles were growing up in the later middle ages. In two substantial regions of Europe, Iberia and eastern Europe, the nobility recovered and strengthened their position in the course of the fifteenth century. In large parts of Germany, east of the Elbe and Slavonic Europe the effect of depopulation seems to have been no less spectacular than it was elsewhere. But whereas in the West disused lands were filled up by freer peasant farmers, in the East the nobility retained their control over them and began in the later fifteenth century to set up the wide grain-producing estates worked by serf labour which were to be characteristic of Prussia and Poland in later centuries. In 1412 the Grand Master of the Teutonic Order accepted the request of the Prussian nobility that peasants who fled from the lands of their lords should not be received into towns. About the same time maximum wages for farm labourers were fixed. Legislation of this kind in favour of seigniorial landlords

was very common in Europe in the century following the
Black Death – the English Statute of Labourers of 1351 is an
example of it. But, whereas in north-west Europe this legislation represented the attempts of the *seigneurs* to retain an
economically untenable position and became ineffective, in
Prussia and elsewhere in the East it marked the beginning of a
successful seigniorial reaction against a peasantry which had
been relatively free in earlier days. In the course of the fifteenth
century it gradually extended to the establishment of more
widespread serfdom.

The wider divergencies in the history of the European
nobilities such as between those of Germany, west and east
of the Elbe only became apparent after 1450. They are also
probably inseparably connected with divergencies in the
industrial and commercial sectors of the economy. In much
of eastern Europe trade and industry were little developed
and grew relatively weaker; in north-west Europe trade and
industry became more important in the course of the fifteenth
century. Hence there developed a symbiosis of the grain-
producing estates of the East with the industrial towns of the
Netherlands which they fed with grain. This pattern accentuated the social contrast between eastern and western Europe
and contributed to the phenomenon known in the Slav world
as the 'second serfdom.' In the fifteenth century however this
was in its infancy. For the period 1350 to 1450 the weakening
of the social control of the lay and clerical nobility was a
general phenomenon, prominent in most parts of Europe and
strongly affecting the whole of its social and political life.

iii *The industrial and commercial world*

Many of the towns and cities of medieval Europe suffered a
decline in population and size quite as spectacular as that
which took place in the countryside. Florence, for example,
which has been credited with a population of 110,000 before
the Black Death probably shrank to about half that number
after the Plague and did not recover its old size during the
fifteenth century. There and in many other places the town

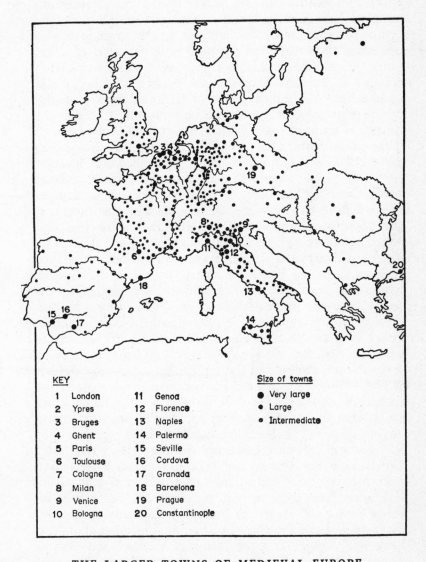

THE LARGER TOWNS OF MEDIEVAL EUROPE
(after N. J. G. Pounds, *An Historical Geography of Europe, 450 B.C. -
A.D. 1330*, Cambridge, 1973, p. 348)

walls which had been rebuilt with wider circuits to contain growing populations in the thirteenth and early fourteenth centuries later enclosed areas which were not occupied by houses. The shortage of manpower in the towns was also frequently shown by local attempts to fix the level of wages and by the proliferation of organizations of artisans created to promote their interests against the leaders of industry and trade in the older guilds. So far as scanty medieval statistics can be relied upon it seems that many cases of decline in the volume of trade and of production at the old centres can be found in the century following the Black Death.

Nevertheless the industrial and commercial world does not present the same picture of general decay as the seigniorial world. Given the nature of the surviving evidence this impression is difficult, probably impossible, to justify statistically. It is impossible to quantify wealth or economic activity at this period except for very restricted groups, places and times. The impression however is strong. In the most obvious sense cities such as Florence, Venice, Bruges, London or Nuremberg acquired a prominence in the world of the early fifteenth century in terms of material and artistic sophistication and political power apparently greater than they had enjoyed earlier even though they were smaller communities. A document put together at Venice in the mid-fifteenth century compared the revenues of the various European powers. The author, whoever he was, put the four monarchical powers of France, England, Castile and Burgundy at the head of his list, estimating that each of them once had an ordinary annual revenue of two or three million ducats, in each case considerably reduced by wars in recent decades. He credited the Venetian republic with a revenue of 1,100,000 ducats in 1423 since reduced by 'great wars and destruction of commerce' to 800,000. This put Venice in his league table of powers in below France and Burgundy but above England and Castile. Florence, Bologna and Genoa came lower down but above the King of Portugal and the dukes of Brittany and Savoy. Though the author's figures are unexplained and of course are not to be taken too seriously, his list does indicate the Venetians' own estimation of their relative position in the world and the relative wealth of the city state powers. A better known document of Venetian self-satisfaction is the death-bed speech attributed to the doge Tommaso Mocenigo who died in 1423, recommending his fellow citizens not to imperil their prosperity by war. 'In peace time this city puts a capital of ten million ducats into trade throughout the world with ships and galleys so that the profit of export is two million, the profit of import into Venice is two million, export and import together four million . . . You have seen our city mint every year one million two hundred thousand ducats in gold, eight hundred thousand in silver, of which five thousand marks go annually to Egypt and Syria, a hundred thousand ducats to your places on the mainland of Italy, to your places beyond the sea fifty thousand ducats, to England a hundred thousand ducats [presumably for English cloth and tin] and the rest remain in Venice.' These figures and others like them occur in a rhetorical composition and do not prove anything. But like so much evidence from the Italian cities, especially Venice, in the first half of the fifteenth century they convey the impression of a booming commercial city, proud of its statistics. It is not an accident that the history of Venice which more than any other community depended for its existence solely on the commercial arts was the greatest political success story of the fifteenth century.

In very general theoretical terms it is not difficult to see how the commercial and industrial sectors of the European economy may have acquired a greater relative importance in a period of contracting population. If we assume that early fourteenth century Europe was so heavily populated that it was difficult to produce enough food to keep a large part of the population above the subsistence level then it is likely that the retreat from marginal lands which were agriculturally unrewarding would lead to higher average standards of living and to surpluses of food. This interpretation is supported by the evidence which shows that cereal prices remained low and that more attention was paid to raising animals. It is a reasonable hypothesis that in these circumstances relatively more people would become involved in manufacture and trade which would become more widespread and diversified. This is what seems to have happened. One of the key statistical series available for late medieval Europe, the figures of English exports of raw wool and cloth (exceptional because national figures of this kind are extremely rare) are probably significant for the economic trends of Europe as a whole. They show that from the middle of the fourteenth century a decline of wool exports set in, which continued very gradually through the fifteenth century; at the same time exports of manufactured cloth rose sharply in the late fourteenth century, fluctuated at a higher level in the early fifteenth and rose again later in the century. Behind these figures must lie a considerable shift of activity in England, hitherto one of the economically more backward parts of Europe, from agricultural and pastoral to industrial pursuits. It is very likely that the same picture fits large parts of continental Europe: a geographical extension and diversification of commerce at a time of stagnation in volumes of trade. Thus, although it may be correct to call it an age of depression, it was also a period when industry and trade became more widely characteristic of European life.

The trading patterns of the Italian cities were already well established. It is possible to find symptoms of decline here. The Florentine cloth industry declined. No Florentine firm of the fifteenth century, even the Medici, seems to have been as large as the Bardi and Peruzzi. On the other hand there are aspects which indicate a healthy state of affairs. The Venetian state galley system, developed through the fourteenth century, reached its widest extent in the middle of the fifteenth, with galleys sailing regularly to the Black Sea, the Aegean, Palestine, Alexandria, the Maghreb, Marseilles, Barcelona, Seville, London and Bruges. There is little sign that the Venetian dealers in spices and textiles found the times hard in western Europe or that their trade with the East was seriously upset by the increasing domination of the Ottoman Empire over the eastern Mediterranean. The silk industry, catering for an increasingly sophisticated market, became more widely established in the Italian cities. The commercial records of a Venetian merchant, Andrea Barbarigo, for the year 1431-2 show the extent and character of the trade in which he engaged. He bought a quantity of English cloth, sheepskins and canvas which he dispatched, in the care of a business associate, together with two bags of silver coins on a Venetian ship sailing to Acre. With the money and the proceeds of the sale twenty-six sacks of cotton were bought for him and sent back for sale at Venice. With a bill of exchange he ordered a consignment of gold thread from Constantinople. Nearer home he sent money to an agent at Fermo in Italy for the purchase of 1000 bushels of wheat for sale at Venice. He wanted to buy English cloth for export to Syria. Since the sailing of western galley fleets was suspended because of war he arranged to buy twenty English cloths at Bruges through a German merchant who sent them overland.

The most famous commercial family of the fifteenth century, the Medici, established a network of branches at Rome, Geneva, Bruges, London, Lyons, Naples and Milan. The Medici were mainly experts in the international exchange business, transferring money by letters of exchange from one part of Europe to another, rather than dealers in commodities. For a time they established a control over a large share of the international exchanges at the papal court which gave Cosimo de' Medici a legendary reputation for wealth. In this particular, highly successful specialization they were peculiar and also rather dependent on political circumstances. The international exchange business however was also essential for the more mundane commercial intercourse between countries. For example, an account book of another Florentine firm, the Borromei, doing business at Bruges in the 1430s, shows that their services were being used by Netherlandish and English merchants in the ordinary trade in wool and other commodities. Though others, South Germans, Flemings, Hansards, played some part in international banking the Italians still dominated this field. The Medici were unusual in some respects but the geographical extent of their operations was by no means unusual for Italians of the time: Venetians, Genoese and Lucchese concerned with trade in goods as well as exchange, could be compared with them. A letter written by the manager of the Bruges branch of the Medici bank to Cosimo in 1464 is typically Italian in its European oversight of the commercial world. He refers to his hopes of recovering debts from the

Duke of Burgundy and to difficulties at the London branch, whose books were to be sent back to Florence on the galleys, and to money owed by an English lady for a payment made on her behalf by the Geneva branch. Then he refers to some snags in the sale of alum (a material used in the finishing of cloth) which was being dispatched from the papal mines at Tolfa to the Netherlands and to silk cloth sent from the Medici workshop in Florence. After that there are references to the Florentine and Venetian galleys just arrived in northern waters, to shipments of wool from the Bruges branch to Milan. The letter ends with a fragment of political news from England. Only Italian merchants, supported by world-wide commercial contacts, had this general grasp of European affairs and it grew stronger rather than weaker in the fifteenth century.

The other classic area of medieval industry, Flanders, was harder hit by economic changes. The big cities were more dependent on the basic textile industry and their predominance in that field was overthrown by the developing industries of England and Holland which could produce simple cloths more cheaply, probably because their labour costs were lower than those of the highly organized industry of the Flemish cities. Ypres was the greatest casualty; it had declined severely by the late fourteenth century. Fourteenth-century Flanders contained striking examples of attempts by towns to protect their share of business by prohibiting industry outside in the surrounding countryside. Nevertheless the decline of the big centres was in fact compensated by development in the smaller towns and countryside – around 1400 for example we find cases of Italian merchants encouraging cloth making in the smaller places near Ypres – and also in towns of other parts of the southern Netherlands such as Brussels and Louvain. The Flemings also responded to the crisis by diversifying their industry. The production of heavy woollen cloth was replaced by light serges and by other more complex products. Until late in the fifteenth century Bruges retained its position as the commercial centre of north-west Europe, the point at which the commercial systems of the Italian cities and the Hanseatic towns met. In the later part of that century the leadership passed from Bruges to Antwerp. Antwerp, unlike

Bruges, was important not chiefly as a port and a major industrial centre but as a place where international fairs were
held. It was a meeting place for merchants dealing in the
international trade in English cloth, German metal, eastern
spices. The passage of supremacy in finance and commerce
from Bruges to Antwerp therefore signified that the industrial
importance of the southern Netherlands had suffered a
relative decline. In spite of the decline however, the southern
Netherlands remained in the fifteenth century the outstanding
area of urban civilization in Europe north of the Alps.

The network of Italian commerce did not extend very much
to the northern part of Europe. Bruges was its terminal point.
North of the Alps and east of the Rhine was the extensive
network of trade dominated by the German merchants associated with the Hanseatic League. The Hanse itself was a very
loose political confederation of German towns which cam into
existence in 1367 in order to counter the threat posed to the
interests of the North German ports by King Waldemar III
of Denmark (see above, p. 53). The agreement made by
seventy-seven towns meeting at Cologne in 1367 was the start
of many diplomatic campaigns waged on behalf of the interests
of German towns in a desultory manner through the fifteenth
century. But the Hanse was an extremely unwieldy confederation with a shifting membership and little community of
interest between its members which included such diverse
elements as the great Rhineland metropolis of Cologne, the
northern seaports like Lübeck and the towns of East Prussia.
The League itself did not organize trade. German commerce
did not develop during this period anything comparable with
the world-wide companies and elaborate financial systems
characteristic of Italian commerce. It was very much simpler
and on a very much smaller scale. The typical Hansard was an
individual trader who travelled with the goods which he had to
sell. Nevertheless Germans dominated the commerce of
northern Europe in the fourteenth century. During the earlier
centuries of medieval expansion they had established th m-
selves as the main commercial intermediaries between East
and West. From Novgorod to Bruges it was they who traded
and reaped the profits of trade rather than the Flemings,

English and Poles who produced or consumed many of their goods. Their trade was carried by sea through the Baltic, by land from the mouth of the Rhine into eastern Europe. It involved vital products on which the life of northern Europe depended. In one direction Russian furs, Prussian corn, Baltic timber, North Sea herrings; in the other French wine and salt, English and Flemish cloth. Later on the Hansards had to face competition from the emergent trading areas of England and Holland which made serious attempts to break their monopoly of import and export in the Baltic. The early fifteenth century was a period of intense rivalries between national groups of merchants. Piracy was closely related to trade all along the western coasts of Europe and this period ended with one of the most catastrophic episodes in Hanseatic history, the capture by English pirates of the annual fleet carrying salt from the Bay of Bourgneuf through the Channel in 1449. On the whole, however, the Hansards succeeded in keeping their hold. At the end as at the beginning of the period they were masters of northern trade.

The essential 'commercial revolution' – the invention of international firms and of methods of accounting and exchange – which made possible the commercial world of the late Middle Ages had taken place earlier, in the thirteenth century. In this respect the years 1320–1450 were not a period of innovation. In the whole agricultural world the period seems to have been marked by little technical progress. The general tendency to divide the land into smaller units as the seigniorial demesnes broke up may have led to technical regression. In the industrial field, however, there are reasons for regarding this as a much more inventive and adventurous period. Medieval Europe in 1300 was in some respects well advanced technologically in comparison with earlier and contemporary civilizations. For example mills of various kinds driven by water power or wind, for grinding corn or fulling cloth, were a normal feature of the countryside. The application of water power in the iron industry was also common. Spinning and weaving and the building of huge cathedrals had also involved a great deal of technical ingenuity. Nevertheless the succeeding century and a half saw important developments.

Most of them are not obviously spectacular. One field in which they can be detected easily however is the art of war. Explosives were an importation from Asia, not a European invention; but the development of effective guns took place in Europe during this period. The first cannon, made of forged iron, appear in the 1320s. Before the end of the fourteenth century they were being used extensively. The English were battered out of their strongest fortress in Normandy in 1375 by the use of big guns, specially ordered by King Charles V. By this time cast bronze cannon were in use; by the late fifteenth century cast iron was being used. Almost any collection of medieval book illustrations will demonstrate the development of body armour from the mail, formed of hundreds of linked rings, which was normal in the early fourteenth century, to the technically much more ambitious jointed steel plates of the late fifteenth century. For a large part of the late fourteenth and early fifteenth centuries one of the dominant weapons was the newly developed steel crossbow. Warfare might appear from one point of view to become an increasingly effete exhibition of pseudo-chivalry. The ritual of the tournament was much more elaborate by the late fifteenth century and, in northern Europe at least, the heroes of the tiltyard were also the captains of war. But this is in part an illusory impression. In war itself the effectiveness of properly equipped soldiers was much greater than it had been in previous centuries and kings could be frighteningly powerful.

The developments in war were largely connected with the technology of metals. Although the total production of metals probably declined during the great depression, the techniques of producing and working them improved. Larger iron-smelting furnaces were being used in the early fifteenth century than before and water-driven bellows were applied to them. In the mid-fifteenth century there were advanced iron industries in northern Italy and in the other great industrial cockpit of Europe, the Rhineland-Netherlands area, for instance at Namur and Liège, ready for the period of expansion to come.

The most epoch-making new development, one which was

again dependent on metals, was printing. Simple pieces of printing, playing-cards for example, were quite commonly produced in Venice and Germany in the early fifteenth century. An enormous leap was made from that to the Gutenberg Bible of the 1450s, a large text printed with moveable type. Whether or not John Gutenberg of Mainz deserves the main credit for the invention – the earliest stages in the history of printing are very hazy – there can be no doubt that it was a great and original achievement of combined technical skill, in making the type and in printing, and business organization, in setting up the complex workshop long in advance of the profits. It is conceivable only in a society which accepted a close connection between technical experimentation and commercial investment and is the best possible testimony to the existence of such a society. This was all done in a West German city by ordinary citizens. By this time there was also a widespread paper industry. Paper became common and began to replace parchment in the later fourteenth century.

Though it did not have an immediately important impact, like the development of guns or printing, it is remarkable how much interest was already shown in western Europe at this period in machinery and in the problem of the transmission of power. One of the most extraordinary creations of the later Middle Ages was the astronomical clock, showing the movements of the solar system as well as the time and the feasts of the religious year, constructed by Giovanni de' Dondi in 1348–64. Large mechanical clocks became fairly common about this time. These were weight-driven. Early in the fifteenth century clocks driven by a coiled spring were introduced, probably in the Netherlands, and clock makers had to grapple with the problem of maintaining a constant time with variable motive power. About the same time, and also in the Netherlands, the first experiments were apparently being made with another basic mechanical invention, the crankshaft.

In 1450 European trade and industry were still overshadowed by the general stagnation of population. The great quantitative expansion was still in the future. But within this globally depressed economy shifts of emphasis towards the commercial and industrial sectors of society were taking place. A Greek visitor, Bessarion (see below, p. 311), writing about 1444, was one of the first external observers to express his admiration for the technical competence of the western Europeans. He had seen 'wood cut by automatic saws, mill wheels moved as quickly and as neatly as can be'; he reported that 'in the smelting and separation of metals they have leather bellows which are distended and relaxed untouched by any hand, and separate the metal from the useless and earthy matter'. Bessarion must have seen these things in Italy. There and in the north-west advanced technical inventiveness in the use of power and the treatment of metals was allied with business enterprise in a way which was peculiar to western Europe. While the agricultural world stagnated city populations were increasingly wealthy and aspiring.

iv *The Social Rebellions of the Fourteenth Century*

In the very long run fundamental changes in the structure of society resulted from the population decline of the late fourteenth century. The manifestations of these changes appeared clearly in the mid-fifteenth century, when the seigniorial structure was generally and massively weakened. Medieval society first felt the strains resulting from a decline in population, however, in the half century immediately following the Black Death. During that period there were several violent but temporary clashes of class interest. These revolutionary episodes were not in themselves effective in producing social change, but they were symptoms of the underlying stresses in society.

The classic example of late fourteenth-century social rebellion was the English Peasants' Revolt of 1381 which deserves a place in any history of European society not only because it was violent and widespread but also because it left a deposit of records in which the aims of the rebels are more clearly expressed than in the records of other agrarian revolts. The Peasants' Revolt was sparked off by indignation about an experiment in taxation, the attempt to levy a Poll Tax which involved taxation by head, with comparatively little

variation in the burden, as a substitute for the taxation of the
more well-to-do according to their property which had
hitherto been the normal form of taxation levied from the
laity by parliamentary grant. This attempt to shift the incidence
of taxation down the social scale was bitterly resented by the
new taxpayers. It also took place at a time when the economic
effects of population shortage were being felt. Landlords were
trying to cling to their old rents, fighting against the shortage
of labour, holding on to their jurisdiction over their unfree
tenants. The tenants were conscious of the new power which
the shortage of manpower had given them, they were probably
in general better off than their fathers had been and therefore
more restive about the judicial bonds which continued to
buttress the control of the *seigneurs.* The chronicler Froissart,
who observed the rebellion with the distaste of a devotee of
aristocratic society, was correct in his well-known remark
that it was 'all because of the ease and riches that the common
people were of, which moved them to this rebellion'. As he
also correctly reported 'A custom in England and also in
other countries is that the nobles have great jurisdiction over
their men and keep them in serfdom, that is to say, that they
ought by law and custom to work the lords' lands, to gather
and bring home their corns, and put them in the barns to
thresh and to fan, and by labour services to make their hay
and hew their wood. . . . These unhappy people . . . began to
stir because they said they were kept in too great servitude,
and in the beginning of the world, they said, there were no
bondmen and could not be any unless they were traitors to
their lords like Lucifer to God. They said they were not like
that for they were neither angels nor spirits but men formed
in the same mould as their lords and now they were treated like
beasts, which they said they would no longer suffer, for they
would be all one, and if they laboured or did anything for
their lords, they wanted wages for it.' For a few days in June
1381 widespread revolts took place in eastern England, partly
directed against local manorial lords, partly against the
government which supported them and culminating in a brief
occupation of London. Prominent among the rebels' demands
were the abolition of serfdom, low rents and higher wages.

The English Peasants' revolt took place against a background of political weakness which had undermined public confidence in the crown's leadership. A boy king, Richard II, succeeded a senile king, Edward III, and in these circumstances the government's financial difficulties, which were also caused partly by social changes which undermined the traditional system of taxation, became more scandalous and intolerable. The combination of political weakness and social conflict was essential. Similar ingredients were present in the French crisis of 1358 which produced the revolt of the *Jacquerie*. The French monarchy suffered a devastating crisis after the capture of John II at Poitiers in 1356. The government was led by a young Dauphin whose position was threatened by a relative, Charles of Navarre, who would have overturned the monarchy if he could. The court's financial policies, involving heavier taxation and currency debasement, brought it into conflict with the bourgeoisie of Paris under the leadership of Etienne Marcel. Marcel's followers tried to control the levy of *aides* and the appointment of the Dauphin's councillors. Their conflict with the court brought them into temporary alliance with Charles of Navarre and culminated in February 1358 in an irruption into the royal palace. Within these two years from 1356 to 1358 we can observe the court and the nobility being attacked and counter attacking. The Estates of Languedoil in October 1356, following Poitiers, introduced scales of taxation according to which the proportional contribution of the nobles was increased, that of the non-nobles decreased. The estates of Champagne and Compiègne in the spring of 1358 increased the burdens on non-nobles and reduced them on nobles. Both nobles and burgesses were of course smarting under the effects of labour shortage and war taxation. The conflict between the two pillars of the crown's financial system weakened and discredited still further the king and nobility who had so obviously failed in war. These events were more spectacular than the financial scandals and embarrassments which dominated English politics between 1376 and 1381. Like the later English events, however, they were a striking case of military and financial failure leading to a situation in which more radical social upheaval could take place.

The revolt of the *Jacquerie* took place in the Paris region, mostly to the north of the city, in May and June 1358. The word *Jacquerie* appears to have been derived from *Jacques Bonhomme*, a traditional symbolic name for a typical peasant and it appears to have been essentially a movement of bands of peasants directed against members of the seigniorial class. It differs from the English Revolt in its lack of clear aims, at least so far as is revealed by the surviving records. It also differs in its extreme manifestations of physical violence. Bands of peasants arose in a number of places, pillaged houses, killed lords and ravished ladies. There is no clear indication that they had any purpose beyond the satisfaction of their hatred and contempt of their social superiors, the gentry. As the movement rapidly grew it acquired some sort of organization under the leadership of a man called Guillaume Carle whose army is said at one time to have numbered several thousand. Marcel's Parisian bourgeoisie was for a time uncertain whether to ally with them or to oppose them but in any case there was little time for political attitudes to develop. On 10 June, Charles of Navarre destroyed the main force of *Jacques* near Clermont. Marcel's attempt to exploit the situation to his own advantage collapsed. In the end the main beneficiary of the movement was Charles of Navarre who gained increased power and prestige.

Though the *Jacquerie* of 1358 was perhaps the most bloody of the social rebellions of the fourteenth century, the most dense concentration of political upheavals with a prominent social content is to be found in the years 1378–82 which saw the revolt of the *Ciompi* at Florence (1378), the risings of the weavers at Bruges and Ghent (1379–82), the Peasants' Revolt in England (1381) and the rising of the *Maillotins* at Paris (1382). The point of time – around 1380 – is significant. In thirty years the demographic effects of the plague had become acute but social structures had not yet adapted themselves. They cracked easily under the stress of war and political failure. None of these crises was purely a matter of class conflict. All of them were connected with difficulties in the management of conventional politics by traditional ruling classes and sprang in part from the political and financial problems of traditional state structures. But in all of them the resentment of relatively subservient classes against their masters was prominent. Taken together they might be said to constitute a general crisis of medieval society. None of them was effective. The old order recovered its stability. But the general crisis foreshadowed the general weakening of seigniorial society and the gradual levelling of the social pyramid which was to be characteristic of the next seventy years of European history.

The revolt of the *Ciompi* came at the end of the War of the Eight Saints between Florence and the papacy and was able to take place because the normal fabric of Florentine political life broke down under the intense strains caused by the prosecution of the war, heavy taxation and autocratic behaviour by the ruling oligarchic group which was identified with the war. In May 1378 an enemy of the oligarchs, Salvestro de' Medici, a political not a social enemy, achieved a commanding position in the government. He instituted a policy which was not only hostile to the war leaders but also favourable to the lesser guilds and to the politically unrepresented *Popolo Minuto*, that is to say the artisans and employees who were not organized in recognized guilds. When the policy was in danger of rejection in June, Salvestro and his friends conjured up a mob which assembled outside the *Palazzo* crying 'Viva il popolo, viva la libertà' and then ran riot for two days attacking the houses of prominent citizens, releasing criminals and sacking convents. This led to the usual Florentine expedient of setting up a *balìa* to restore order. The *balìa* itself was moderate in complexion but it also took action against obscure dissidents in the city. A month later this produced a second, more radical rebellion which broke out on 20 July and led to the seizure of power by politicians who really did represent or spring from the *Popolo Minuto*. The rebels were a mixed lot and it has been shown that the revolt cannot be regarded simply as a rising of wage-earners against their capitalist employers. But the tyranny of the Wool Guild was certainly an important object of the rebels' hatred. It was resented not only by wage-earning employees but also by the independent artisans of trades subsidiary to the cloth industry, such as dyeing, who also thought of themselves as being members of the *Popolo Minuto* and were equally excluded from economic and political authority. The difficulties of the cloth industry in Florence, once supreme, now in decline and suffering from the shortage of labour, was a contributory cause of the revolt. The rebels were called *Ciompi* – wool carders. The most prominent rebel leader, Michele di Lando, was a wool carder, therefore in some sense a proletarian of the textile industry, but he was also, like several of his associates, an old soldier and it is very likely that the taste for physical violence and its fruits was another element mingled with economic grievances. At the time of their seizure of power the rebels presented a petition which gives some indication of their formal aims. They wanted a reorganization of taxation with a new and fairer assessment of tax burdens and the abolition of the state debt which was maintained by the payment of interest to share-holders. They called for the abolition of the official of the Wool Guild who was responsible for the maintenance of its disciplinary orders against workers. Most remarkably they wanted a new guild of the *Popolo Minuto* which would give those classes previously excluded a formal position within the constitution of the city and they wanted its members to be eligible for certain offices. The rebels imagined themselves as obtaining power by creating not a new kind of constitution but an extension of the old one which would give them the same political and social rights as the patricians of the old guilds. For a few weeks the leaders of the *Popolo Minuto* terrorized Florence. Three new guilds – of Dyers, Tailors and *Popolo Minuto* – were created. The old lists of citizens eligible for offices were burned. But the rebels had no staying power. At the beginning of September reaction set in, the guild of the *Popolo Minuto* was abolished and Florentine politics quite quickly returned to normal. The events of 1378 were regarded with horror by subsequent historians as a unique and terrible interruption of the natural order.

The troubles in Flanders were caused by the urban resent-ment of comital power which had often been an important factor at various points earlier in the century. They were sparked off in 1379 by the decision to build a canal linking

Bruges with the River Lys. The project had the approval of
the count but it would have diverted trade from Ghent, so it
had complex political and economic implications. It provoked
violent reaction first from boatmen in Ghent who joined with
the weavers of the city to wrest control from the governing
group in the city which supported the policy of the count. The
count's officers had also offended against city liberties by
arresting a bourgeois. This led to a general upheaval in both
Ghent and Bruges in which the leadership was taken by the
weavers and which was aimed both against the patricians of
the city and against the count as an enemy of city autonomy.
Peace was patched up at the end of 1379 but Ghent held out
defiantly. The man who eventually became leader was Philip
van Artevelde of Ghent. Like his father before him he became
involved in a most complex dispute in which the issue of
municipal liberties was inextricably bound up with the
international triangle of power between France, Flanders and
England (see above, p. 47).

Contemporaries thought that there was a close connection
between these disorders and the troubles which broke out in
France after the death of Charles V (September 1380). With
the powerful hand of Charles removed, the French court's
demand for taxes provoked widespread resistance in French
towns, notably in Rouen where it turned into an attack on the
richer citizens by the poorer. This unrest culminated in the
revolt of the *Maillotins* at Paris in March 1382. The events
were described thus by a Florentine businessman and adventurer Buonaccorso Pitti who was at the French court at the
time:

'In 1381 the people of Ghent rebelled against their overlord, the count of Flanders, who was the father of the
duchess of Burgundy. They marched in great numbers to
Bruges, took the city, deposed the Count, robbed and killed
all his officers, and dealt in the same way with all the other
Flemish towns which fell into their hands. Their leader
was Philip van Artevelde. As the number of Flemings
rebelling against their overlords increased, they sent secret
embassies to the populace of Paris and Rouen, urging them

to do the like with their own lords, and promising them aid and succour in this undertaking. Accordingly, these two cities rebelled against the King of France. The first insurrection was that of the Paris mob, and was sparked off by a costermonger who, when an official tried to levy a tax on the fruit and vegetables he was selling, began to roar "Down with the *gabelle*." At this cry the whole populace rose, ran to the tax-collectors' houses and robbed and murdered them. Then, since the mob was unarmed, one of their number led them to the Chatelet where Bertrand du Guesclin, a former High Constable, had stored 3000 lead-tipped cudgels in preparation for a battle which was to have been fought against the English. The rabble used axes to break their way into the tower where these cudgels or mallets (in French, *maillets*) were kept and, arming themselves, set forth in all directions to rob the houses of the King's representatives and in many cases to murder them. The *popolo grasso*, or men of substance who in French are called *bourgeois*, fearing lest the mob (who were later called *Maillotins* and were of much the same kidney as the *Ciompi* in Florence) might rob them too, took arms and managed to subdue them. They then proceeded to take government into their own hands and, together with the *Maillotins*, continued the war against their royal lords.'

The Count of Flanders appealed to his son-in-law and heir, Philip the Bold Duke of Burgundy, effectively the most important person at the French court. It was in the French interest to help him both to suppress the dangerous fires of city rebellion and to ensure the integrity of Philip's inheritance in Flanders. So a French army defeated and killed the Flemish rebels at Roosebeke in November 1382. Even then Ghent did not give in. Temporary and ineffective support was given in 1383 by an English invasion, a repetition of the pattern of 1340, called the 'Crusade of the bishop of Norwich' because it pretended to be a religious intervention in favour of the legitimate pope against the one at Avignon, but this melted before a French army. In 1384 Louis de Male the last count of independent Flanders died but the Ghenters were still holding out against Philip and when he finally made peace with them in 1385 to complete his acquisition of the county he confirmed all the city's old privileges.

This ended the cluster of violent revolutionary outbreaks in western Europe. The greatest of all medieval revolutionary movements, that of the Bohemian Taborites, was to arise forty years later and in a different setting. As far as England, France and Italy are concerned the worst storm was over. The movements had been on the whole unsuccessful. They have however an important symptomatic character. All over western Europe peasants and townsmen were going to become more free of seigniorial authority in the next fifty years, to achieve by the processes of social evolution what the rebels of 1378–85 had failed to achieve by rebellion. The century after 1385 was one of gradual adjustment to the new demographic and economic conditions.

CHAPTER IV

THE FOURTEENTH-CENTURY WORLD
OF IDEAS

i *Universities and Courts*

In medieval Europe, far more than at any time since, intellectual life was dominated by the universities. The only other institutions which dealt in higher education to any great extent were the schools of the religious orders and they were largely extensions of the university system, purveying the same sort of learning in order to raise the intellectual standards of their own members. Broadly speaking, if a man wished to acquire the training to deal with philosophy, science, mathematics or theology or an advanced expertise in the learned professions of law (which in most parts of Europe meant Civil or Roman Law), or medicine, he had to attend a university. There were notable exceptions, such as Dante and Chaucer for example, but these men both possessed a degree of learning which was unusual for an autodidact and has led scholars to speculate whether they had been to a university even though the evidence is against it. The countries of southern and western Europe were fairly well provided with universities by the early fourteenth century. Italy had famous ones at Bologna, Padua and several other cities; Spain had Salamanca; France had Paris and Montpellier and several more; England had Oxford and Cambridge. Germany and central Europe had none until princely patronage led to the foundation of Prague (1347) and Cracow (1364), Vienna (1365), Heidelberg (1385) and several more in the next century. But the university world was cosmopolitan and Germans and Netherlanders went in substantial numbers to Paris and elsewhere. The numbers of university trained men were, by this time, large both inside the church and among the laity. They formed quite clearly an international, intellectual élite of graduates. Paris at its height, in the early fourteenth century, may have had a university population of 3000 to 5000. The graduate élite in Europe as a whole must have numbered many thousands. The purpose of university education was to give the student a grasp of certain crucial texts and to train him to think precisely about them. Universities were devoted essentially to the exercise and development of the reasoning faculty. Broadly speaking, they were not interested in original research in the modern sense and certainly not in physical experimentation (which was rare) or history (which was not a university subject); nor were they interested in literature or the fine arts. Within the limits imposed by their choice of subjects and methods of teaching, however, their achievements were immense, not only in producing the famous treatises of scholastic philosophy but also in carrying out the continuous social function of training a large proportion of the ruling classes in rational analysis.

Like modern universities, the medieval ones were divided into faculties. Though not all of them were represented in every university, there were four faculties: Arts, Theology, Law and Medicine. The Arts Faculty provided both the basic university education for students who intended to go no further in specialization and the preparation for the other Faculties. Its educational importance was, therefore, very great. Its curriculum was originally supposed to cover the *trivium* and *quadrivium*, derived from late Roman education, (grammar, logic, rhetoric, arithmetic, geometry, astronomy, music), but by the fourteenth century two developments had transformed it unrecognizably. The linguistic element had been much reduced: students still, of course, had to know the Latin language in which all higher education was conducted but it had degenerated into a technical language and Latin literature was little cultivated. At the same time, the arts course was swamped by the books of Aristotle. Translations of his works into basic Latin acquired enormous popularity in the universities during the thirteenth century and came to provide most of the prescribed texts for the Arts courses. A diligent student, therefore, would become well acquainted with Aristotle's writings on Logic, Psychology, Natural Science and Metaphysics. The overwhelming importance of Aristotle in late medieval education and thought, a dominance unrivalled by any writer in modern Europe, was due to the fact that his books seemed to provide such good accounts of the subje ts studied in the Arts Faculty that from the late thirteenth century they ousted most others.

Academic Medicine also depended heavily on Aristotle, being the study of texts rather than the study of living or dead bodies, but it also depended a great deal on Latin translations of Galen and Hippocrates and Muslim scientists. Civil and Canon Law were naturally based on the Digest of Roman imperial legislation and the Decretals of popes. The queen of the sciences, however, was Theology. The Faculty of Theology provided a long and arduous course which could hardly be completed by a student until he was well into his thirties, and the doctorate in Theology was the crown of academic life. The studies for it were based on the Bible, which had to be thoroughly examined and on the twelfth century theological textbook by Peter Lombard called the *Sentences*. In studying these basic texts, the student would also, of course, be led into the whole field of theological and exegetical literature embracing the Fathers, Augustine and earlier medieval writers such as Bede and Anselm, in addition to the vast theological literature produced by the universities themselves since 1200.

By the early fourteenth century this structure of higher education was very well established and many of its greater literary creations had already been achieved. It did not change very significantly between 1320 and 1450. It continued with similar curricula to train the intelligentsia of the clerical and also, to some extent, of the lay world. But though the institutional structure did not change very much, the more original minds among the theologians continued to grapple with the insoluble philosophical problems which that structure created. The problems of medieval academic thought sprang partly from the fact that it had two supreme authorities which were difficult to reconcile, the Bible and Aristotle. Obviously, they might be regarded as corresponding to the abstract realms of faith and reason which would have to be handled in any religious philosophy but the problem was particularly acute and persistent in the medieval universities because the divergent approaches to truth were institutionalized in the courses of the faculties of Arts and Theology.

The great university thinkers of the thirteenth century, culminating in St Thomas Aquinas (d. 1274) and Duns Scotus (d. 1308), were concerned to produce a simple consistent scheme of philosophy and theology in which the two sets of ideas given by human reason and divine revelation were shown to be consistent. This involved showing that essential tenets of the Christian faith, such as the existence of God and the immortality of the soul, could be demonstrated by reason as well as by reference to the Bible. This synoptic approach produced great masterpieces of thought which continued to have much prestige. The idea that reason and revelation were in harmony, naturally tended to have the backing of ecclesiastical authority, provided that reason was not allowed to modify accepted doctrines, and Aquinas's system was widely accepted as authoritative. Among the original thinkers of the fourteenth century, however, there was a tendency for this single, all-embracing system, harmoniously justifying Christian doctrine, Greek science and established lay and ecclesiastical society, to be abandoned. In its place were erected partial structures of thought which were sometimes explicitly inconsistent with other parts of university learning which had been fitted into the thirteenth century syntheses.

The anti-synoptic tendency manifested itself in various ways. The medieval users of Aristotle were heavily dependent for the interpretation of difficult Greek texts, translated into dog Latin, on the helpful commentaries of the Arabic philosopher, Averroes, which were also translated into Latin and much easier to understand than Aristotle. But Averroes's interpretations made Aristotle incompatible with Christian doctrines. In the faculties of the universities, other than that of Theology, therefore, developed an 'Averroist' line of thought which accepted Aristotle as an authority for such subjects as logic, biology, physics and metaphysics without reference to the orthodoxy of the views derived from him. Averroists were prominent at Paris in the early fourteenth century and in the Italian universities, especially Padua, throughout the fourteenth and fifteenth centuries. Some of them proclaimed that ideas like the eternity of the world were well founded in Aristotle. The Averroists were a little like the deists of the French Enlightenment: they did not denounce Christian doctrines directly but they did maintain the rationality of non-Christian ideas. It was not an accident that some of them, notably the Parisian master, Jean de Jandun (d. 1328) and his associate, Marsilius of Padua (see below, p. 146) were political enemies of the papacy. More positively, Averroism was an essential accompaniment of Paduan medicine which had to take pagan theories seriously without concern for their incompatibility with Christianity.

The most important individual thinker of the northern university world in the fourteenth century was the Oxford philosopher and Franciscan, William of Ockham, who left the university in 1324 to defend his suspect views at the papal court. He later fled from Avignon to join Lewis the Bavarian, whose political position he defended against the papacy in several works before he died in 1349. Though important in the political controversies of the time, Ockham was primarily a logician and metaphysician. He examined the propositions of his predecessors and decided that the rational defence of Christianity was not tenable. The proof of the existence of God as a prime mover was 'probable, that is more probable than its opposite, but not demonstrated'. He also very much discounted the real existence of ideas, as opposed to individual, contingent objects and events, which had been important to his predecessors. Thus, the ordered hierarchy of being from animals through greater degrees of rationality and ideas in man and angels to God became less convincing. Men, he thought, had only an intuitive knowledge of individual things, of white things, not of a universal quality of whiteness, so that they could only form scientific hypotheses, not discover general principles which were necessarily true of the whole of Creation. Though associated with a condemned enemy of the papacy, Ockhamism was a powerful force among the original minds at both Oxford and Paris in the mid-fourteenth century. The interest in logical difficulties and in concrete particulars, rather than in the more uplifting metaphysical speculations of, for instance, Aquinas, was a marked tendency. It turned some minds towards mathematics and natural science. This did not lead to a flowering of experimental science – though one Ockhamist at Paris did proclaim that modest advances in the understanding of cause and effect could best be obtained 'if men turned their minds to things and not to the understanding of Aristotle'. It did, however, lead to some serious attempts to modify and examine Aristotelian science, especially in the realm of the mechanics of moving bodies. These advances are particularly associated with Jean Buridan, rector of Paris University in 1328 and 1340, and another Parisian, Nicholas of Oresme, who died as Bishop of Lisieux in 1382. Their works are stages towards the later developments of Leonardo da Vinci, Copernicus and Galileo who were greatly dependent on these medieval predecessors.

Another English thinker who illustrates, from a different angle, the break-up of the scholastic world-picture, is John Wycliffe. Wycliffe was no Ockhamist, on the contrary he was a keen believer in the reality of abstract ideas. He used his dialectical skill in the years 1376 to 1384, when he died, to defend the view that the true Church was an entirely spiritual body made up of those who were in a state of grace. He demolished the philosophical and theological validity of the visible church and all its panoply of religious orders and Canon law, substituting all-powerful lay authorities. One of the first acts of the papal curia after it returned from Avignon to Rome in 1377 was to condemn opinions expressed by Wycliffe which denied the whole basis of ecclesiastical government. Wycliffe was a curiously insular figure in his lifetime, deeply involved in Oxford disputes but totally without influence outside England. Thirty years after his death, however, in a manner almost reminiscent of Marx's influence in Russia, he provided the ideological basis for the astonishingly successful reformation movement of the Hussites in Bohemia. His heresies were condemned again and more strongly at the Council of Constance in 1415.

The Averroists, Ockhamists and Wycliffists of the fourteenth century lived for the most part within the existing framework of university and church. Down to the Great Schism the containing structure of the visible church remained, as the administrative history of the Avignon papacy shows, immensely strong. In some respects the most characteristic representative of the orthodox Christian tradition at the end of the century was Jean Gerson (1363–1429). Gerson, the son of a peasant in Champagne, was a brilliant theologian and became chancellor of the University of Paris in his early thirties, but he was profoundly critical of the prevalent fashion for abstract speculative argument. In his long and influential career he was famous for two things. Firstly for his advice to the Christian world to go behind the scholastic structure to a simpler mystical moral theology. This involved him incidentally in the defence of orthodox positions against theological radicals and he attacked the mystical excesses which he thought he detected in the writings of the Netherlandish ascetic Ruysbroeck (see below, p. 165). Secondly for his involvement in the ecclesiastical politics of the Great Schism, especially at the Councils of Pisa and Constance as a moderate conciliarist trying to bridge the offensive divisions within the church. Gerson represented the main stream of Christianity in northern Europe which was to survive the storms of the late fourteenth and early fifteenth centuries. But already before his career started the disputes in the university world had shown the difficulties not only of harmonizing faith and reason within one metaphysic but also of reconciling the temporal power of laymen and churchmen. The dualism in medieval society was nicely balanced at the beginning of the fourteenth century. At the beginning of the next century it was to break up, with large consequences for religion and thought.

The dualism in economic and political power, the division of authority between the clerical and lay nobilities, which was so characteristic of the medieval world, was accompanied by a kind of dualism on the intellectual plane. Though sophisticated learning was largely in the hands of the priests there was also a culture of the lay nobility and the lay court which was equally international and which to some extent propagated a

different set of values. In literature it centred on the cele-
bration of the two ideals of chivalric prowess and courtly
love, which, in the world of the nobility of the time, were not
fantasies but the objects of actual ambitions. For example, one
of the servants of John de Montfort, Duke of Brittany (d. 1399),
who had a tempestuous and on the whole successful political
career attempting to recover and hold his duchy in the face
of the French crown's jealousy and the English crown's
interference, wrote an account in verse of his master's warlike
exploits. Nobles saw themselves as living out the role of the hero
of chivalric legend. Marshal Boucicault, a French captain who
played a prominent part in various episodes in Charles VI's
reign – the Crusade of Nicopolis, the French occupation of
Genoa, Agincourt – was the subject of a biography which
made him into a paragon of piety, chastity and valour. There
are many other examples of the fusion of the ideal with actual
life. In northern Europe at this time the hagiography of
chivalry was perhaps even more prominent than the production
of lives of religious saints.

The world of chivalry and courtly love is most easily evoked
for the English reader by the name of Geoffrey Chaucer and
its ideals are fully mirrored in his *Troilus and Cressida* and in
some of the *Canterbury Tales*. Chaucer was essentially a court
poet. France had no single writer of his stature but in general
it had a much richer culture and the ideals of the European
nobility were most fully expressed in the French language in
the courts of the Valois kings and in those of the great royal
dukes of Burgundy, Anjou and Orleans. One of the royal
dukes, Charles Duke of Orleans (d. 1465), who was captured
by the English at the battle of Agincourt, was in fact himself
the leading French poet of his generation. His highly accom-
plished, melancholy verse contains one of the last great
elaborations of the courtly love ethos. A good representative
of the ideals of aristocratic society in the fourteenth century is
the chronicler Froissart. Jean Froissart (c. 1338–1410) was
also a poet but of course he is chiefly remembered for his long
account of the Anglo-French wars which is indeed the most
considerable piece of history produced in northern Europe at
this period. Froissart saw political and military history very

largely as a succession of chivalric encounters and this was no doubt how his patrons saw it.

The poetry of the late fourteenth and early fifteenth century is known to the modern reader chiefly in its short lyric forms of which Christine de Pisan, Charles d'Orleans and others were masters. But there was also a vast production of lengthy romance poetry by poets more or less closely connected with the courts. Froissart the chronicler also wrote a long poem of the romantic love and noble deeds of an imaginary Hermondine, daughter of the King of Scotland, and Méliador the knight of the golden sun, which he read to Gaston Phoebus, Count of Foix, in 1388 during a succession of sleepless nights. The only important woman writer of this age, Christine de Pisan, was also a courtier poet. She was an Italian by birth married in adolescence to a court official of Charles V. She turned her hand to writing in French during her long widowhood and was thus able to live on the patronage of such great men as the dukes of Burgundy and Orleans. She wrote among other things a panegyric life of Charles V. Romance was designed to serve the role of courtly entertainment; it had the function in that society which has been performed for much larger audiences in more recent societies by the novel and the film. But though it was more frivolous in purpose than the theological writings of the university men it gave expression to the standards by which the leaders of lay society lived, which were to some extent alternatives and rivals to the ideals of the church.

ii *The Beginnings of Renaissance Ideas*

The poet who has come to be accepted as the greatest literary genius of the medieval world, Dante, died at Ravenna in 1321. As everyone knows, Dante was a poet with a passion for philosophy. He wanted to understand and devoted a large part of his life to absorbing and recasting the aspects of contemporary thought which were available to him. For that reason, his works can serve as an introduction to the world of thought in which he lived. But one must be careful to identify that world. It was not, as is sometimes mistakenly thought, the world of scholasticism. Dante was a citizen of Florence until his exile in 1302 and probably never travelled outside northern Italy. As a politician, a poet, a friend of lords, he knew the world of the Italian communes thoroughly, the rest of Europe only by hearsay. The hearsay was extremely important to him because the scholastic thought which had been developed mostly at the University of Paris was one of his main inspirations. It was amalgamated in his mind with other intellectual influences from Italy. The combination was typical of the Italian city world of the fourteenth century. This is the context in which Dante must be placed and which makes his work a good starting point for this section.

The most striking cultural innovations of the Italian cities were, of course, aesthetic. At this period, the name which comes to mind first in this field is the painter, Giotto (d. 1337), like Dante a Florentine, whose school set art on a new course of realistic representation. The scenes in Giotto's great fresco series about the life of Christ in the Arena chapel at Padua and about the saints in the Bardi and Peruzzi chapels, which he decorated for two great merchant families in the church of Santa Croce at Florence, broke new ground both in making the spatial setting realistic and in depicting dramatic emotional scenes. They have something in common with the many real people whose predicaments and crimes are shown to us in Dante's Divine Comedy, with which they are roughly contemporary (Arena chapel *c.* 1306–9, Comedy *c.* 1310–21, Bardi and Peruzzi chapels *c.* 1325). The Arena chapel frescoes are in a style which already embodies many of the characteristics of later Italian Renaissance painting. Giotto took pains to improve the sense of space by setting events within architectural frameworks which could be made fairly realistic with simple perspective. His figures are not, as in earlier medieval painting, symbolic emblems of biblical persons but men and women with perceptible body and weight, displaying visible emotions which bring the stories to life in a realistic manner. Of course the elements of symbolism and allegory were still very important; all biblical stories were loaded with traditional allegorical meanings and all had acquired conventions of pictorial representation. But Giotto established a new balance between symbolism and realism which is characteristic of Italian painting.

In the realm of ideas the Italian cities were most notable not for philosophical or scientific speculation but for the cultivation of literature, and particularly for their interest in the models provided by the Latin writers of antiquity. This interest has been a feature of many periods in European history in many countries – it has been given the general name 'humanism' – but it has an exceptional and central importance in Italian Renaissance civilization which is unparalleled. There are clear reasons why it should have been particularly prominent in fourteenth-century Italy, reasons which are bound up with the development of urban civilization. Unlike the cities of northern Europe in general, the Italian cities contained large numbers of professionally educated laymen. The clerical class, the class of professional writers, was not as in northern Europe, an extension of the clergy. The chronicler, Villani, tells us that in 1339 there were three kinds of schools for laymen at Florence teaching firstly basic reading, secondly arithmetic and thirdly grammar and logic. Every Italian city by this time contained large numbers of merchants who could write letters and keep accounts and smaller numbers of lawyers and of notaries. The notaries, who, for example, numbered about 600 at Padua in the early fourteenth century, wrote documents, everything from wills to new laws. At Florence they were joined with the lawyers to form one of the city's seven major guilds. The result of this general lay education was a fairly widespread interest among laymen in the writing of Latin because the ability to draft an impressive document or oration was a valuable professional qualification. And out of this lay intelligentsia sprang, among a few people, a lively interest in Latin literature. In the early fourteenth century the most important centre of classical interest was Padua, where a local poet, Albertino Mussato, first had the idea of reviving the classical ceremony of coronation with the laurel in 1315. Dante was first and foremost a poet, writing in Italian like many contemporaries. But he was also an expert rhetorician and one of the decisive experiences of his life was reading Virgil's *Aeneid* from which he took the idea of a journey through the underworld. In the first two books of his *Divine Comedy*, Virgil was his imaginary guide through Hell and Purgatory.

One of his other main experiences was the discovery of scholastic philosophy. The home of scholasticism was in the northern universities. Though it was practised with distinction in the Italian universities, it was to the educated city dweller a separate intellectual tradition which had been imported into the Italian world. It had very little to do with the study of Latin literature for its own sake. Though the great system builders of scholastic thought worked mostly at Paris, however, there were important centres of this learning in Italy too, at the Universities of Padua and Bologna and in the *studia* of the Dominican order, and a number of leading scholastics, including Aquinas, had been Italian. It was through the local and derivative centres that Dante, like many other Italians, got to know about scholastic thought.

Considered simply as a body of ideas, Dante's writings are a strange mixture of these two sets of ideas, amongst others. The plan and the poetry of the *Divine Comedy* are much affected by Virgil. The approach in the poem to scientific and philosophical questions like embryology or free will, comes from university scholasticism. In another book on *Monarchy*, Dante, bitterly resentful of the turmoil of Italian politics which made him a rootless exile from his native city, tried to formulate a political philosophy. It is also a curious mixture of traditions. He justified his belief in the necessity of universal peace by an Aristotelian argument that man's supreme capacity was reason and that he must enjoy peace for the full realization of this potentiality. But he then named as the proper instrument of universal peace a world monarchy in the hands of the Roman Emperor, using Virgil's *Aeneid* to show how this authority had been divinely ordained. Except as a poet Dante was not an influential writer and his idea of a revived Roman Empire as a world power was wildly anachronistic. But his work in the *Monarchy* as well as the *Divine Comedy*, does show the Italian mind beginning to grope towards the creation of new systems of thought, different in kind from those developed in the North and springing out of the circumstances of Italian life. A century later the Italians were beginning to achieve a real intellectual autonomy.

Another great mind which grappled with the intellectual dualism of Paris and Italy was that of Marsilius of Padua, who in 1324 completed his *Defensor Pacis*. Unlike Dante, Marsilius was a university man; at one time he had been a student at Padua, at another he was Rector of Paris. He was expert in the Aristotelian learning of his time. He was also a Paduan patriot and his attachment to the cause of that city's independence led him to support the German King, Lewis the Bavarian, against the pope, John XXII (see above, p. 97). The *Defensor Pacis* drew together these elements in his life. It was a theory of the city state, based on Aristotle, such as could have been conceived at that time only by an Italian, accustomed to city states with full sovereignty. It was an onslaught on the temporal power of the papacy, which Marsilius, like Dante, saw as the great enemy of peace in Italy, because of its greed for political power. It was an argument conducted in the language of the university scholastics. As an example of his precocious thought, here is Marsilius's statement of the idea of popular sovereignty within a city, which remarkably foreshadows modern theories along the same lines:

'The legislator, or the primary and efficient cause of the law, is the people or the whole body of the citizens, or the weightier part thereof, through its election or will expressed by words in the general assembly of citizens, commanding or determining that something be done or omitted with regard to human civil acts, under a temporal pain or punishment. By the weightier part I mean to take into consideration the quantity and the quality of the persons in that community over which the law is made. The aforesaid whole body of citizens or the weightier part thereof is the legislator regardless of whether it makes the law directly by itself or entrusts the making of it to some person or persons, who are not and cannot be the legislator in the absolute sense, but only in a relative sense and for a particular time and in accordance with the authority of the primary legislator.'

When he came to the problem of the spheres of temporal and spiritual authority, Marsilius systematically cut the clergy off from any right to temporal jurisdiction or property. There were in his view, no ecclesiastical laws which were enforcible by priests and no property rights which were vested in churches as such. The evangelical law which could be deduced from the Bible was a matter of conscience and divine judgement. Any earthly enforcement of it was entirely a matter for decision by laymen; no independent authority whatever was held by the church as a hierarchy of priests and the pope was no more than the president of a priesthood dependent on the approval of laymen.

With one leap, Marsilius therefore produced a theoretical conception of a secular state which was typically a republican city state of the Italian pattern. This was an extraordinarily sudden advance. He used the armoury of Aristotelian scholasticism to construct a theory which was in most respects, the opposite of the previous constructions of university political theory. It was popular instead of monarchical, its state was unitary and secular. It is an elegant theory and it is surprising that it did not become more popular. But it was too bold in its direct confrontation with the scholastics' ingenious adaptation of Aristotle to monarchical, theocratic ends. In fact, Renaissance social ideology was going to advance by another route, by abandoning scholasticism entirely, rather than by adapting it to the city-state environment.

The man who did most to create a new intellectual framework for the Italian mind, and who was perhaps the most original thinker of the fourteenth century, was Petrarch. Paradoxically, he spent most of his life outside Italy. His life, 1304 to 1374, coincides almost exactly with the Avignon Papacy and was fairly closely bound up with it. He was the son of a Florentine notary who had been banished soon after Dante suffered that fate and he was born in exile. In 1312 his father emigrated and established a practice at Avignon. Between 1316 and 1326 he studied law at the universities of

Montpellier and then Bologna. He therefore knew the university world from the inside. His father presumably intended him to follow in the same profession or the higher reaches of it as a notary or as a lawyer, but while he was at the university Petrarch decisively turned his attention towards other things; to the composition of Italian verse and to the study of Latin literature. In 1330, some time after the death of his father, the economic position of Petrarch's family collapsed. He might have been forced to take up some lucrative profession such as law if he had not found a source of patronage through his connections at the papal court at Avignon which enabled him to achieve a unique position in the European world. His patrons were two brothers of the Roman Colonna family, Giovanni and Giacomo, one a cardinal the other a bishop. In 1330, Petrarch got his first income as domestic chaplain to Cardinal Colonna. In 1335, he was appointed canon in the cathedral of Lombez in Gascony of which Giacomo Colonna was bishop. In 1341 came the famous ceremony of his coronation with the laurel at Rome, which was arranged for him by King Robert of Naples. In 1342–3 Petrarch wrote *Secretum*, an imaginary autobiographical dialogue with St Augustine which was perhaps his most original work. By this time, it is clear that he was well established as an employee of the papal court and a recipient of papal favours, but established in a peculiar way. His position depended on his skill as a writer. He was by now the author of many Italian poems and Latin letters. His assured income came from ecclesiastical benefices but he never became a priest and he lived as a virtual layman. His home was a house in the country near Avignon, from which he observed the papal court with distaste and frequently with scorn which he expressed very scathingly in some of his letters. He had put into letters his low opinion of Pope Benedict XII while that pope was alive and did not hesitate to do the same for later popes. His role, if it can be called that, was altogether a very anomalous one. His essential expertise as a writer, a stylist rather than a scholar, gave rise to reflections of a more general kind which simply did not fit into the familiar patterns of philosophical and theological debate and were, therefore, much freer for being in an intellectual framework on which there were no constraints. His social position as a great writer was both very privileged and very irresponsible. He walked the corridors of power without feeling that he had any compelling loyalty to the owners of the building. He was a new kind of man and he set the fashion for a new breed.

There was one point at which rather obliquely Petrarch did confront the world of earlier medieval controversy. He detested scholasticism. There is a short passage in *Secretum* which brings this out. 'Few', says Petrarch, 'really know the definition of man although in every school it is repeated so often that the ears of pupils must be exhausted with it and the columns of the building worn down.' This is one point on which he elicits agreement from his imaginary Augustine who replies: 'This endless garrulousness of the dialecticians is full of definitions of this kind and glories in giving rise to eternal disputes, but they do not know what they are really talking about. If you ask one of this herd for the definition of man or anything else the reply is ready but if you probe further there will be silence or, if the habit of disputation has given him an easy and audacious way of speaking, he will show that he has no real knowledge of the thing he has defined. Against this sort of people, so disgustingly superficial and so uselessly ingenious, it is proper to cry: why do you go to such trouble in vain and apply your intellect to such pointless snares?' This is not just an idle comment. The one point at which Petrarch did place himself in the intellectual world was in audaciously stating his preference for literature over Aristotelian philosophy. It comes out in a work which he composed in 1352-5, 'An Invective against a Physician'. A physician was offended by Petrarch's criticism of the ineffectiveness of the medical treatment given to the dying Clement VI and attacked poetry. Petrarch replied with an attack on medicine, partly on the ground that it was associated with the pagan Averroes, and an attack on pagan schools of philosophy in general. The connection of university medicine with the study of ancient natural philosophy in the works of Aristotle, Galen and others, made this a fairly natural association. Petrarch expressed his attitude more systematically in a work which he composed late in life in 1367, 'On his own and many others' ignorance', directed against four Venetian Aristotelians, a full-scale attack on the study of Aristotle for failing to provide any real understanding of the human soul both because of the nature of Aristotelian thought and because of the unfruitful dialectical method of schoolroom question and answer which the moderns used in interpreting Aristotle. The true wisdom which Petrarch opposed to this sterile activity was the ethical insight of Cicero, St Paul and St Augustine.

Cicero had overwhelming importance in Petrarch's intellectual world. Cicero was the supreme rhetorician, the master of style. He was, therefore, the technical professional master whom rhetoricians like Petrarch aspired to imitate. But Cicero's writings were not merely stylistic masterpieces. They embodied reflections on philosophy and morality of an acute and captivating kind. The rhetorician was easily carried on from one aspect of Cicero to the other. Petrarch could see from his reading of the Confessions, that this was what had happened to Augustine too in his pre-conversion days and it was one of the reasons why Augustine was at least partly a sympathetic authority. Early in *Secretum*, Augustine reminded Petrarch of Cicero's demonstration that it is virtue that makes men happy. Petrarch says he remembers, 'but you are calling me back to the doctrines of the Stoics which are out of step with popular opinion and closer to abstract truth than to practical usage'. Augustine retorted effectively saying that Petrarch must not allow himself to follow the mob, an appropriate appeal to his aesthetic snobbery. Some pages later on, Augustine pointing out how the union with the body enfeebles the soul, so that during life men cannot understand properly and, in effect, death is to be welcomed as a release for the soul, admits that he first got this idea from Plato and that he was led to it by a passage in Cicero. When they are talking about the adverse effects of sensual indulgences on the soul, Plato comes up again and Petrarch this time admits that he has been impressed by the Platonic view, again made known to him by Cicero. Petrarch refers, at this point, to his unsuccessful attempt to learn Greek in 1342. Most of Plato's works were inaccessible to Petrarch as they had been to the medieval world in general because they had not been translated. Apart from the *Timaeus* and a few other things, he was known to the medieval world only through quotation and reference in other writers. In the case of Petrarch who in fact never succeeded in learning Greek, Plato was mainly known as he was represented by Cicero.

The choice of Cicero as an all-purpose philosophical authority, supplanting Aristotle who dominated scholastic philosophy, was accepted enthusiastically by later humanists. It was an important innovation because the philosophical structure built around the new authority was bound to be quite different. The approach which was founded on Cicero discouraged any attempt at a systematic coverage of all aspects of philosophy. It was rather indifferent to logic, uninterested in the philosophy of nature, powerfully drawn towards ethical and moral questions. This approach was adopted from Petrarch even by later humanist writers who had much more natural interest in philosophy but who still started from his standpoint rather than the scholastic one. Petrarch, therefore, introduced a new intellectual style, which had the effect of turning philosophical thought away from logic, metaphysics and natural science towards ethics and politics.

A more precise theme which Petrarch made popular was the role of *Fortuna*, fortune, in human affairs. This comes up in *Secretum* when Augustine tells Petrarch that he is suffering from the psychological condition of depression which in the medieval world was called *accidia*. Petrarch agrees and describes rather graphically the symptoms of despair from which he suffers, his sensation of being surrounded by dangers and enemies, and complains that he is badly battered by fortune. Apart from telling him that he is self-centred, Augustine points out to Petrarch that the remedy for his mental disease is to be found in the writings of Seneca and Cicero, where they show how a man must face the world by cultivating mental virtues. Treatises of one kind and another on this theme of the relationship between interior virtue and exterior fortune abound in later humanist literature. For modern taste they make very dull reading indeed. Seen against the medieval background, however, they can be recognized as a new and more realistic kind of psychological analysis, an attempt to analyse everyday psychological problems of the reflective man, something which was missing from the philosophical or the devotional literature. *Secretum* ends with Augustine urging Petrarch to abandon the literary work on which he was engaged, his epic poem, *Africa*, and devote himself to the proper business of meditation on death. Petrarch is not willing to do this. He still hopes that the two are in some way compatible. *Africa*, which Petrarch went on writing all his life is about Scipio Africanus Major, the Roman general who recovered Spain for Rome and defeated Hannibal in the Second Punic War, only to be attacked by his enemies on his return to Rome and to retire unselfishly. Scipio was also used by Cicero as the mouthpiece for an account of the relationship between the earthly body and the immortal soul. Petrarch was continually fascinated by Scipio whom he selected from the heroes of antiquity as especially an embodiment of the life of the good man, combining genuine glory and genuine virtue. What held Petrarch in his attachment to Scipio was the idea that there could be a supremely good earthly life which combined glory with virtue, which in a sense reconciled the conflicting ideals. He was attempting a kind of classical, secular hagiography. This also was important for future humanists. Petrarch did not have much to say about political philosophy and what he did say was said obliquely in the medium of classical biography. But he clung to the ideal of the possibility of virtuous achievement in political life and this attitude like the others, was taken up.

Petrarch never resolved the problems which he opened up in *Secretum*. He went through the rest of his life clinging to the classical ideal but wondering whether perhaps he ought to follow the same path as his brother, Gherardo, who became a monk, unable to complete *Africa*, changing and adding to his biographies of the lives of illustrious men of antiquity. The failure to complete the great works did not matter. The important thing was the idea, the stance he adopted in the world, the picture he gave of himself. The educated layman, taking his independent lay intellect seriously and surveying the problems of humanity without feeling obliged to fit them into a system, had arrived. This was what Petrarch meant in the long run. More precisely, he provided an intellectual framework for the Italian lay intelligentsia, with enormous success because a vast undernourished public of educated laymen was ready and waiting for his message. By this influence, he introduced a great new cleavage into Italian intellectual life. Petrarch himself was not very interested in politics or society but his literary compositions and his exploration of his own psychology produced a new ideal type, the lay scholar-gentleman, a new way of writing about affairs in Ciceronian terms and a heightened passion for antiquity. His writings laid the foundation for a view of society in secular terms without religion or metaphysics, something unimaginable in the scholastic environment. For the time being the new attitudes to society were incipient and half-expressed but Petrarch's imitators in the fifteenth century were, as we shall see, to produce a new social ideology.

The Italian intellectual world, in which Petrarch was immediately influential, was different from the northern. At a simple level the historian sees a clear distinction if he compares Froissart's chronicles with the history of Florence written by Giovanni Villani (c. 1271–1348). Instead of the noble exploits which fill Froissart's pages, Villani is concerned with the mundane political problems of a bourgeois republic; their assumptions about the aims of politics are different. At the literary level the realistic stories of Boccaccio's *Decameron*, written in Florence in the 1350s, some of them about real people, are very different from the stories of romance legend. So different were the social assumptions of the French *seigneur* and the Italian citizen that the impact of the Italian novelties in the north could only be superficial. Avignon was a great meeting place of the two cultures. It was however more effective in spreading Italian art forms than Italian ideas. Simone Martini, the Sienese painter, who worked at Avignon in the 1340s, is the most famous of the Italian artists who were brought into direct contact with France through the patronage of the papal court and transmitted to the north some of the new realistic devices. Boccaccio's stories had some influence. But in essence the Italian cities were to remain for a long time a distinct cultural section of Europe.

iii *Religious Movements*

In spite of its enormous power, the established Church did not control all religious life in the fourteenth century. On the contrary, the records of the period abound in evidence of independent religious activity of varying kinds, ranging from orthodox movements which the Church controlled imperfectly to outright rebellion against its authority and blatant heresy. As at all times religion was ambivalent in its role in society. The same scriptural formulae could be used in a traditional church, whose outward function was to cement and confirm existing social relations, or in a subversive sect which turned its back on contemporary society. This distinction and paradox was particularly evident in medieval and Renaissance Europe because of the massive economic and political power of the established Church. Most of Europe most of the time was content to support the established religious order. The cathedrals of Prague (c. 1344–85) and Milan (begun 1386) and the fifteenth-century city churches of Coventry and Nuremberg were built by the beneficiaries of seigniorial and urban society to the glory of the traditional church. During the same period, however, a whole range of religious movements inspired by a more original and impatient piety, linked in many cases with new social classes, sometimes orthodox and loyal, sometimes heretical and hostile to the Church, rose and fell in various parts of Europe.

A papal bull, issued in 1318, which opened with the words *Gloriosam Ecclesiam* (Glorious Church) accused a heretical group of believing in the existence of 'two churches, one carnal, oppressed by wealth, flowing with luxury, stained with sins, over which the Bishop of Rome and other inferior prelates are said to rule; the other spiritual, refined by temperance, decent with virtue, trimmed with poverty, in which only they and their accomplices are contained'. During this period great numbers of Europeans, more or less obedient or rebellious in their attitude to authority, were inspired by some version of the distinction, stated here in an extreme form, between the way of life of the clergy who had an honourable role in normal society and the impulse towards a life of religious perfection.

Apart from this constant incongruity between ecclesiastical normality and evangelical idealism, the division between conformists and non-conformists was very much affected by the degree of success which the Church had in various parts of Europe in adapting itself to the conditions of local society. In the course of the twelfth and thirteenth centuries, the Church had become highly centralized and exclusive. To a large extent it had imposed uniformity in diocesan and parish organization and in canon law. It was very reluctant to allow the formation of new religious orders or to tolerate religious organizations which were not controlled by priests. Uniformity was an enormous strength in some ways but it also made it difficult to incorporate the devotional instincts of people who happened, through variations and changes in social structure, not to fit into the organization. Crowds of pious townswomen, who could not afford to enter orthodox monasteries, formed themselves into *béguinages*; pious countrymen whose ignorant parish clergy preached no sermons to them, listened to Lollard hedge preachers instead. Some dissident religious movements were composed of people who had been left out.

The question of 'Reformation' in the usual sense of the word, that is the rejection of papal authority by a whole section of the Church, is a separate issue. The Reformations of the sixteenth century were political as well as religious acts. In the fourteenth century such action was for the most part unthinkable, not because of a lack of religious dissent, which was often common, or because kings had no quarrels with popes, but because the European unity of ecclesiastical organizations – the flow of authority from Rome, the flow back of money and obedience from the provinces – was real and accepted, a living social organism, and the economic strength of the Church was great enough for most people to accept a basic dualism in society. The Great Schism weakened that unity and power and the Hussite upheaval in Bohemia in the early fifteenth century has much resemblance to the sixteenth-century Reformations. It would be a mistake, however, to see the dissident religious movements of the fourteenth century as leading straight to the sixteenth-century Reformation. On the contrary, with the large exception of the Hussites, the fifteenth century was a much quieter period in the history of the Church; for the most part the ecclesiastical establishment managed to quell or absorb the troublemakers and retained its powers on a diminished scale.

The medieval religious movements are a difficult subject to approach. The basic difficulty is the relationship between religious ideas and religious *movements*. Information about dissident movements comes mostly from inquisitors and other hostile witnesses. The concept of 'heresy', which governs the evidence is a very unsatisfactory one for the historian. It is based on abstract criteria of belief and therefore encourages historians to treat religious movements as episodes in the history of thought, which is misleading in the same way as a history of socialism masquerading as a history of the modern working class. On the whole, the radical religious movements of this period were largely separate from the history of academic religious thought; but there are connections which are often difficult to define. Some of the Rhineland pantheists claimed the authority of Eckhart, who was condemned for statements resembling theirs, but he was certainly not the source of their movement. The English Lollards were inspired by Wycliffe and adopted vulgarized versions of some of his theories, but an explanation of the existence of Lollardy must obviously depend mostly on understanding why thousands of Lollards quarrelled with the established Church. Ockham, a clearer case, joined an existing unorthodox movement which he had done nothing to create. The language and ideas of popular religious movements are usually banal and uninteresting; it is the movement and its circumstances that matter.

By far the most remarkable of the many attempts to wrest the medieval church back into the way of the Apostles was the establishment of the Franciscan Order in the thirteenth century. Its members were sworn to a life of poverty, begging and homelessness. By the fourteenth century the expansion of the order into a great European organization had long made practice of these conditions limited. The Franciscans, like the other main 'Mendicant' order, the Dominicans, were an important and ubiquitous part of the life of late medieval Europe, but most of them lived in comparative comfort and stability and some became bishops and cardinals. There had always been, however, a section of the Franciscans who hankered for the absoluteness of the strictest interpretation of the Rule. This 'Spiritual' wing of the order was very prominent in the early fourteenth century in central Italy and in Provence. Its adherents were characterized by a desire to interpret the Rule of St Francis in its most rigorous sense and, also, in many cases, by acceptance of the visionary millennialist ideas which were derived from an earlier medieval thinker, Joachim of Fiore, and which led them to believe that the world was approaching a holocaust in which the coming of Antichrist would eventually lead to the destruction of all but the elect. This powerful combination of the apostolic and millennial visions, characteristic in various forms of many European religious movements, was naturally regarded with hostility by ecclesiastical authority especially when it found many supporters among laymen.

In the early fourteenth century, the Spirituals of the Franciscan order and their lay sympathisers, known as *Béguins*, were particularly strong in Provence, around the towns of Marseilles and Narbonne, uncomfortably close to the seat of the papacy at Avignon. In Pope John XXII (1316–34) they had an enemy who was determined to stamp them out. His most important statement was the Bull *Cum Inter Nonnullos* of 1323 which authoritatively destroyed the whole basis of the strict interpretation of the Franciscan Rule by declaring that it was heretical to deny Christ the right of property. He also condemned the millennial theories. In the course of the 1320s he virtually stamped out the Franciscan Spirituals in Provence.

The necessity to support orthodoxy against extreme and subversive opinions had always inclined the papacy to side with the sections of the Franciscans which favoured more relaxed interpretation of the Rule. This offensive against the Spirituals brought John XXII into conflict with the moderate opinion which at that time, governed the Franciscan Order. As a result of this, the theological dispute became entangled with the high politics of the relationship between pope and emperor. When, in the years 1327-8, John's enemy, the Emperor Lewis the Bavarian, marched on Rome, he took with him as anti-papal propagandists, several Franciscan supporters of the strict Rule. John XXII countered him by imprisoning the Minister General of the Order in Avignon. He escaped with a small party including William of Ockham, the most outstanding philosopher of his age, who was, at that moment, at Avignon to face charges about the unorthodoxy of his academic opinions. They fled to the camp of Lewis of Bavaria.

This irruption of the problems of the Franciscan Order into politics initiated a politico-theological pamphlet literature about poverty which lasted some twenty years. William of Ockham defended the doctrine of the poverty of Christ and the Apostles and was, incidentally, led on by his Franciscan conflict with the papacy to the treatises on political philosophy exalting the lay power at the expense of the papacy, for which he is better remembered. Pope John XXII, in one of the oddest moments in the history of medieval thought, played into their hands by preaching a wildly unorthodox sermon on the beatific vision. In 1350 an Anglo-Irish Archbishop, Richard Fitzralph of Armagh, composed a denunciation of Franciscan theories, 'On the Poverty of the Saviour', which was later to be one of the main sources of John Wycliffe's ideas and is, thus, a kind of link between two different ages of theological dispute. The poverty issue was, thus, converted into a subject of scholastic debate. But by this time, the dispute was for practical purposes dead. William of Ockham had submitted in 1348; the moderate majority in the Order had taken control with papal approval. The dispute about poverty, nevertheless, with all its scholastic elaboration and political unreality, contained a kernel of genuine importance, a disagreement about whether property was in itself a good which would form part of a perfect world or whether it was a necessity of the temporal world to be shunned, if possible – this was a dispute which potentially divided two radically opposed interpretations of man. Groups of *Fraticelli* (little brothers) outside the Order but claiming to be the only true descendants of St Francis, survived in Italy long after, into the fifteenth century. Their characteristics were adherence to the old ideals of rigid poverty and the expectation of the millenium. The most famous of their number, Fra Michele, was brutally executed in Florence before the Franciscan Church in 1389. But the movement had had its day.

The original breeding ground of the Fraticelli and the area in which they flourished longest was the mountain country of central Italy where the traditions of remote ascetic hermitages and of holy men and women venerated by small communities were powerful factors in ordinary religious life. The Franciscan Order, by this time, was a vast European organization and the asceticism of the Apennines was only one, though it might claim to be the original one, of the ways of life which it embraced. In the Italian cities, in contrast to the countryside, the late medieval church had made its most successful adaptation to new social conditions. The mendicant orders had been largely responsible for this by taking over the organization of city religion in the course of the thirteenth century. By 1320, it centred around huge city churches like the Franciscan Santa Croce at Florence or the Dominican SS. Giovanni e Paolo at Venice, where preachers addressed very large congregations. The mendicants also had 'tertiary orders' attached to them, that is to say, organizations of lay men and women who pursued an ordinary lay life but satisfied their piety by wearing habits and following strict rules and were regarded as semi-religious. The mendicants, therefore, produced, especially in Italy, a form of organization which was extremely well adapted for canalizing the religious instincts of a huge urban population of lay men and women; fulfilling a function which would have been impossible for the parish organization. The Italian cities also had a mass of lay confraternities of various kinds, organizations of laymen, usually attached to churches, which performed religious and charitable duties and also observed strict rules.

Apart from the *Fraticelli*, therefore, Italian society in the fourteenth and fifteenth centuries is notable for the successful absorption of an effervescent religious life into orthodox organization. The capacity for constant renewal of religious enthusiasm without breaking out of the orthodox framework is very striking. It is worth looking briefly at two prominent examples. The first is a Dominican. The Dominican Order, also dating from the early thirteenth century and based on a similar obligation of poverty to the Franciscans, had on the whole, a less turbulent history. It produced no movement like the *Fraticelli* and it was more settled in its concentration on preaching and learning; otherwise, it had a similar role in Italian society. St Catherine of Siena entered the Dominican tertiary order about the middle of the fourteenth century as a girl, went through an ecstatic religious conversion and, though living with her family, devoted her life to the care of the poor and the sick. Her extraordinarily powerful personality brought her out into a prominent position in the last years of her life from 1375 to 1380. In these years, she preached a crusade at Pisa and then went to Avignon to exhort Gregory XI to do his duty by returning to Rome. Gregory, in fact, needed no persuasion and she probably had little practical effect but she made a profound impression on the Curia and after the pope's return, undertook missions to Florence on her own initiative to preach and try to draw that city into peace with the Church. Among the people profoundly affected by her was her confessor and biographer, Raymond of Capua, who became Minister General of the Dominicans in the year of her death. He initiated the system of setting up Observant convents, to be populated by those brothers who wished to observe the original rule of the Order more strictly than had been customary in the recent past. Catherine was obviously a very extraordinary woman, but, while Joan of Arc, for example, seems totally unparalleled in her environment, Catherine's life is a magnified version of a common type in Italian society.

S. Bernardino was also formed in the society of Siena at the end of the fourteenth century, as a member of a confraternity, a hospital organizer during a plague and then a

Franciscan. In 1403 he started his dual life's work, the pro-motion of Observant houses within the order and popular preaching which occupied him until his death in 1444. He was extraordinarily successful. The number of observant houses was said to have risen from 20 to 230 in his lifetime. His long, emotional, puritanical sermons made an impression throughout northern Italy. Like Catherine, Bernardino was an Italian type of the period, the mendicant revivalist. In contrast to the apparent inertia of religious life in large parts of northern Europe during the fifteenth century, early Renais-sance Italy was the scene of a number of popular revivals, usually connected with the orders and distinguished by puritanism within an orthodox framework. The most famous of the evangelists, Savonarola at the end of the fifteenth century, was a natural successor, who reminds us that intense religious puritanism was still more characteristic of Renais-sance Italy in general than the secular humanism with which it is usually associated.

In the cities of northern Europe the Church was less success-ful in dealing with contemporary society. Northern towns also had great numbers of mendicants and confraternities but there were probably more novelties in the North in the fourteenth century and the Church was less flexible than it had been a century earlier. Whatever the reason, most of the dissident or fringe manifestations of the fourteenth-century church are to be found in the towns of the Low Countries, the Rhineland and central Europe. A common feature of the life of these towns were pious men and women who devoted themselves to an apostolic life. Unlike the members of religious orders, they were not organized under any rule or ecclesiastical discipline. They were commonly called *beghards* (men) and *béguines* (women). The women tended to organize them-selves in houses but the men were often mendicants and the word *beghard* seems to have been synonymous with *turlupin* (more common in France) and with 'Lollard' which was later in the century imported into England as an imprecise general designation for every sort of religious radical. The *béguines*, who were commoner, were regarded as dangerous by priests because they aped the religious orders and talked theology.

They were very numerous: by 1320 there were about 100 *béguine* convents in Cologne alone. They were denounced by the papacy in one of the decrees of the Council of Vienne in 1311 (*Cum de quibusdam mulieribus*) which complained that 'certain women commonly called Béguines, afflicted by a kind of madness, discuss the Holy Trinity, and the divine essence and express opinions on matters of faith and sacraments contrary to the Catholic faith, deceiving many simple people. Since these women promise no obedience to anyone and do not renounce their property or profess an approved rule, they are certainly not "religious", although they wear a habit and are associated with such religious orders as they find congenial'. Most of them, no doubt, were animated by the ordinary instincts of pious spinsters and widows who could not afford or did not like husbands. In fact, as the century progressed, many of the houses adopted rules and they ceased to be regarded as a menace. The reason for their adoption of their way of life was fairly clearly that society and the Church did not otherwise provide for them.

A quite different problem was posed by the only genuine widespread, organized heresy of this period, the *Waldensians* or *Vaudois*, descended from the disciples of the late twelfth century evangelist, Peter Valdes. The *Waldensians* were very widely spread in the fourteenth century. Proceedings against them were numerous, especially in Lombardy, eastern France, Germany and central Europe. They belonged to the country-side and the small towns rather than the cities. Like the later English Lollards, they seem to have been mostly simple men who rejected the established Church as spurious and professed a hard, quietist life of religious poverty which probably suited their social condition. They read the gospels in translation, they thought oath-taking of any kind sinful, they rejected legal jurisdictions, they thought the Eucharist valid only for those free of sin, they rejected purgatory and images together with most of the normal church organization. But they were not isolated, conscientious objectors. They recognized the authority of a class of sinless *perfecti* devoted to a mendicant life after a ceremony of initiation; like other later nonconformist organizations, they had established their own counter-church, a hierarchy formed according to their alternative standard of devotion to the apostolic life. They were not militant and in most times and places ecclesiastical authorities did not take the trouble to root them out. In most areas they eventually died out or were absorbed into later reformed churches, including the Hussite movement of which they were probably important precursors in Bohemia and Austria.

Yet another type of religious manifestation is provided by the Flagellants. Flagellation as a form of penance was a very widespread phenomenon in Mediterranean Europe. In Italy many of the confraternities of the towns, thoroughly respectable organizations composed of ordinary citizens, included flagellation by their members as a regular penitential exercise. There were brief periods, however, both in Italy and in northern Europe when mass hysteria produced penitential movements in which violent and repeated self-infliction of wounds by flagellation played a large part. The most important of these movements spread from Hungary across northern Europe at the time of the Black Death in 1348–9. Its adherents developed rituals of public flagellation, often performed in the middle of towns, moved about the countryside and also sang hymns in the vernacular. Evidently, a number of factors entered into the movement: the psychological effects of the plague, anti-clericalism, anti-semitism (Jews were massacred in some of the German towns), millennarian expectations. The movement was condemned by a papal bull. In most places it vanished fairly quickly. In 1399 processions of *Bianchi* (so called because of their penitential white clothing) moved about the towns and countryside of Italy. Many of these also were Flagellants. The movement was unexpected and surprising though the millennarian significance was one factor in its origins. It died away as mysteriously as it had arisen.

At the same time as the denunciation of *béguines* in 1311, Pope Clement V issued a decree condemning *béguines* and *beghards*, also to be found according to this document in Germany, who believed that it was possible for men to attain to a sinless perfection in this life which freed those who achieved it from obedience to laws of church or state. This condemnation was followed in the fourteenth and fifteenth centuries by a number of trials of individual laymen and women who were supposed to have claimed that they had attained god-like perfection, identification with God, freedom from earthly imperfections, or that such things were attainable. This is what has been called the heresy of the 'Free Spirit'. There is no evidence that there was an elaborate organization of such a heresy. It appears however that there were a number of people – mostly women – in the towns of the Netherlands, the Rhineland and Germany who practised asceticism outside ecclesiastical control and developed unorthodox theories about what could be done by ascetics. For example, a woman in a community at Schweidknitz in Silesia, which was investigated in 1332, was supposed to have said, 'just as God is God, so she was God with God, . . . when God created everything . . . I created everything with him'. It is very difficult to know how much of the content of reports like this is to be attributed to insanity, how much to religious exaltation, how much to inquisitorial methods. The 'Free Spirit' was a state of mind, not a church or a doctrine, but it does seem to have existed fairly often in some parts of Europe.

The Netherlands and Rhineland also produced a school of mystical writers which includes the great names of Master Eckhart, Johann Tauler, Heinrich Suso and Jan Ruysbroeck, and which constitutes the most striking link between popular religion and sophisticated thought. Eckhart (1260–1327) was a Dominican friar who rose to high rank in his order as Minister Provincial of Saxony and was also a highly educated theologian. He became famous through his preaching in Strasburg and Cologne in the later years of his life. The inspiration which he tried to convey to his hearers was a mysticism which owed much to the tradition of Christian neoplatonism stretching back to Antiquity. Eckhart may have been orthodox in intention but the unusual language which he used (e.g. 'we are transformed totally into God and converted in him in a similar manner as in the sacrament the bread is converted into the body of Christ') and the alarming impact of his sermons led to his condemnation for heresy at the end of his life in the course of John XXII's thorough-going witch hunt. Eckhart preached to the laity an extreme and daring enterprise of individual perfection – the soul was to empty itself of concern for worldly things and by an effort of intellect come to an understanding of God. Among other things Eckhart preached sermons and wrote treatises in German; his works were a most unusual meeting of ecclesiastical learning and the vernacular. Some of his statements are difficult to distinguish from 'Free Spirit' theology. The opening of such vistas to a non-clerical city populace by such a great master of the spiritual life was novel and to ecclesiastical authority perplexing. Tauler (*c.* 1304–61) was also a Dominican chiefly active at Cologne and Strasburg. Suso (1295–1366), another Dominican, wrote an account of his own life which is an early modern example of autobiographical conversion literature. Tauler was active chiefly as a preacher both to convents of Dominicanesses and to laymen. It was Tauler's works rather than those of the greater Eckhart, tainted with the suspicion of heresy, which survived in circulation to inspire Luther. And Tauler's connection with Rulman Merswin, the Strasburg merchant founder of houses of the Friends of God, has naturally been regarded as symbolic of the link between learned theology, the special province of the Dominican Order, and the piety of women and laymen. The relationship between university theology and religious life in general through the later Middle Ages is a strange one: high learning was for the most part the preserve of an élite but in sermon literature, as for instance in the works of Wycliffe and Hus, it could enter in a diluted form into the unlearned world. The works of the Rhineland mystics were perhaps the most fruitful adaptation of the university tradition to the spiritual needs of the unlearned. A large proportion of their sermons and writings were in German, not Latin. They are the first considerable body of religious literature in northern Europe in a popular language.

There is some similarity between this position and that of their contemporary Jan Ruysbroeck (1293–1381), who wrote entirely in Flemish and spent the whole of his life in Brabant. Until 1343 he was a fairly ordinary priest in Brussels. Then he set up a small and unpretentious religious community under the Augustinian rule in the country nearby at Groenendael.

Ruysbroeck is now generally regarded as one of the great mystical writers of the Middle Ages. One of his main pre-occupations in his writings was to point out the errors of the 'Free Spirit' enthusiasts whom he had encountered in the city of Brussels. According to a biographer he grappled especially with a woman from one of the patrician families of Brussels who had acquired great prestige in the city as a religious oracle, making pronouncements to her followers from a silver throne. Ironically, twenty years after his death, in the first decade of the fifteenth century, Ruysbroeck's own writings came under the scrutiny of the great theologian of Paris University, Jean Gerson. Gerson found in them unsound theories about the possibility of union between the individual and God. Like Eckhart, though to a lesser extent, Ruysbroeck's ideas appeared to ecclesiastical authority to be dangerously tinged with the unorthodox enthusiasm which was endemic in the lay city world around him.

Ruysbroeck had some influence on the origins of a more widespread orthodox movement in the Netherlands. One of his disciples, Gert Groote (1340–82), also an enemy of heresy, and a disciple of Groote called Florens Radewijns, were the founders of two connected movements which were to influence the later religious life of north-west Europe considerably. The Brothers of the Common Life were loose communities of priests and laymen aiming at an approach to the apostolic life without strict rules or withdrawal into the cloisters. They were similar in aim to the mendicant third orders. From Deventer and Utrecht they spread widely over the Netherlands and western Germany. The Canons of Windesheim on the other hand were an enclosed order aiming at a very severe observation of the monastic life in reaction against the laxity of the old orders of Benedictines and others. The Brothers of the Common Life were devoted as part of their austere life to education and one of their members was perhaps the most famous religious author of the later Middle Ages, Thomas à Kempis (1380–1471) a Rhinelander who joined the Brothers at Deventer in 1392. The style of Kempis's *Imitation of Christ,* which he completed by 1424, – personal, literate but uncompromisingly ascetic – is probably a faithful echo of the ideals of the Brothers. The organization springing from the work of Groote and Radewijns came nearest to providing the towns-people of north-west Europe with an approach to religion, foreshadowing that of the Calvinists and Puritans, which was appropriate to their way of life.

The turbulent spirit of fourteenth-century Europe was controlled by an overwhelmingly powerful church and papacy which commanded the respect if not the love of lay authorities. At the end of the century however the structure of the Church was radically weakened. This led to a period of instability in institutions and ideas during the early fifteenth century in which some of the ideas mentioned in this chapter emerged from the corners and shadows of society into positions of prominent and even dominant importance.

CHAPTER V

THE CRISIS OF THE PAPACY
AND THE CHURCH

i *The Great Schism*

Pope Gregory XI left Avignon on 13 September 1376 to embark on a painful journey back to Rome, after which only schismatic popes were to reside at Avignon. At that time the popes had been established at Avignon for some sixty-eight years. So strong had the connection become that it was only with the greatest persistence in the face of strong opposition from the King of France, the majority of the cardinals, and even his own family, that Gregory was able to tear himself free of Avignon and carry through his entirely conscientious project to restore the papacy to its proper see at St Peter's. The tears which were shed when Gregory left Avignon and the desperate attempts which were made to keep him there showed the strength of the connection. The papal connection with Avignon and all that it entailed had become so deep-rooted, such a network of customs and relationships and vested interests had grown up around it, that Gregory's move, which might seem in a very long historical perspective to be the most natural restoration of the papacy to its proper sphere, seemed to his contemporaries to be a revolutionary step. To some influential cardinals and nobles it appeared as wanton adherence to a revolutionary idea in the face of the natural continuity of politics. From a practical point of view it could only be regarded as a most unwise move. The city of Rome itself was in decay. Some of the titular churches of the cardinals themselves lacked roofs. The palace at the Vatican was uninhabitable. The return would be enormously expensive. As a papal capital, Rome, even after Albornoz, was much less secure than Avignon. It was only the inflexible will of the Pope opposed to material advantage and prudential policy that carried through the enterprise. Its historical results, the severance of the papacy from northern Europe and its return to the Mediterranean, were enormous and they represent a striking case of vast consequences following unexpectedly from the will of one man.

Gregory XI had a predecessor in Urban V who made a temporary return in 1367. Both were ecclesiastically minded popes more than ordinarily concerned about the scandal of absence from Rome. Urban V was a monk who tried to keep up a monastic regimen as Pope, living frugally and devoting himself solely to proper ecclesiastical concerns. Gregory XI, though a nephew of Clement VI and a cardinal at the age of nineteen, born to the purple in a great Avignon dynasty, was by training and inclination a scholar: he had studied law at Perugia and he assembled a famous library. Urban's attempt to return had underlined the difficulties. It was opposed by the French court which sent a special embassy to resist it. When Urban had got as far as Viterbo fighting broke out between his following and the local people and there was a rising. In Rome he was received with great enthusiasm by the populace but the political situation in the State soon became menacing. One of the magnates, Francesco di Vico, rose in Tuscia. Further north the city of Perugia rose. Bernabò Visconti of Milan threatened to invade. After retiring from Rome for the late summer heat in 1369, Urban did not return. But if Rome was unattractive then it was far more so in 1376 when Gregory's plans matured, for instead of the optimistic aftermath of Albornoz's efforts this was a time when the papal position in Italy was more insecure than it had been for half a century.

Contrary to the legend that he was shamed into adopting the return to Rome by St Catherine of Siena, there is every reason to suppose that Gregory embraced it as the chief objective of his policy as soon as he was elected in 1370 and never abandoned it. To his misfortune, however, his pontificate happened to be filled with the kind of turmoil in central Italy which was most unfavourable for his plans. From 1372 to 1375 the pope who dreamed of directing a united Christendom from St Peter's in a crusading effort against the Turks, a true inheritor of medieval ideals, was forced to devote the best part of his efforts to fighting a war in Italy often against his own immediate subjects. These years saw a particularly bitter conflict between the papacy, defending its position in the Italian state, and an aggressive Milan under Bernabò Visconti. To fight such an enemy the pope was forced to adopt methods which were particularly destructive of his idealistic position in Europe. Throughout the Church he imposed particularly heavy taxes, the last effective attempt to maintain the fiscal powers of his predecessors. In Italy he taxed his subjects in the states oppressively and engaged the help of English and French mercenaries, notably the companies of John Hawkwood and Enguerrand de Coucy, thus associating himself with some of the most distasteful aspects of the Italian political scene.

After the end of the Milanese war in 1375 Gregory was faced by a new outburst in the papal state which was even more harmful to his Italian position. The new trouble was caused by mounting hostility to the papacy in Florence and in the towns of the papal state. This was largely the result of the war effort against Milan during which his taxation had pressed hard on his towns and had been imposed by an unloved French administration. After the war had ended, transalpine mercenaries, associated in the popular mind with the papacy, were still more dangerous to local people because they were unemployed. Friction produced mounting hostility which in the later part of 1375 exploded into successful rebellion in many towns of the state and warfare between the pope and Florence. The war with Florence was particularly bitter. The great commercial republic did not have the military capacity of Milan but it had great wealth at its disposal. It was also able to adopt an ideological position as the champion of Italian republicanism against barbarian mercenaries, the defender of 'Liberty', which it used to inflame the revolts of the papal cities. In Florence itself the war excited very strong anti-papal feeling and some consequent seizure of ecclesiastical property. In memory of eight officials connected with this seizure it came to be called the 'War of the Eight Saints'. Gregory imposed an interdict on Florence and released other Christians from their debts to Florentine merchants. The war dragged on into 1378 and indeed received a new impetus at the beginning of 1377 when Hawkwood's English mercenaries massacred the innocent civilian population of the town of Cesena.

It took Gregory XI four months to travel from Avignon to Rome which he reached in January 1377. The difficulty of the journey which was attended by almost every conceivable misfortune, including shipwreck, presaged the storms to come. Gregory returned to a very divided and hostile patrimony. He died in Rome in March 1378. On his death sixteen of the twenty-three cardinals were at Rome to take part in the election. Six Frenchmen were still at Avignon so that the French voting strength was rather diminished. Of those at Rome seven belonged to the 'Limousin' party (stemming from Limoges), five were French but not Limousin and four were Italians. This distribution of interests really determined the progress of the fateful election which took place in May 1378. The French participants were so equally divided that the small number of Italian cardinals held the balance. This, combined with the intimidating pressure of the Roman mob calling for the election of an Italian, made that outcome possible. One may reflect ironically that if the six French cardinals still lingering in Avignon had come to Rome they might have secured a French election which would have led to a return to Avignon and thus perpetuated the Avignon papacy. As it was, however, the conclave resulted in the election of an outsider, Bartolomeo Prignano Archbishop of Bari, as Urban VI.

Most of the cardinals in Rome accepted Urban, a learned and austere non-cardinal. They might have continued to do so if he had not very quickly proved himself to be also a tactless and provocative Puritan. He attacked the luxurious eating habits of the cardinals, their neglect of their titular churches, their acceptance of bribes from laymen and he reproached them in public. Urban did not understand the ways of the papal court and his intolerable behaviour opened the way for the Schism. The Schism was made possible by two things. Firstly the hostility of the majority of the College of Cardinals to Urban VI, not only a personal dislike, but also a rooted objection to the return to Rome which most of them had disliked from the first and would have prevented if Gregory XI had not been so inflexible. Secondly a distribution of interest among the lay powers of Europe which made the division into two obediences politically attractive. During the summer of 1378 the cardinals, repelled by Urban VI, drifted away from Rome and congregated in the nearby papal town of Anagni. From there they eventually denounced Urban's election as invalid and finally in September elected one of their own number, Robert of Geneva, as anti-pope with the title of Clement VII. During recent years Clement had been in charge of the papal mercenaries in central Italy. These mercenaries, many of them French, were still present in considerable numbers in and around Rome and in the early months of the Schism their support for the French cardinals was crucially important. Urban VI had at first no effective power at his disposal with which to squash his enemies. Only in 1379 was he able to defeat and disperse the French troops. By that time the first phase was over; the Schism was beginning to be established on a broad European basis.

The first two powers to give support to Clement VII were Queen Joanna of Naples and King Charles V of France. The reason for the decision of the Queen of Naples is obscure and puzzling because Urban was her subject and might have expected help. For whatever reason Joanna came fairly quickly to the decision to favour Clement. This was important because Neapolitan help was near enough to be immediately useful. It also determined that the Italian peninsula should be torn between the two obediences throughout the Schism period. More important in the long run was the attitude of Charles V of France, the most powerful prince in Christendom. Although he made a gesture to Urban VI, Charles seems in fact to have favoured the dissident cardinals from the beginning and to have encouraged their independence covertly even before they had announced their denunciation of Urban. The French desire for the Schism antedated it. The natural wish of the French crown to perpetuate the favourable circumstances of the Avignon papacy, the profitable *entente* between Avignon and Paris, was the main substantial reason for the beginning as it was for the continuance of the Schism, the rock on which the Avignon papacy continued to be built. Charles V quickly accepted Clement VII. The inclination of the French court was strengthened by the personal interest of Charles's brother Louis Duke of Anjou, a wealthy prince in search of a kingdom, who helped Clement VII with money on the understanding that he was to have papal support for intervention and conquest in Italy. At this stage the intention was probably that he should take over the Visconti dominions, usefully removing the Church's most dangerous Italian enemy while satisfying his own personal ambition. But the link with Clement VII was to lead in the end to the revival of the old French interest in the kingdom of Naples and thus introduce an important theme in Italian politics of the fifteenth and early sixteenth centuries. In the summer of 1379 Clement went from Naples to Avignon to continue the Avignon papacy.

During the next few years, partly by the natural operation of political reactions, partly through the activities of diplomatic envoys sent out by Urban and Clement, the main lines of a political division of Europe into two obediences were worked out. Urban's chief acquisitions were the Luxemburg Emperor Charles IV, quickly followed after his death in 1378 by his son King Wenceslas, and England, both motivated no doubt mainly by opposition to France. Urban was also fairly successful for the same reason in the Netherlands and was theoretically though luke-warmly accepted in northern Italy. Clement VII, apart from France and Naples, was most successful in the Iberian peninsula where both Aragon and Castile eventually rallied to him. These main lines of division persisted until the Schism began to break up in the early years of the fifteenth century. They do not complete the picture because there were many small political units, propaganda activity was often intense, and allegiances were most uncertain and shifting in areas of most political fragmentation like the Rhineland and central Italy. There had been many schisms and anti-popes in the past. This one was different because it involved not merely a dispute about the headship of the Church but the division of Europe into two genuine and fully developed ecclesiastical structures. The ecclesiastical and administrative organization at Avignon had not been fully transferred to Rome. It was easy for Clement VII to resume and continue it. Urban VI could use the administration transferred to Italy by Gregory XI. After the apostasy of Clement VII he was left with only a handful of mainly Italian cardinals. He created a new college naturally consisting mainly of Italian cardinals and his cause was served increasingly by Italian administrators. Thus two papacies and two central administrations were created, one mainly French and one mainly Italian.

The Schism lasted from 1378 to 1415, for a whole generation. Its unedifying political squabbles and the dull legalism of the propaganda issued by both sides have made it an unpopular subject for modern historians and a forgotten episode in European history. In its effects, however, it is very important. The obvious deduction is the true one: the Great Schism began the destruction of the medieval papacy. Gregory XI, albeit with difficulty and against resistance, had directed the machinery of the high medieval papacy in all its grand and powerful complexity. There was no thought of contraction during his pontificate; the papacy was still expanding its medieval powers. His collectors gathered money from clerical subsidies all over Europe. He supervised the appointments to major ecclesiastical benefices, bishoprics and abbeys and collected Services from them. He influenced appointments to a great many minor benefices by collation and reservation. His cardinals mediated with some genuine effect between the Kings of England and France. From distant Avignon he could direct armies to operate effectively in the Romagna. After Gregory XI, that machinery was never properly restored. There are two reasons for this. One is the general social transformation which was then occurring in European rural society: the decline of the power of rural landlords which ultimately weakened the tax-collecting governments dependent on these landlords. The papacy in the late fourteenth century met, and would in any case have met even if the Schism had not taken place, increasing resistance from the clergy who were less willing to pay subsidies because their own rent income was harder to collect and from laymen who were less willing for the papacy to appoint its nominees to their benefices. The Church was so dependent on landed wealth that the crisis of seigniorial landlordship in the period 1350–1450 permanently reduced its standing in European society. Thus it is probable that even if the Schism had not happened the high medieval form of papacy would have been difficult to maintain. But it would have been less difficult. The second reason was the Schism and this was decisive. When there were two popes each one was fatally weakened in his relationship to his political supporters. It was impossible for either of the popes to maintain the full vigour of their systems of taxation and appointment. The popes of the Schism period on both sides were poor and impotent in comparison with their predecessors. By the time the Schism was healed in 1415 this change was too generally accepted for it to be possible to return to the old ways.

Urban VI reigned until 1389. His remote allies in England and Germany were of little practical value to him and during this period the Roman branch of the papacy returned to the position of extreme insecurity and vulnerability in the stormy world of Italian politics which had been the lot of many early medieval popes before the prosperous days in Avignon. Urban also showed himself to be a tough, grasping and vindictive man. The central question, as for so many earlier and later popes, was his relation with the kingdom of Naples, because it could mean security or insecurity in Rome, close to the frontier with Naples, and also for the less fundamental reason that Urban as a south Italian himself hoped to endow his family with lands within the kingdom.

The return of the papacy to Rome increased the importance of its relationship with Naples. In considering the history of the papacy in the period of the Schism and the Councils, the subject of this chapter, the actions of the popes have to be understood in two contexts: their general relation to Latin Christendom and the local political pressures which affected them in the papal state among which the influence of Naples was always particularly important. The history of the papacy in this period will therefore involve sketching also the history of southern Italy. Queen Joanna of Naples supported Clement VII and, being childless, she adopted as her heir Louis Duke of Anjou, his keenest French supporter. But there was another more successful claimant to the Neapolitan throne, a remote relation, Charles of Durazzo, who invaded the kingdom in 1381, defeated the forces of Joanna's fourth husband and imprisoned her. Joanna, like Charles of Durazzo, was ultimately descended from Charles Count of Anjou who invaded Naples in the thirteenth century; they both belonged to the old Angevin line of Naples and Hungary. The new French claimant, Louis, was also, fortuitously and confusingly for the modern student of history, Duke of Anjou, but the title does not indicate a relationship; he established a new Angevin line. Louis of Anjou's descent into Italy in 1382 was supported by Bernabò Visconti who was at that time playing for a marriage alliance with France and thus initiated a policy of using French intervention in Italy. The expectation of French invasion may have inspired Charles of Durazzo to murder Joanna; at any rate her body was exhibited to prove that she was no longer an alternative ruler. Louis of Anjou's invasion seemed likely to succeed in winning Naples for him and this intensified the political conflict associated with the Schism. Urban VI, the Roman Pope, in reaction to the Angevin claimant to Naples, gave full support to Charles of Durazzo and moved into the kingdom of Naples himself. In 1384, when his prospects seemed good, Louis died, but the kingdom of Naples was immediately conferred by the Avignon Pope on his son Louis II of Anjou, who invaded Italy in 1390.

Thus the new tradition of Angevin intervention had been fully established and Louis II was deeply embroiled in Naples. Urban was incapable of managing his own candidate. His policy culminated disastrously in 1385 with the torture of six of his own cardinals and Charles of Durazzo besieging him in Nocera on the borders of the papal state. Urban then retreated from Naples and spent most of the rest of his life in exile in Genoa, Lucca and Perugia, planning ineffectively a new incursion into Naples whose political life was once more thrown into confusion by the death of Charles of Durazzo in 1386.

Urban's successor Pope Boniface IX (1389–1404) was also a Neapolitan but from the temporal point of view a man of less quarrelsome and narrow-minded tendencies with some of the qualities of a constructive politician. Unlike Urban, Boniface made serious attempts to restore the shattered finances of the Roman papacy. He was not successful in getting the co-operation of northern monarchs in raising taxes from their kingdoms. But some of the more humble financial expedients which were to be found useful by later Renaissance popes can be traced to his pontificate and the Curia returned to a more ordered way of life. Boniface made his political cornerstone an alliance with Ladislas of Naples. Charles of Durazzo, who had taken the kingdom of Naples from Joanna, was killed in Hungary in 1386, when trying to make good his claim to the throne of that country also. Ladislas his son was a boy and the kingdom relapsed into the semi-anarchy of magnate rule which was always near the surface. In 1390 Ladislas was crowned king by the new Pope Boniface IX. The relationship now established between the papacy and Naples was a curious one and was to be very important in future years: the king needed papal recognition because he was threatened by a French rival for the throne, the pope needed Neapolitan friendship because without it his position in Rome was extremely insecure. In the same year that Ladislas was crowned Louis II of Anjou invaded. The duel between them was to last throughout Ladislas's life. For the first decade Ladislas was fighting to recover control of the kingdom. Louis had landed at Naples and controlled the territory around the capital. Some of the Neapolitan nobility supported him. It was not until 1399 that Ladislas entered Naples itself. By then Louis of Anjou had been weakened by the cooling of French enthusiasm for the Avignon papacy and the abandonment of his cause by some of the leading Neapolitan nobles, including the Sanseverino family. In 1402 to 1403 Ladislas turned aside from Naples and tried, like his father, to recover the kingdom of Hungary, which since 1382 had been in the hands of Sigismund of Luxemburg. He was able to get the support of Venice and its invaluable power along the Adriatic coast and got so far as to have himself crowned at Zara. But he then wisely abandoned the enterprise and devoted the rest of his life to aggression in Italy. The popes of the Schism period were all more or less insecure in Rome, vulnerable to uprisings by the populace or the nobility; Ladislas could advance his power by intervening on one side or the other. He helped Boniface IX to put down a rebellion of the Roman populace in 1394, and a revolt led by a member of the Caetani family in 1399. Although he suffered a great deal from the hostility of the Romans, who more than once forced him to flee the city, Boniface's position was generally more secure and his control over the papal state better than Urban's had been.

At Avignon Clement VII reigned in a contrasting atmosphere of comparative security and affluence under the protection of the French crown. The claim of John of Gaunt to the throne of Castile made it relatively easy to persuade the king of the largest Spanish kingdom to accept the French pope at a council at Medina del Campo in 1381. He was followed by the kings of Aragon and Navarre in 1389 and 1390. Clement therefore enjoyed a large and geographically unified obedience which was easier to manage than Urban's group of scattered and uncertain followers. The end of his life however was disturbed by a different kind of threat. Many scholars in the University of Paris thought that the Schism was a religious scandal which ought to be ended, even at the expense of the resignation of the Avignon pope, by the submission of the dispute to the judgement of a general council of the Church and in 1394 – the year of Clement's death – the promoters of this plan, called the *Via Cessionis*, the 'Way of Surrender', found a degree of favour at the royal court. In the days of the masterful Charles V the French court would have been united and more likely to be solidly behind its pope. King Charles VI was a prey to the policies of his great noble relatives, the most powerful of whom was Philip, Duke of Burgundy, ruler of an area of divided ecclesiastical allegiance where rigid adherence to one side was not such an attractive policy. The decision of Charles VI to give some support to the ideologists of the university was in a sense the first move in the process which was eventually to bring the Schism to an end, the first serious sign that the power blocks might dissolve and realign.

ii *The Age of the Councils*

The practical division and enfeeblement of papal authority which resulted from the Schism had profound implications in the world of ideas. The medieval church was a partially centralized monarchical system. The theoretical structure which had been created to match it was even more monarchical in conception. It depended of course fundamentally on the pope's role as Christ's vicar on earth in succession to St Peter. The Church as a whole constituted a mystical body which was identified with Christ, but within that body the power to regulate the Church on earth resided in its head. As an early fourteenth century theologian, Augustinus Triumphus, expressed it: 'The pope succeeds to Peter in personal administration . . . he succeeds to Christ however in office and in universal jurisdiction because Peter in the person of all the pontiffs received universal jurisdiction from Christ.' In the view which had come to be widely held by the fourteenth century, the pope was the head who controlled the body of the Church; the body did not legislate for itself, the pope legislated for it. There were of course analogies between this theory and the theories of lay monarchy which was often understood as a head controlling the body politic. But lay monarchies were in practice much more limited by assemblies of their subjects and, in theory, their powers were commonly related to a 'natural law' to which they were supposed to conform. The power of popes was limited in practice by no assemblies representative of the whole Church except very infrequent general councils (none met between 1311 and 1409) and in theory the supernatural origins of the office provided strong arguments for its unique authority. The monarchical power of the pope within the Church was therefore theoretically more impressive than that of kings in their kingdoms. It had theoretical and practical expression in the canon law. This was the body of law which regulated the lives of clergy and the relations of laymen to the Church, and was used in ecclesiastical courts throughout Europe. It had grown up mostly in the twelfth and thirteenth centuries. It consisted essentially of the decrees and decisions of popes. Being the product of a monarchy's jurisdiction, it naturally provided theoretical support for the monarch. Its arguments had been elaborated and sophisticated by two centuries of canon lawyers who had included many of the ablest minds of Christendom.

The Schism made it much more difficult for people to believe that the government of the Church could be left to popes. It therefore encouraged intellectuals to develop an alternative conception of the nature of the Church and of the source of authority in it. In many quarters of course, the opportunity given by the Schism to cut down the theoretical stature of the papacy was seized with enthusiasm because many churchmen disliked the practical centralization of the papacy. The result was the development of a body of doctrine which emphasized the corporate authority of the whole Church and the governmental role of representative councils against the idea of the pope as a clerical king. This is 'conciliar thought'. From an early stage in the Schism it was suggested that the only way of reuniting the Church was to override the authority of the conflicting popes by summoning a general council. By the end of the Schism period the notion of the power of a general council to act for the whole Church, even against a pope, was being elaborated by leading authorities at the very heart of the Church's ideological tradition. The leading writers were Jean Gerson and Pierre d'Ailly, both of whom were leading Paris theologians (d'Ailly was a delegate to the council of Pisa and both attended the council of Constance), and Francesco Zabarella, an Italian canonist. D'Ailly and Zabarella were both made cardinals by John XXIII. Gerson and d'Ailly both wrote in defence of the Council of Pisa, arguing that the whole body of the Church represented in a council could override a particular pope. About the same time Zabarella wrote a 'Treatise on Schism' in which he marshalled technical canonist arguments to support the view that the Church should be properly regarded, in legal terms, as a corporation of which the pope was the temporary head, not a monarchy. These ideas were preserved and developed by canonists and theologians in the next generation. The most memorable of the stream of writings on the theme is the *De Concordantia Catholica* (On Catholic Concord), published in 1433 by Nicholas of Cusa, a German philosopher and bishop who was at that time an enthusiastic supporter of the Council of Basle though he later changed to the papal side and was made a cardinal by Nicholas V. Nicholas of Cusa argued that the government of the Church ought to be a balance between the various parts, not a concentration of power in the one part.

As it turned out, conciliar thought was ultimately a blind alley as far as the history of the papacy was concerned. The idea of transferring authority in the Church to councils died out because the political circumstances which favoured such councils came to an end. After the middle of the fifteenth century conciliar thought was of little importance. For about fifty years, however, it was a flourishing and apparently promising line of ideas. Its popularity at that time reflected the fact that at some periods, especially the first decade of the fifteenth century, before and during the Councils of Pisa and Constance, and the fourth decade, during the heyday of the Council of Basle, it really looked as though the monarchical papacy was doomed. In fact it was to survive the crisis in a greatly altered form. Though the conciliar movement produced an extraordinary quantity of elaborate theory, its political history depended very largely on the shifting attitudes and fortunes of lay powers and the relations of these with various papal courts. The effective beginnings of the movement are to be found in the political impoverishment of the two rival popes by loss of lay support, which eventually persuaded their cardinals that a joint desertion of their pontiffs was a more promising policy than persistence in bankrupt claims of legitimacy.

Clement VII's successor Benedict XIII, elected in 1394, had been as a cardinal the main architect of the Avignon obedience in Iberia, but as pope he never enjoyed the enthusiastic support of the French court. From 1395 onwards, the court, under the influence of the clergy and their spokesmen at the University of Paris, hostile to the papacy for the usual reasons of objection to taxation and centralized control of benefices (Avignon cardinals were no less greedy pluralists after 1378 than before), clearly adopted the policy of the *Via Cessionis* with its political advantages for relations with the Low Countries and Germany. In 1398 a council of the French clergy at Paris proposed the withdrawal of obedience and this was for the time being accepted as royal policy. Benedict found himself, with even his Spanish support falling away, besieged in his palace at Avignon by French troops, his plight now no better than that of his Roman rival. In the next few years his support in France improved for the keenness of the political opposition depended substantially on the Netherlandish interests of the Duke of Burgundy and, as the influence of that prince at court waned, enthusiasm for a solution to the Schism by abdication waned also. The new bearer of the Angevin claim to the kingdom of Naples, Louis II of Anjou, was a natural ally of Avignon. But the attitude of both the court and the French clergy had become quite unreliable and in the early years of the new century Benedict was drawn into a new approach to his problem. In 1405 he moved to Genoa which had recently been converted to his cause by a French army, hoping that he could gain a decisive victory in the heartland of the rival obedience, and aggressively rejecting any suggestion of compromise. It was in that area, as it turned out, that the first effort to resolve the Schism was to reach its climax.

His rival, Innocent VII, the successor of Boniface IX, far from vindicating his claims to the obedience of Christendom, was unable to secure proper control of the city of Rome. The Roman papacy was overshadowed by the rising star of the Italian political scene, Ladislas of Naples. When Boniface IX died in 1404 there were renewed tumults in Rome, the Colonna family calling on Ladislas to intervene. The new pope, Innocent VII, was a subject of Ladislas who entered Rome two days after the election, establishing himself as the arbiter of the city, and was made rector of parts of the papal state. The pontificates of Innocent VII (1404–6) and Gregory XII (1406–9) were dominated by Ladislas. He was strengthening his hold over his own kingdom, confronting the greater nobility – several members of the Sanseverino family were strangled and the castle of the Orsini princes at Taranto besieged. Strong in Naples itself, Ladislas's aim seems to have been to use opportunities to increase his power in the papal state and beyond, posing as the champion of the Roman papacy against that of Avignon. At the election of Innocent's successor, Gregory XII, in 1406, the sense of powerlessness in the Roman Curia became a force for reconciliation equal to the French pressures on Avignon. Before the conclave, each of the cardinals agreed that if elected he would not enlarge his own College and would be willing to join the Avignon pope in a double abdication. During 1407 there were negotiations between the two courts. Then a new intrusion of Ladislas of Naples into Rome drove Gregory out of his palace to seek refuge in Siena. The two popes were now within a short physical distance of each other, both impotent or dependent on the support of uncontrollable lay powers – Ladislas on the one hand, the French army in Genoa on the other – each maintaining a farcical insistence on the total legitimacy of his position under the eyes of an increasingly sceptical or in-different Christendom. In May 1408, the next phase was precipitated by eight of Gregory's cardinals who deserted him because he had broken his promise by promoting four more loyal colleagues. In June, nine Roman and six Avignonese cardinals assembled at Pisa within the territory and under the cynical aegis of the ecclesiastically neutral republic of Florence. From there they proposed the holding of a general council of the Church in the same city.

The Council of Pisa met from March to August 1409. It was representative of a very large proportion of Latin Christen-dom. Several hundred bishops, abbots and proctors of lower rank represented the national churches of most parts of Europe and a number of lay rulers sent envoys. The absentees were not negligible. Aragon stood by Benedict XIII and he had taken refuge there. Gregory was supported by Ladislas of Naples and some other minor powers in Italy, outside by two German princes whose ecclesiastical policies reflected their secular aims: Rupert of the Palatinate, anti-king of Germany, was a Rhenish alternative to the Bohemian King Wenceslas; Sigismund, King of Hungary, was Wenceslas's brother and also hoped to supplant him. The council rested on the local support of two powers which wished to restrain the aggressions of Ladislas, Florence and the Cardinal Legate of Bologna, the northernmost part of the papal state, Baldassare Cossa; more widely in Europe it rested on those lay powers which had no interest in the claims of either pope and on the clergy in general who were happy to acquiesce in any movement which would produce a more peaceful and less exacting papacy. In addition to the main business of the Schism, there was a good deal of talk about reform and reduction of papal intervention, talk which produced little practical result. The council did, however, achieve its main purpose. It deposed the two existing popes and the cardinals of the combined colleges then elected a new one, Peter Philargis, Cardinal of Milan, a learned Cretan who became Alexander V.

Alexander V survived his election for less than a year and was succeeded by Baldassare Cossa, the determined Neapolitan nobleman who had become Legate at Bologna and now took the title of John XXIII. The other two popes both retained enough support to enable them to reject the verdict of Pisa. The next four years, in which Europe had three popes, were therefore only an interval before another attempt was made to heal the Schism by council. Gregory and Benedict had little capacity for effective action. John XXIII, supported by Florentine money and by Louis of Anjou, took up the duel with Ladislas of Naples, the most immediate and dangerous opponent of the Council of Pisa and its popes. The resolution of the Schism was anathema to Ladislas because his plans demanded above all a pliable pope at Rome. When Gregory XII had left Rome, Ladislas, with the support of the Colonna, had taken over. It now became a serious possibility that he would get control of all the papal state and become a danger farther north. When the Council of Pisa met, Ladislas advanced into Tuscany as far as Arezzo. He now became a menace to the whole peninsula and provoked a grouping of forces against him, at the heart of which was Florence. Florence joined with Siena, Baldassare Cossa and Louis II of Anjou and engaged the best available mercenaries. Ladislas withdrew. The allies occupied Rome. A fleet brought by Anjou from Marseilles was defeated by Neapolitan ships in a battle off the island of Meloria and for a while Florence was forced into peace with Ladislas. But the new pope of the Pisan obedience, John XXIII, was a formidable politician. He formed a new army including *condottieri*, which not only occupied Rome, but pressed into the kingdom to defeat Ladislas at Roccasecca in 1411. But Ladislas recovered, the pope's *condottieri* quarrelled, some passing to the service of Ladislas. In 1413 Ladislas occupied Rome again and gave it up to sack by his soldiers. John XXIII fled to the north. Ladislas pursued him. He seemed to be threatening Bologna and Florence, when in 1414 illness struck him down and once more Italy could breathe again. Before he died, however, he had made John XXIII's position in Italy hopelessly insecure and driven him into the arms of King Sigismund. The idea of the Council of Constance was born out of the plight of John XXIII and the ambitions of Sigismund who was now claiming the crown of Germany against his brother Wenceslas and wanted a friendly and universally accepted pope to validate his own position as Holy Roman Emperor in Germany and Italy, and to bring ecclesiastical unity to central Europe. In 1413, Sigismund persuaded John to accept the plan of a council at Constance. John would have been wise to refuse to attend the council but, with misgivings, he crossed the Alps in the autumn of that year.

The character of the Council of Constance is symbolized by the fact that it proceeded simultaneously and with similar ruthlessness against Pope John XXIII and against the Bohemian heretic, John Hus, who were respectively deposed and burnt in May and July 1415. The council was equally hostile to the heretic who defined the Church as the community of the regenerate and to the pope who misused the wealth of the clergy for his private purposes. The council was the voice of the solid majority of the European clergy. It was for reforming the head, but was profoundly conservative about the body of the Church. It stood for the hundreds of bishops and thousands of incumbents who wished to remain in the enjoyment of their offices undisturbed either by the turbulence of radicals, or by the exactions of the papal court. It was a vast and impressive assembly. It lasted for four years, from November 1414 to April 1418, it was attended by thousands of clergy and by King Sigismund and, while it lasted, its proceedings were the focus of European diplomacy in something akin to the manner of the peace conferences and international organizations of the twentieth century.

The early months of the council were occupied by the confrontation between Pope John XXIII, with his large following of Italian clergy, and the generally unfriendly churchmen of northern Europe. John had hoped to dominate it but the council showed quickly that it was not willing simply to accept him as head and, as he would have wished, to proceed with general questions of reform of the Church on the assumption that Pisa had completed the work of ending the Schism. On the contrary, it showed every disposition to start by reopening the question of the headship of the Church. This approach was reinforced when King Sigismund arrived in December 1414 and refused to support John's pretensions, preferring the views expressed by the French theorists Cardinals d'Ailly and Fillastre. A decisive step was taken when it was agreed that the members of the council should not be voted by head but by 'nations': the representatives were divided into the four nations of Italy, France, Germany and England, which were to debate separately before presenting common views in full assembly and this procedure robbed Pope John of the advantage of the numerical superiority of the Italians and automatically gave the advantage to the ultramontane churches. John was forced to agree to abdicate on condition that Benedict and Gregory, who were not present at the council, agreed to do the same. When he was pressed to make his abdication unconditional, John fled from Constance under the protection of Duke Frederick of Austria, an enemy of Sigismund. This forced the council to assume the power to continue its work as the embodiment of the will of the Church without the authority of a pope. It did not dispute the headship of the Roman Church, which was energetically supported in their own interests by the cardinals, but it inevitably behaved in practice as though there were no limitations to conciliar authority. John was brought back to the neighbourhood of Constance and formally deposed in May 1415.

Gregory XII added his abdication without much fuss. Benedict XIII was obdurate and, in his anxiety to remove all hindrances to the reorganization of the Church, Sigismund himself journeyed to the south of France to negotiate at Perpignan with the remaining Spanish supporters of the Avignon pope. Though Benedict would not yield, and lived without yielding until 1423, his supporters agreed in December 1415, to abandon him and participate in the general council as the Spanish Nation. Sigismund followed up his success with a long diplomatic trip to Paris and London and did not return to Constance until the beginning of 1417. During his absence the council had made little progress, partly because it was pre-occupied with the destruction of the Bohemian heretics, Hus and Jerome of Prague, partly because it lacked a force to produce decision out of its desultory and divided deliberations. Since the summer of 1415 a small reform commission had been sitting and had considered numerous proposals for the improvement of ecclesiastical behaviour and the limitation of papal authority. But its work was bedevilled by divisions including the bitter national division between France and England which followed Henry V's invasion in that year. As a deliberative body, the council was paralysed by its unwieldiness and by the serious division of interest which cut across its members: between the cardinals who had vested interests in papal supremacy and the other clergy who wanted to reduce papal influence, between the English and French clergy representing the lay political interests of their kings, between the English and Germans who were most willing to limit papal powers and the other nations which were less critical of them. However, the impatience of Sigismund and the political alliance between him and the English delegates of Henry V, was effective in bringing matters to a climax in the autumn of 1417. Two important actions were taken. The first was the publication of the decree *Frequens* which proclaimed that general councils should be held at regular intervals – though it proved to be ineffective, this was a victory for conciliarism. The second was agreement on a method of electing a pope, by a majority of two-thirds of the cardinals and two-thirds of the representatives of each of the nations. A cardinal of the Roman obedience

Oddo Colonna, was elected pope as Martin V by this system.

After the election of Martin V, the council lost nearly all its impetus and never recovered the cohesion which would have been necessary for an attack on the general question of reform. The issues which had been discussed under this head at Constance and which in varying degrees agitated the representatives of the various national churches included such ma ters as papal powers of taxation, pluralism, papal appointments to benefices, or organization of the college of cardinals and the power to grant indulgences. Theoretically the council might have legislated about these things in such a way as to curtail severely the rights of future popes. The proceedings of the council included many varied expressions of opinion on this issue, mostly voicing the desire of the clergy to limit papal power. But the council never presented anything like a united front. With the complete resolution of the problem of Schism, it would be natural to proceed to reform. Martin diverted the dangerous elements by issuing his own reform programme in January 1418, a moderate series of promises to observe the proper forms in such matters as taxation, sale of indulgences and elections of bishops. The council ended with the acceptance of three concordats for the English, French and German nations which again contained piously moderate rulings on the usual points at issue. Ecclesiastical Europe was for the time being too exhausted to press its advantages: the council was finished and in a sense the papal court had won.

Martin V (1417–31) is commonly and justly regarded as the precursor of the Borgias and the Della Rovere, the first pope who successfully adopted in outline the polity which was to become characteristic of the Renaissance Papacy. Essentially the new papacy was built on an acceptance of the forces destructive of the medieval papacy which had become irresistible during the Schism, primarily the refusal of ultramontane Europe to tolerate papal domination in the old manner. Martin had not given away very much in the concordats of 1418, but that was deceptive: whatever continuity there was in the rules, northern Europeans would no longer tolerate papal taxation or appointments as they had done in the past, and Martin was quite unable to force them. Positively, the Renaissance Papacy meant the creation of a new foundation for papal power in the control of the papal state which, starting from the ruins of the Schism period, was built anew in laborious stages and with huge setbacks over the century to come from the pontificate of Martin V to that of Julius II. Martin V was a Colonna, of the oldest Roman nobility, deeply versed in the politics of central Italy and a man of hard and unsentimental temper. He was admirably equipped to create an Italian papacy and he did so.

Martin was able to return to Rome by 1420 and to regard himself as fairly secure in the papal state by 1424. This success was achieved partly by good luck which set his enemies against each other and exterminated some of them. Rome and the papal state had been left in extreme disorder by the death of Ladislas and the flight of John XXIII and the succeeding interregnum caused by the council. Rule over it was divided between Ladislas's sister, Joanna II, and the great condottiere Braccio da Montone who secured control of a good part of the papal territory. Joanna was a childless, middle-aged widow with a tendency to give political power to her lovers. Her reign was in some ways a return to the conditions of Naples under the first Joanna. Martin decided wisely that her help was needed if he was to recover Rome and he joined with her in employing another great condottiere Muzio Attendolo Sforza. In this way he got back to Rome and secured a base there though Braccio remained powerful for the time being in the rest of the state. Then there was the problem of the succession to Joanna. Martin favoured the Angevin candidate, Louis III of Anjou, Joanna at first favoured Alfonso V, King of Aragon who came to Naples in 1421 and was adopted as her heir. Then she changed her mind and adopted the Angevin. The *condottieri* were also ranged on two sides, Muzio Attendolo Sforza and then his son, Francesco for the Angevin, Braccio for Alfonso. They finally fought it out at a great battle at Aquila in 1424; Braccio was killed and his death left Martin in control. Thus by 1424 Alfonso had retired from Italy and both Braccio and the elder Sforza had been removed by death: the recovery from the chaos of the period of the Council of Constance had been remarkably rapid. In these circumstances it was relatively easy to secure two other objectives. One was the re-establishment of a proper papal administration over the whole of the state. Martin's grasp of it was better than anything which had been achieved by previous popes since the days of Albornoz. The one major flaw in his control was that he was unable to subdue the city of Bologna at the northern tip. It rebelled and he fought a long and rather unsuccessful war against it in the later part of his pontificate. His rule was fairly secure over most of the rest of the dominions which he claimed to control. The communes, even Perugia, were reintegrated into the papal state, as were the lords, even the great Malatesta of Rimini. Income from dues paid by subject lords and communes began to expand, partially replacing losses in other parts of Europe: it has been estimated that 80,000 out of 170,000 florins received by the pope in 1426–7 came from the papal state. As a Roman nobleman Martin reverted to the dynastic policy of pre-Avignon popes, linking aggrandizement of his relations in Italy with the establishment of papal power. His brother became prince of Salerno in the kingdom of Naples while other members of the family received substantial grants in the papal state around Rome.

In the Church as a whole Martin's other objective was to avert the dangers of conciliarism which might flow from observance of *Frequens*. He allowed a council to assemble in Pavia and then Siena in 1423–4. It was poorly attended by the northerners and treated casually by the pope. It faded away and conciliarism did not seriously trouble him again until the end of his pontificate. Unlike his predecessors, Martin was able to establish a thorough domination of his cardinals who, according to observers trembled in his presence. Though he did not have much success in persuading the northern kings to accept papal taxation or in extending control of benefices, in Italy he was almost completely successful.

Martin's successor, Eugenius IV (1431–47), a Venetian ecclesiastic without political astuteness, was entirely unfitted to carry on his policy. He began his pontificate inauspiciously with a quarrel with Martin's family the dangerous Colonna, displeased by the termination of their influence, which threw Rome into disorder. But though he mismanaged the position in Italy his failure was also due to the misfortune that the beginning of his pontificate coincided with the beginning of the Council of Basle. The assembly at Basle was partly motivated by the same anti-papal feelings as had appeared in the reform commission at Constance. It was given real strength and momentum of a kind which Constance lacked by the success of its negotiators in dealing with the Hussite menace (see below, p. 209). The lay and ecclesiastical powers of central Europe were determined to promote and prolong the council chiefly because of the Hussite menace and its efforts and final success in this sphere were the background to the council's growing prestige in the years 1431–4. They were also the main reason for the patronage of Sigismund who wanted to resolve the Hussite problem in order to be able to take over his kingdom in Bohemia. Eugenius was extraordinarily insensitive to pressures in favour of the council in northern and central Europe. He tried at first to dissolve it but it would not be dissolved and indeed his papal legate in Germany, Cardinal Giuliano Cesarini, realizing that it was essential for dealing with the Hussites, defended it. The council set up its banner by declaring that its authority was independent of the pope and proceeded to declare him and the cardinals contumacious for not appearing in answer to its summons. Eugenius was forced in 1433 to abandon his stand of non-recognition. The council was not satisfied and wanted complete submission and recognition of its autonomous authority. Eugenius again submitted in the Bull *Dudum Sacrum* and withdrew all his reservations under a threat of deposition.

In 1433 Eugenius had been humiliated in Italy by the plundering of the papal state by the condottiere Francesco Sforza, which he could not prevent and which he was forced to end by granting Sforza a substantial portion of his state, the march of Ancona, for life. In 1434 the papacy descended to a new trough of impotence. The invasion of the state by other *condottieri* in the pay of Milan led to a revolt in Rome from which Eugenius was forced to flee in disguise. For nine years, 1434–43, he was an exile mostly in Florence. Effective control of Rome and the state was made impossible firstly by the hostility of Milan and secondly by the condition of Naples which after the death of Joanna II, the last of her family, in 1435, was torn between the ultimate victor Alfonso V of Aragon and the French candidate René of Anjou, whom Joanna had named as her heir. After the death of Joanna, Alfonso V came quickly from Aragon to claim his inheritance, while Eugenius unfortunately felt obliged to support the much less effective René. Alfonso was defeated and captured by the Genoese in a sea battle at Ponza in 1435, but Genoa was at this time under the control of Milan and in exile Alfonso made an alliance with Filippo Maria Visconti. With Alfonso and Filippo Maria, the two strongest Italian powers, ranged against him, Eugenius was in a poor position. He sent his soldier Cardinal, Giovanni Vitelleschi, into the kingdom of Naples in support of the French claimant in 1437, but without effect. Throughout these years Alfonso was gaining ground until he completed his conquest by taking the city of Naples itself in 1442.

In this period of general powerlessness Eugenius had one victory which, if not a substantial achievement was at least a *succès d'estime*. The mid 1430s saw a new consciousness both in Constantinople and in Europe of the pressure of Turkish advance threatening the extinction of Byzantium and the invasion of the West and a revival of plans for the reunion of the eastern and western churches in response to the threat (see below, p. 226). From 1434, the pope and the council were engaged in rival negotiations with representatives of the Greek church. In this dispute the pope had a geographical advantage and it was his plan for a council of the two churches at Ferrara in 1438 which was accepted by the Greeks. The council was attended on the Greek side by the Emperor John Paleologus, the Patriarch of Constantinople, and a number of bishops. In 1439 it moved to Florence, where the commune was willing to contribute to the crippling expenses. Eventually a Decree of Union was accepted by both sides which contained a compromise solution of the chief doctrinal difference (whether the Holy Spirit proceeded as the Latins claimed from the Son as well as the Father, the '*Filioque* clause') and a limited acceptance of papal supremacy by the Greeks. The Decree of Union was in effect a concession by those Greek prelates who thought it a fair price for western aid against the Turks. It was not accepted when they returned home and led to no lasting reconciliation or co-operation. Nevertheless, it brought considerable temporary prestige to the pope.

During the preparation and sitting of the Council of Florence, however, relations between the pope and the Council of Basle deteriorated from bad to worse. In 1435 the council proceeded to the abolition of all payments to the papal court on appointments to benefices, a measure which if carried into effect would be the most serious blow which could be dealt to the material position of the papacy and represented the most extreme interests of the ordinary beneficed clergy. In 1437 the majority at Basle, increasingly under the leadership of the extremist French Cardinal Louis Aleman, having issued a denunciation of Eugenius for his personal and public conduct and defiance of the council summoned him to appear before it. Cesarini who had been throughout the best hope of a continued link between pope and council left in disgust, in January 1438, and in the same month the pope was declared suspended. Eugenius eventually proceeded in 1439 to excommunicate all those who took part at Basle and the remains of the council elected their own pope making the strange choice of an elderly, pious lay prince, Duke Amadeus VIII of Savoy, who took the title of Felix V.

When the Council of Basle took its most extreme step its prestige was already in decline. The Hussite menace had receded and the council's only really enthusiastic supporters among the lay princes were Eugenius's enemies in Italy, Filippo Maria Visconti of Milan and Alfonso V. But in most parts of Europe it continued to be treated with respect and of course was everywhere a valuable counter-balance to the papacy. It was this period rather than the age of the Schism which gave birth to the most extreme European reaction to the medieval papacy. In Italy this was the time when Lorenzo Valla, in the service of Alfonso V, wrote his book on the Donation of Constantine, demolishing with humanist scholarship the legendary gift of temporal sovereignty to the papacy. In France, Charles VII took the opportunity in 1438 to issue the Pragmatic Sanction of Bourges which acknowledged the council, and abolished papal authority in ecclesiastical appointments and the levy of annates. Although Charles VII like most princes was in practice quite half-hearted in his attitude to Basle this document was in line with the attitude of the extremists there; it represented the general reaction of the northern European clergy to medieval papalism which had now reached its most unrestrained point. Its practical long-term effect, like that of Basle, was small. The truth was that the papacy had already lost the battle for northern Europe. The Reformations of the sixteenth century were to be in many respects only the recognition and completion of this process. When the personal passions of Basle had died away the rest of the fifteenth century was a quiet period in ecclesiastical history.

Eugenius recovered his position at the end of his pontificate largely as a result of a diplomatic revolution in Italy in the years 1442–3. René of Anjou finally gave up the attempt to win Naples and Eugenius at last accepted the *fait accompli* and recognized Alfonso V. Eugenius also came to terms with the Duke of Milan and his condottiere Piccinino, with whose help he had some prospect of disposing of the chief threat to the papal state, the condottiere Francesco Sforza. In 1443 Eugenius returned to Rome; his exile ended.

The Council of Basle was by no means finished. Felix V did not abdicate until 1449. Its story from this time, however, was a decline and from 1443 the papacy can be regarded as having passed its crisis. Eugenius's successor Nicholas V (1447–55), had a very different career. The political situation in Italy entered a phase which was much more favourable to the papacy. Filippo Maria Visconti died five months after Nicholas was elected. Sforza had turned his attention from the papal state towards Milan (see below, p. 298). The alliance with Sforza and Florence provided the papacy with an effective counter-balance to Alfonso V. Although Nicholas had to endure a republican rebellion in Rome in the tradition of Cola di Rienzo, led by an idealistic soldier, Stefano Porcaro, in 1453, it was easily put down and on the whole he was not troubled by political insecurity. In northern Europe the healing wounds caused by the Council of Basle was symbolized by the Concordat of Vienna which was arranged with the Emperor Frederick III and other German princes in 1448.

With Nicholas V we can say that the transition from medieval into the Renaissance papacy had taken place. One element in that metamorphosis was the essential acceptance of the Italian base. To grasp the full extent and significance of the change other things have to be taken into account. Nicholas was an Italian prince in a cultural as well as a political sense: he accepted the ideals of classical humanism. He also ruled over a Christendom which had already lost one kingdom, Bohemia, to reformation.

iii *The First Reformation: the Hussite Movement*

While the popes of the conciliar period struggled to re-establish their position in the European Church and the Italian political scene, the unity of Latin Christendom was broken in a novel way by the secession of a whole people. The Hussite Movement which surprised and frightened traditional Europe in the first half of the fifteenth century played a role in European affairs curiously similar on a smaller scale to the Russian Bolshevik movement in the twentieth century. From 1420 to 1434 it loomed menacingly in the East driving rulers and priests into plans of counter-revolution or conciliation and generally providing the established order throughout Europe with a bogeyman. The Hussite Movement was an isolated phenomenon in the fifteenth century. It belongs to the same class of phenomena as the sixteenth-century reformations: a religious reorganization initiated for reasons of state, but drawing inspiration from both popular feeling and learned theology. The general background conditions for such a movement were the traditions of religious radicalism, the divisions in scholastic thought and the weakness and division of the papacy. The decline of respect for the universal church and of the willingness of lay princes to tolerate papal supremacy were general tendencies of the early fifteenth century. Nowhere else however were they carried to the point of actual reformation. The Hussite movement was produced by a local coincidence of favourable circumstances.

Hussitism sprang from a dual parentage, a native movement of popular pietism and a school of university radicals largely dependent on foreign inspiration. The father of the Czech reformation is by general consent a priest called Milíč of Kroměřiž who in 1363 abandoned a successful career of ecclesiastical pluralism to become an evangelical preacher and moral reformer, significantly using as his vehicle of exhortation the Czech language. Milíč attacked the usual butts of fourteenth-century evangelism but he also believed that the struggle with Antichrist prophesied in the Book of Revelations was about to take place and that he was the man to lead a company of disciples in that struggle. The Emperor Charles IV tolerated and protected his pious work in the city of Prague. In 1367, he went to Rome intending to greet the returning Pope Urban V with the news that he was Antichrist. This naturally led to his condemnation. But he had made an impression at Prague by founding a new 'Jerusalem' for training evangelical priests in an old brothel district, by his criticism of the clergy and by his encouragement of frequent communion by the laity. The second great evangelist, Mathew of Janov, was a disciple of Milíč and also a university man who had been at Paris. He wrote a book called 'The Rules of the Old and New Testaments' which was in some ways the most influential and characteristic piece of writing in the whole Hussite movement. It commends the pious individual and the observance of biblical precepts against false professors of Christianity whom Mathew clearly identifies with the established Church. He favoured the abolition of monasticism and much else in the contemporary Church. Before the end of the fourteenth century there was a well established tradition of lay anti-clerical pietism in Prague, not very peculiar in its tendencies but probably stronger than in most places and linked with the cultivation of the Czech language. In 1391 a well-to-do Prague merchant founded the Bethlehem Chapel as a centre for popular preaching in the city and it was through his appointment as resident preacher there in 1402 that John Hus first rose to prominence and influence in the city.

In the 1390s the influence of Wycliffe began to be strongly felt in the University of Prague and like pietism acquired overtones of local national protest. Since its foundation in 1349, the members of the university had been divided into Saxon, Bavarian, Polish and Czech 'nations', corresponding to the university's central European catchment area. The division became less realistic with the foundation of other German universities. By the early fifteenth century the Czech masters and students were more prominent than their quarter-share of the government of the university would suggest but not dominant in numbers and in the faculty of Theology which had the most prestige they were still rare. The Czechs thus became a large dissatisfied minority in a university mainly controlled by Germans. In the very first years of the fifteenth century Jerome of Prague began to bring back from Oxford the theological writings of Wycliffe containing the heresies which had been condemned. It was about the time that Hus, already a university master, decided to enter the Theology faculty and also became preacher at Bethlehem. After this the philosophical and evangelical trends began to link up with politics.

The development of Hus's ecclesiastical attitudes and his political importance were very much affected by the policies of King Wenceslas IV of Bohemia (1378–1419), which really provided the opportunity for a reformation movement to take root in the country. Wenceslas was King of Bohemia; his brothers, of whom the most prominent was Sigismund of Hungary, held other parts of the Luxemburg inheritance. He had also succeeded his father as King of Germany. Wenceslas was by all accounts a dissolute and ineffective ruler. In 1400 he was deposed by the German electors and replaced by Rupert of the Palatinate. In 1402–3 the many conflicts with his Bohemian nobles, often stirred up by his brothers, culminated in his being temporarily held captive by his brother Sigismund. During his captivity the Roman Pope Boniface IX, in whose obedience Bohemia lay, had recognized Rupert as King of Germany. This was a severe affront and a real injury to Wenceslas and his relations with the papacy were strained. Five years later in 1408 came his opportunity to do something about it. The cardinals deserted both popes and summoned the Council of Pisa. The possibility of a Luxemburg-French alliance in support of the cardinals offered the opportunity to secure the election of a pope who would re-affirm Wenceslas's position as King of Germany. This crisis in the king's relations with the papacy coincided with a crisis in the University of Prague.

The novelty of Hus's approach to religious regeneration and his historical importance in the circumstances of 1409 and after, lay in the fact that he believed in reform of the Church by the state. Earlier religious enthusiasts advocated the same kind of moral purification; Hus believed that the state should enforce it by reforming a corrupt Church. He was fortified in this belief by the writings of Wycliffe whose main historical importance in the Hussite movement was this emphasis on the role of the state, rather than his more extreme heretical opinions about such matters as transubstantiation. The division between those sympathetic and hostile to Wycliffe began to coincide with the division between Czechs and Germans in the university. Most of the Germans came from parts of Germany which were loyal to the Roman pope and would eventually return there to seek benefices; they were therefore orthodox. Czechs were influenced by the breach between King Wenceslas and the pope and more inclined to be critical of ecclesiastical authority. Hus's pronouncements were inspired by both the reforming zeal of the Czech pietist tradition and the academic radicalism of Wycliffe, who was a speculator of far greater strength and originality than any member of the provincial University of Prague. Although Hus was primarily a moralist he was easily seduced into defending Wycliffe's clearly heretical theories about the unreality of transubstantiation and about the Church as the body of the redeemed. Wenceslas began to favour the Czech Wycliffites in the university because they offered him the chance of acquiring an informed, clerical backing for his case as a supporter of the Council of Pisa. In January 1409 he summoned representatives of the university to his court at Kutna Hora to give an opinion about relations with the pope and the cardinals. The Czech 'nation' spoke for supporting the cardinals and the council, the other three 'nations' for the pope. King Wenceslas then solved his problem by changing the constitution of the university, by the Decree of Kutna Hora, so that the Czech nation had three votes and the other three one between them. He declared for the cardinals and received an assurance that they would support his candidature to the German throne. Wenceslas had no taste for heresy – his move was simply political. But his Decree had the effect of denuding the university of Germans and therefore preparing it for its subsequent role as the essentially Czech centre of a native religious movement. In the autumn of 1409 the university declared its independence of ecclesiastical authority by electing Hus as Rector in spite of the suspicion of heresy attaching to him.

In 1410 Wenceslas's rival as King of Germany died and he hoped to recover the crown. But it was his own brother Sigismund, who in fact secured the support of the majority of the electors and elbowed him out of the way. Wenceslas still hoped, in his rather half-hearted way, to get papal support for himself. He was anxious to play down the shameful issue of heresy in his kingdom by persuading both sides to be quieter. Archbishop Zbyněk of Prague would not be quiet. He proceeded to a burning of Wycliffe's writings at Prague and excommunicated Hus The pope, now John XXIII, summoned the offender to appear at the papal court. Hus continued to be defiant, supported enthusiastically by his colleagues at the university, half-heartedly by the royal court. In March 1411, the pope declared him heretic and excommunicate. The king ordered his officials to begin the listing of ecclesiastical property and investigations into the state of the monasteries. The archbishop fled to seek the help of Sigismund. Bohemia was on the brink of Reformation. Zbyněk's successor as Archbishop of Prague was a former royal official. Henceforward the Church in Bohemia was mainly governed by men who were not inclined to oppose the king. This was one reason why the Reformation developed as it did after 1411. Another factor was the continued impact of international ecclesiastical politics, especially the Council of Constance. Also at this stage, Hus received support from certain sections of the Czech nobility which enabled him to retire in safety from Prague and live a protected life in the castles of his patrons in the years 1412 and 1413.

A new crisis broke in Prague in the early part of 1412, again as a result of outside events. Pope John XXIII proclaimed a crusade against Ladislas of Naples, organized the sale of indulgences to those who wished to buy the spiritual advantages of crusading and enlisted the king's assistance with the promise of a proportion of the proceeds. Hus expressed his condemnation strongly. This was a blow to his relations with the king. Hus presented his attack on indulgences in a strictly academic disputation held at the university in June 1412 against the wishes of the dean of the faculty of theology, which denounced his views and persuaded the king and council to issue the decree of Žebrak condemning them. In the week before the issue of the decree excitement was further increased by another crisis at Prague. Three youths who were opposing the indulgence sellers were seized by the city authorities and summarily executed. Their bodies were recovered by demonstrators and carried off to the Bethlehem chapel for burial. For the time being no action seems to have been taken against Hus and his followers who continued to maintain in disputations at the university that excommunication was futile and other subversive ideas. But later in the year a papal legate arrived bearing the strongest condemnation that John XXIII had been able to devise; Hus was excommunicated and any place where he stayed for twelve days was placed under interdict. Hus issued an *Appeal to God and Jesus Christ from the sentence of the Pope* and left Prague. He spent most of the year 1413 and the beginning of 1414 at the castle of Kozí in southern Bohemia under the protection of a nobleman called Ctibor of Kozí. It was here that he composed his most important written works. One of them was a Latin treatise *On the Church*, very heavily dependent on the book of the same title by Wycliffe and maintaining the Wycliffite thesis that the true Church of which Christ is the head is not the same as the visible church headed by the pope so that the latter deserves only limited obedience. He also wrote a Czech treatise on the sin of simony which was also greatly indebted to a book of Wycliffe's with the same title.

In 1414 the Council of Constance met as a result of the arrangement made by Sigismund with John XXIII. For Sigismund the council was a stage in his plans for the development of his power in central Europe. The growing movement towards heresy in Bohemia was also an important factor in those plans, firstly because it offered opportunities for bringing pressure to bear on Wenceslas (who still had the crown jewels in his possession) to accept Sigismund as King of Germany, secondly because it could be foreseen as a possible obstacle to Sigismund's accession in the kingdom of Bohemia after Wenceslas's death. Sigismund therefore decided that the council should tackle the problem of Hus and his movement and in the spring of 1414 sent an invitation to Hus to come to the council. Hus at first refused but in the course of 1414 various pressures induced him to change his mind. Whether it was because he felt himself to be losing support or because he wished to relieve his protectors of the pressures upon them from Sigismund or the pope, in the autumn of 1414 he accepted a renewed invitation with the promise of an imperial safe conduct. When he got to Constance his enemies, particularly the representatives of the Bohemian clergy, were able to work against him in a more favourable atmosphere. In spite of the safe conduct they fairly soon secured acceptance of their argument that as a condemned heretic he should be imprisoned. The accusers wisely based their attack on Hus's alleged adherence to the writings of Wycliffe which were acknowledged to be heretical. There remained the hope that Sigismund would intervene to protect him, but Sigismund, once he had been crowned King of Germany, seemed to lose interest in the fate of Hus and perhaps underestimated the strength of sympathy for Hus and the harvest of hatred of himself in Bohemia which he was to sow by this neglect. Hus was tried and burnt on 6 July 1415.

While Hus was at Constance the reform movement in Prague was beginning to adopt the practice of Utraquism (the taking of communion in both kinds by the laity) which was to become a central feature of the movement. It fitted in with

their admiration for the primitive church and their belief
that the laity should participate fully in religious ceremonies.
Perhaps more important was the beginning of organized
support for this among the Czech nobility. Several letters of
support for Hus were sent by groups of the Moravian and
Czech nobility while he was being tried, the last in the name
of 250 of them. Soon after this period appeared the first signs
of more radical tendencies within the reformist movement.
A letter written in 1416–17 spoke of rumours from the Pilsen
area of people who disbelieved in all rites without biblical
authority. About the same time it was reported that in the
area around Kozí where Hus had been in 1413–14 there were
many people who believed that bishops were unnecessary, that
communion could be given outside the mass and that laymén
could preach and hear confessions in ordinary houses. These
ideas had little to do with the views propagated in university
circles by the Prague masters. They involved a wholehearted
and crude rejection of the customs of the established Church.
They bear a striking resemblance to some of the traditional
ideas of the Waldensians and may well have been derived
from them.

The main radical wing which developed in southern Bohemia
and later centred on the settlement at Tabor was essentially
a peasant movement. The leaders and theorists were priests
but the bulk of the personnel were lay countrymen. In addition
to their criticism of the established church and their primi-
tivism there was a strong chiliastic strain in their beliefs. The
second coming was widely predicted in 1420 and many
believed that the end of the world was near. They were also
social revolutionaries. The establishment of equality, even
communism, and the overthrow of the social order were as
marked as religious reformation among the aims of the early
Taborites. As soon as they were established they became
dangerous enemies of towns and noblemen wherever they
could strike at them. No doubt the millenniarist priests who
led these groups were sometimes products of the Prague
university milieu. The explosive mixture was produced by the
combination of an intellectual impulse with the latent radicalism of the countryside in the conditions of political and

religious unrest which characterized the later years of the reign of King Wenceslas. In its origins up to 1421 Tabor was a revolutionary peasant movement whose ideas had affinities with those expressed by John Ball and Wat Tyler in the English Peasants' Revolt in 1381, directed both against the religious authority of the Church and the social authority of the seigniorial landlord.

At the level of national politics the effect of the Council of Constance on Bohemia was divisive. Hussite noblemen at a parliament drew up a letter to the council alleging that Hus had been burnt without any evidence that he was a heretic. Many of them joined a league, subscribing to a document in which they promised to protect free preaching on their estates and accept episcopal authority only so far as it was consistent with scripture. This was answered by the formation of a catholic league, pledged to the opposite policy and also including some powerful magnates. Resentment against Sigismund and the council was increased by the burning of Hus's friend Jerome of Prague at Constance in 1416. Bohemia was divided; in so far as he took a stand at all, the king supported the position of the most moderate Hussites. This period also saw the emergence of a new inflammatory millenniarist preacher in Prague called John Želivský with a great capacity for stirring up the city mob. Skirmishes began to occur in Prague. Wenceslas tried to bring the situation under control by the appointment of safe Catholic city councillors. In July 1419 their opponents responded: Želivský led a crowd, to whom he had administered communion in both kinds, to the city hall where they threw the Catholic councillors out of the windows. The shock of the 'First Defenestration of Prague' killed the king.

Among the people present at the Defenestration was the man who was to be the central figure of the Hussite movement in the next decade, John Žižka. Žižka was a member of the gentry class, a small landowner and professional soldier who had fought for Wenceslas and was reputed to have been in favour at the court. After the king's death Žižka first emerged as a leader in an attack by the Prague mob on a monastery outside the city. In a more general way, however, the death of

Wenceslas was the signal for the Hussite movement to advance
from the stage of confused dissidence to that of revolution.
Sigismund was the heir. He was occupied by a Turkish invasion in Hungary at the moment, and a large proportion of
the Czech nobility did not want him. The opportunity was
given for Hussitism to become clearly linked with defence of
the liberties of the kingdom and this was the key to the long
revolutionary period. The lead was taken by a senior magnate
and moderate Hussite Čeněk of Wartenburg who summoned
a diet which issued an ultimatum to Sigismund insisting on
political liberties and also on free preaching and Utraquism.
At the same time political disorder encouraged extremism.
The biblical name Tabor was first applied to a hill in southern
Bohemia where a mass meeting was held about the time of the
king's death. Other such meetings were held at Pilsen and near
Prague. In October a conference of moderates and radicals at
Prague divided over the question of whether they should break
the link with the Roman Church altogether by proceeding to
the drastic step of electing their own bishops and the Taborites
smashed images in the churches before they left. Žižka was
by now clearly associated with the more radical wing. Fighting
broke out in Prague between his supporters and those of
Čeněk for control of the royal castles and then Žižka left
Prague to join the Taborites in the country.

In the spring of 1420 Žižka set out with a crowd of enthusiasts from the Pilsen area to join the community which had
been set up at Tabor. They were attacked by royalist nobility
but, astonishingly, won an overwhelming victory at the
battle of Sudoměř, the first sign of the military consequences of
fanaticism which were so often to be displayed in the next
few years. Žižka set about organizing Tabor as a military force
and it began to dominate the territory around it. The work of
Žižka gave rise very quickly to a triangular disposition of
forces in Bohemia. Moderate Hussites wanted to resist the
assumption of power by Sigismund. They found they could
not do this without the help of Tabor which they would have
liked on other grounds to suppress. The balance of power was
demonstrated in 1420 when Sigismund made his first attempt
to conquer the country by a military descent which was also

designated as a crusade against the enemies of the Church. Čeněk, in command of the castles at Prague, pursued a hesitating and ambiguous policy, not wishing to break entirely with Sigismund. The city itself decided on resistance and called for Žižka's help. He came with his Taborite army and decisively defeated the crusaders at the Vitkov near Prague. Prague and the Hussite cause were thus saved, the military inferiority of Sigismund was shown and Žižka was established as the military leader of the Hussites.

In the aftermath of the battle the leaders of the various shades of opinion were able to produce a document, the Four Articles of Prague, which stated the minimum beliefs on which they were all agreed. They were (1) Freedom of preaching by priests without supervision of ecclesiastical superiors, (2) Utraquism, (3) Abolition of excessive clerical wealth, (4) Punishment of those who committed mortal sins. Apart from the proclamation of Utraquism the articles were studiously vague. The Hussite movement now contained a wide spectrum of parties which were incapable of positive agreement. Tabor itself rejected most church ceremonies and monasticism. But here also there was a conservative wing, to which Žižka and his eventual successor Prokop the Bald belonged. The central body of Taborites included a man called Nicholas of Pelhřimov who was accepted as their bishop, which made a complete break with the orthodox church. Taborites mostly rejected transubstantiation. The more radical wing came to be known as the *Pikardi* and regarded the eucharist as a mere commemoration. The left wing of the Taborites seem to have included an assortment of antinomian and millennarian beliefs. The Hussites therefore ranged from those whose beliefs were barely distinguishable from Catholicism to wild rebels.

From 1420 to 1434 the greater part of Bohemia was in rebellion both against the Roman Church and against its king. It remained in a state of successful reformation and revolution which has no parallel in medieval Europe and foreshadows the movements of the sixteenth century. During the period 1420 to 1424 repeated disorder and conflict between the various parties led to the establishment of Žižka's general dominance.

In 1421 the political motives and plans of the rebels received expression at the Diet of Čáslav. This was a parliament of the broad type found in Bohemia as in other princely states, normally of course summoned by princely authority. The Diet of Čáslav was a parliament without its head (not unlike the assemblies which deposed Edward II and Richard II in England in 1327 and 1399), attended by the non-Catholic magnates and a number of knights and representatives of towns of both Bohemia and Moravia, in which Hussitism had also taken root by this time. Sigismund sent envoys to the assembly, but they met with very little sympathy and the Diet formally deposed him. It showed on the whole a remarkable sense of national unity in the face of the common enemy, issuing non-partisan documents and laying down that religious disputes were to be referred to Želivský and a conservative theologian, representing the two extremes of opinion which were to be tolerated. It set up a regency council of twenty representatives of the estates (five magnates, four Praguers, four other town members, five esquires and two Taborites of whom Žižka was one). The politicians of Čáslav, or most of them, did not envisage this as a permanent arrangement. The assumption that kingship was the natural order of things survived the revolution. But in fact Bohemia was ruled by councils of this kind for the next sixteen years. About the same time a synod of Hussite clergy set up a committee of four churchmen representing different points of view to administer the church under the archbishop. Later on in the same year a diet at Kutna Hora proceeded to choose another king to replace Sigismund: the choice was the Jagiellon Prince Witold of Lithuania.

The autumn of 1421 brought the second crusade against the Hussites. This time it was a combined effort by a Hungarian army brought by Sigismund from his other kingdom and an army supplied by his subjects in his kingdom of Bohemia. The emergence of a revolutionary society in Bohemia was a cause of well-justified alarm in neighbouring regions. The princes and towns of southern Germany feared the effects of the Hussite example on their own subjects. The practical difficulty of organizing the princes and towns of Germany to undertake any effective action was, however, very great because of the lack of any central authority to co-ordinate efforts. There was soon added a natural fear of the extraordinary fighting qualities of the Czech armies. The crusade of 1421 was a substantial effort but it was a complete failure. After thrashing Sigismund, Žižka turned back into Bohemia to assert his power, based on the army, over extremists who had got control in Prague during his absence. Witold of Lithuania sent his nephew Sigismund Korybut as Viceroy in 1422 to test the ground for the establishment of a Jagiellon dynasty in Bohemia and he was accepted as regent at another Diet of Časlav.

The essential instability of the situation was quickly shown. Sigismund and the pope were able to bring enough pressure to bear on the Jagiellon family to persuade them to withdraw Korybut after less than a year. The Hussites were divided into two main groups: the moderates based on Prague and the towns of the north and west, the Taborites on the centres at Tabor and Hradec Kralove in south and east. But within both wings splits developed. In 1424 it came to open war between Žižka and the conservative Utraquists. He crushed them in the last and most remarkable of his battles at Malešov, apparently fought like the others against heavy odds and won by sheer tactical skill. This restored some unity under Žižka's leadership. Korybut came back to Prague and the reunited Utraquist forces turned their attentions outwards to an invasion of Moravia in which Žižka was killed in 1424. Apart from Hus he is the most remarkable figure in the movement and in a sense the first of the great revolutionary commanders in the European tradition. He appears to have developed the tactical system for which Hussite armies became famous: the use of a barrier of wagons from behind which soldiers fired with crossbows and guns. This mobile cover in the field seems to have been extraordinarily effective against the traditional soldiery of central Europe. The combination of revolutionary fervour, novel tactics and Žižka's severe discipline built up an army which appeared to contemporaries to be invincible. By the end of Žižka's life, however, it had become not only the indispensable bulwark of the Reformation but also the arbiter of Bohemian politics, giving its commanders an arbitrary power which had filled the vacuum left by the destruction of the traditional order.

In the years 1424 to 1427 the situation created by Malešov persisted. Žižka's army called themselves the 'Orphans' after his death and remained a formidable force. Tabor retained a parallel military organization which came under the command of a priest, Prokop the Bald. Internal divisions were no less deep than before but they did not obtrude so much in this period. Korybut remained in Prague until it was discovered in 1427 that he was conducting secret negotiations with the papacy, after which Bohemia became again formally headless. There was a German crusade in 1427 which was promoted by Pope Martin V and planned on an ambitious scale. Such was the reputation of the Hussite army by this time that the news of its approach was enough to turn the crusading army to flight and eventually to produce panic. Internal unity in Bohemia was promoted partly because the Hussite movement was not becoming externally aggressive and expansive. In 1426 and 1427 the Orphans and Taborites were attacking into Silesia in the north and Austria in the south. They were becoming not only a frightening example but also a serious military threat to the whole of central Europe. Between 1427 and 1431 the movement turned increasingly outwards. From 1427 onwards the pattern of every year included raids by the Hussite 'field armies' beyond the borders. The main characteristics of the raids were plundering. The armies of Orphans and Taborites were now autonomous forces which had to be given employment; what they devoted themselves to was in effect widespread raiding, becoming increasingly bold so that they eventually went as far afield as Berlin, Danzig and Hungary. Their manifestoes sent to surrounding countries made them appear as a social menace, especially in southern Germany. The only friends of the Hussites were the members of the Jagiellon family in Poland, whose constant fighting with the Teutonic knights and bickering with Sigismund disposed them to befriend Bohemia even after the departure of Korybut so that the alignment of forces in eastern Europe at this period came to have a large element of Slav-German hostility. It became increasingly clear during these years that the policy of suppression by crusade was hopeless although it was enthusiastically supported by Pope Martin V. The fifth and last crusade was promoted in 1431 under the leadership of Cardinal Giuliano Cesarini who went to Germany as legate convinced that the Council of Basle, which began in that year, would only be effective if its business was preceded by a decisive expedition to wipe out the threat of Hussitism. The German army dissolved in flight leaving its baggage, including even the cardinal's gold crucifix, to be plundered by the heretics. The fiasco of the fifth crusade convinced many people that only compromise could end the Hussite threat. There had been moves in this direction earlier. The fact that the Council of Basle met at all, against Martin V's will, was very largely due, however, to the urgency of opinion in central Europe that the Hussite movement must be dealt with. The defeat of the crusade of 1431 destroyed the assumption that Hussitism must be crushed before its ideas were discussed and in particular convinced Cesarini, the president of the council, that negotiation was the only way.

In the next three years the council achieved its purpose. Its success was a triumph of diplomacy. The council sent its invitation to the Hussites to participate in discussions at Basle at the end of 1431. It was naturally received differently by different wings of the movement; moderates were attracted, Taborites scornful. In spite of the objections of Prokop however a parliament decided to accept the invitation and Prokop himself came round to a more conciliatory position. Hussite leaders met council representatives at Cheb in May 1432 and rather surprisingly agreed not only to go to Basle but to debate the Four Articles by the standards of both scripture and tradition. They actually arrived at Basle in January 1433. The delegation consisted of the most eminent representatives of the various shades of Hussite opinion: John Rokycana, the Archbishop of Prague who had come to the fore as the leader of moderate Utraquism; Nicholas of Pelhřimov, the Taborite bishop; Peter Payne an Oxford theologian and Wycliffite who had fled to Bohemia; Prokop himself. In the next three months the Hussites presented an elaborate defence of the Four Articles and the members of the council

criticized it. In April they returned to Prague with a delegation from the council led by a papal auditor John of Palomar,
who ingeniously and correctly called for a definite exposition
of the Four Articles. This immediately showed up the difference between the various Hussite parties and sowed dissension
between them. Secretly in the house of Rokycana, Palomar
met a group of leading Utraquist noblemen and pointed out
to them the humiliation of their position in their own country,
powerless against men – the Taborites – who were scarcely
fit to be their servants, and on the other hand the advantages
which they would gain from reunion with the Church, a
reunion to which Utraquism was the only serious obstacle
and even that one which might be overcome.

Palomar returned to Basle correctly convinced that the
widespread discontent about the tyranny of Prokop and the
field armies was a weakness which could be developed. A
new conciliar delegation was sent to Prague in the autumn of
1433. After some discussion the papal envoys and the Czech
parliament arrived at the first version of what came to be
known as the Compacts of Prague. This stated that Bohemians
and Moravians would be allowed communion in both kinds
provided that they accepted all other beliefs and ceremonies
of the Church, that punishment of sins was acceptable as
long as only priests punished priests, that there should be
free preaching as long as the authority of bishops was accepted,
that clerical property was permissible. Even moderate Hussite
theologians found them unacceptable but were forced to
subscribe by the weight of the nobility in the parliament.
The unity quickly broke down, Rokycana insisted that in
Bohemia Utraquism should be compulsory. The legates would
not accept this and left Prague without reaching final agreement. The next step was the formation in the spring of 1434
of a league of Bohemian nobles for the establishment of peace
in the country and the suppression of the troops of soldiers
who were plaguing the countryside. The result was the battle
of Lipany in which the forces of the magnates and the city of
Prague defeated the Orphans and the Taborites, destroying
forever the military power of radical Hussitism, and ending the
revolutionary period of the movement.

Sigismund was able to come finally to terms with the Czech nobility in 1435, to enter Prague in 1436 and to rule until his death in 1437. He made his return possible by supporting the Compacts of Prague and insisting – against the wish of council and pope in favour of a more canonical procedure – on the acceptance of Rokycana as archbishop. Thus, formal agreement had been reached and the troubles were apparently at an end. This turned out however to be far from the truth. Other conflicts of a different kind were to continue. There were several reasons for this. In the first place, largely as a result of the genealogical accidents of the history of the Luxemburg and Habsburg families, the succession to the throne was interrupted. After Sigismund's death without an heir his successor was Albert of Habsburg who died two years later and whose death was followed by the long minority (1439–52) and short reign (1452–57) of Ladislas Posthumus. His death once again left the succession uncertain. Secondly the revolutionary period had made a great difference to the Czech nobility and to their political habits. Many of them had added ecclesiastical property to their estates so that the balance of power in the country had probably shifted somewhat in their direction. More than a decade of rule by the nobility had made them accustomed to power and less respectful to kings. These habits were not given up. Thirdly the council and papacy were ultimately unwilling to ratify the Compacts of Prague, the document by means of which the Hussites had been enticed away from reformation. The full recognition of Rokycana was a stumbling block. The council placed the Czech Church under a special commission. Thus instead of the expected restoration of unity there were in practice henceforward two ecclesiastical organizations in Bohemia, catholic and Utraquist, in uneasy juxtaposition.

With the death of Albert of Austria the Czech nobility were once more effectively kingless. They had a military leader named Hynce Ptáček of Pirkstejn under whose leadership the country was divided into areas each controlled by the local nobility. Rokycana was recognized as the head of the Utraquist Church of which the parliament in 1444 confirmed once more its approval while condemning the radical movements which were still centred on Tabor. Ptáček died in 1444. After him the leadership fell to the man who was to dominate Bohemia and indeed to some extent central Europe in the middle years of the fifteenth century, George of Podiebrady. George was a nobleman from eastern Bohemia who had fought on the winning side at Lipany as a boy. A good soldier, a convinced Utraquist, a strong but farsighted politician, he became increasingly the spokesman of his class. His career is a remarkable instance of the fifteenth-century self assertion of the nobility against hereditary royal dynasties of which less spectacular examples could be quoted from other kingdoms. In Bohemia where the weakness of the monarchy was exceptional as a result of the revolutionary Hussite period, the nobility actually raised up their own king. George of Podiebrady assumed the leadership in the late 1440s while Ladislas was still a minor. In 1448 Pope Nicholas V's emissary Cardinal Carvajal visited Prague in the course of his mission to central Europe. He reasserted the papal objections to Rokycana and would not yield. George and the Utraquist nobility occupied Prague and forcibly restored Rokycana to the archbishopric. The leaders of the Catholic clergy who had been dominant in the city for some years fled to Pilsen. Utraquism was once again dominant though the Catholic nobility remained an important party. In 1451 Prague received a visit from Aeneas Sylvius, the future Pope Pius II, acting as the representative of Frederick of Habsburg, King of the Romans and guardian of Ladislas. This led to an agreement by which Frederick consented to the wish of the Bohemian parliament that George should be governor of the country under Habsburg sovereignty.

In 1452 George of Podiebrady took decisive action against the remnant of Tabor. With the approval of the parliament its doctrines were condemned and its leaders imprisoned. This was the end of Tabor, and of religious radicalism as a political force in the country. It was not the end of radical religious sentiment. In the mid-fifteenth century a new group began to form which was to grow into the Unity of the Czech Brethren. The chief inspirer of this movement was the writer Peter Chelčický (*c.* 1380–1470). Chelčický, whose life is obscure, was probably a man of the gentry or yeoman class. He was caught up in the religious movements of the 1420s and 1430s, but played no prominent part in them, though it was during this period that he wrote his chief works. His extensive works written in Czech express a belief in pacifism, anarchism, the law of love and primitive Christianity. Amongst his inspirations were certainly Wycliffe and probably Waldensianism. His views were essentially more radical than any of those maintained by the warring parties. He is the only writer who gave elaborate literary expression to the spirit of peasant piety which must have infused the obscure lives of a great many Waldensians and Lollards in late medieval Europe.

With the extinction of Tabor the religious problem was entirely a matter of the conflict between Utraquists and Catholics. The political field was still dominated by the Utraquist nobility. Even during the reign of Ladislas Posthumus (1452–7) George remained in effective power as governor. After Ladislas's death the nobility asserted their claim to elect a king and chose George in 1458. He ruled until his death in 1471. His position remained ambiguous. Since there were no fully qualified Utraquist bishops he had to import bishops from Hungary for his coronation and to maintain to some extent an equivocal attitude to the Compacts of Prague. He was declared a heretic and deposed by Pope Paul II in 1466. In Bohemia itself he had to face a powerful league of Catholic nobility. Nevertheless he maintained his position in a country with a half-reformed church, uneasily contained within the community of Latin Christendom.

CHAPTER VI

EUROPE AND THE WORLD BEYOND

i *Byzantium and the Ottoman Empire*

For most of the Middle Ages the Balkans, Greece and Asia Minor were dominated by the Byzantine Emperors, who from their great walled capital at Constantinople, preserved for centuries the apparatus of imperial authority, Roman Law, Greek literature and the Christian Church. Between the eleventh and the thirteenth centuries the Byzantine empire disintegrated and a succession of waves of invaders flowed over its territories: Turks and Mongols from the East, French knights and Italian merchants from the West. By the early fourteenth century the old sphere of Byzantium contained a remarkably variegated debris of small states which had been left by the conflicts of the previous centuries: the Slav kingdoms of Serbia and Bulgaria, small states in Greece established by French and Catalan adventurers, fragments of the commercial empires of Venice and Genoa, a variety of Turkish sultanates in Asia Minor. No state commanded a dominant position in this power vacuum and it was quite unclear what the political structure of the future would be. The history of the area in the period 1320–1450 seems in retrospect to be essentially the story of the rise of one of these contending powers, the Ottomans, to fill the position once occupied by Byzantium, but the history of their rise is a long and complex story.

The Ottoman emirate which was governed by Osman in the early fourteenth century was one of a number of small Turkish states in the western half of Asia Minor whose rulers were devoted to the prosecution of the *ghaza*, the holy war against non-Muslims. These were the marchlands between the Muslim and the Christian worlds. As the Christian warriors of Castile and Prussia acquired merit by their crusading activities, the Turkish frontiermen also justified their plundering on religious grounds. The Ottomans like the other rulers of Asia Minor, and indeed of the whole northern Muslim world, including Iraq, Persia and India, were originally Steppe dwellers and invaders of Islam, but they had embraced the Muslim faith with ardour and identified their role with its promotion. Among the Turks of Asia Minor the Ottomans were outstanding *ghazis*, because they were nearest to the remnants of Christian Byzantium. Osman was succeeded in 1326 by Orkhan, the first of the great Ottoman expansionists.

In the Balkans, Bulgaria, though obviously a primitive area, had a Tsar, and an administrative system in which the titles of the officials were copied from the grand Byzantine words. Bulgaria was in decline, Serbia on the other hand, under King Milutin (d. 1321) was a vigorous and expansive power which was to play a large part in the fourteenth century. In Greece two Latin principalities governed much of the main-land, the duchy of Athens controlled by the so-called Catalan Company of adventurers who had appeared in the Levant only at the beginning of the century, and the principality of Achaea, ruled by the family of the Angevin kings of Naples. The Byzantine administration still had a foothold in the Morea, Euboea and Crete were in the hands of the Venetians, Samos of the Genoese. Genoa had a trading station at Galata, across the Golden Horn from Constantinople, rather like the 'treaty ports' of the Western powers in nineteenth century China, and with the Venetians they exercised an imperialist domina-tion of the trade of the city which had once claimed world empire.

In 1326 Orkhan captured Brusa, thus virtually bringing to an end the rule of the Byzantine empire in Asia Minor. The separate Greek 'empire' of Trebizond still survived (and continued to survive even to 1461) on the south-eastern shore of the Black Sea. But Byzantium itself was henceforward confined to Europe, clinging to a fluctuating area of Thrace and Macedonia. Though the glory of the great city was unimpaired, Byzantium under the Paleologus family, which now held the throne, was small, poor and divided, its taxation system always inadequate to support its army and its central authority threatened by magnate landowners. The middle years of the fourteenth century were a period of destructive civil wars within Byzantium which facilitated the advance of its dangerous neighbours to east and west, the Ottomans and Serbia. It started with quarrels in the 1320s between the emperor Andronicus II and his grandson, and heir, Andronicus III. Andronicus III was supported by a powerful and very able magnate who played a large part in the destiny of Byzantium, John Cantacuzenus. In 1328 Andronicus III occupied Constantinople and forced his grandfather to abdicate. Andronicus III (1328–41) was a failure against the Ottomans who completed the conquest of north-west Anatolia. Elsewhere he was fairly effective and considerably enlarged the empire. He made skilful use of alliances with non-Ottoman Turkish emirs against the Genoese, recovering in this way the islands of Chios and Lesbos. He was fairly successful against Serbia and Bulgaria. Above all he recovered Thessaly and Epirus, the greater part of modern Greece. At his death the Empire seemed to be in a much healthier state.

But the death of Andronicus in 1341 was unexpected and unprepared for and it led to a disastrous civil war which accelerated the ruin of Byzantium in several ways. The heir, John V, was a minor. His mother, Anne of Savoy, was determined to secure his succession. The most powerful man in the empire was John Cantacuzenus. He appears to have been conscientiously determined to play the role of elder statesman and protector to the boy emperor, but the empress mother was persuaded by others to exclude Cantacuzenus from power. They controlled Constantinople. Cantacuzenus had himself proclaimed emperor in Thrace, with no intention of ousting the Paleologus heir, but rather of acting as co-emperor and regent. The disorder of civil war which followed was not only weakening in itself but was also compounded by the intervention of the most dangerous external powers and by social conflict in the empire itself. The social conflict was the work of the so-called Zealots who seized control of the city of Thessalonica and for a time established an independent republic there. This appears to have been a movement based on opposition to the great landed aristocracy, of which Cantacuzenus was an outstanding member, and the support of the urban poor. It weakened the position of Cantacuzenus in the part of Greece which he controlled. It happened also that the empire was rent at this time by particularly bitter religious controversies arising from disputes about the practices of a school of monastic contemplatives who claimed that they could attain to a vision of the divinity or the divine light by spiritual exercises. The supporters of their theology, of whom the most prominent was called Gregory Palamas, were condemned as unorthodox by other theologians. The relations between the ecclesiastical and the political worlds in Byzantium were traditionally very different from what they were in Latin Christendom. The orthodox church did not have an independent and articulated hierarchy like the western church. It was in some ways more individualistic and also assumed that laymen would take part in theological debates, particularly that the emperor would preside at church councils. The controversy about Hesychasm, the disputed contemplative system, therefore easily became entangled with political issues. Roughly speaking Cantacuzenus became identified with the Hesychast party while the Patriarch of Constantinople who was an opponent of the Hesychasts was a bitter rival.

Cantacuzenus turned for support to the ambitious ruler of Serbia, Stephen Dušan, who was happy to help him but did so at the price of increasing Serbian influence in Byzantine territory. He also turned for help to friends among the Turkish emirs. The Emir of Aydin and Saruchan who ruled the mainland behind Smyrna sent help to him in Thrace several times. He married one of his daughters to the Ottoman Orkhan. Thus Cantacuzenus who was one of the most conscientious of Byzantine rulers was responsible for the introduction of the Turks to Europe. For the time being, however, the greater threat came from the Serbs. Dušan's state extended right down to the Adriatic. It was naturally in most respects a barbaric kingdom but it was more powerful than Byzantium and it included many Greeks as well as Serbs. Dušan posed another threat to Cantacuzenus by ambitiously having himself crowned emperor in 1346. In the following year 1347, however, Cantacuzenus was able to bring the civil war to an end by occupying Constantinople and establishing himself firmly as emperor. He still hoped to rule without prejudice to the eventual rule of the Paleologus heir, John V, but the struggle had helped the empire's enemies.

The reign of John VI as Cantacuzenus now called himself, starting in 1347 (when Byzantium was hit by yet another disaster, the Black Death), lasted until 1354. He had his successes. He recovered Thessalonica. He had some success in challenging the supremacy of the Genoese on the sea and in the trade of Constantinople. But his plans for the Byzantine state did not work. By marrying John V Paleologus to his daughter, Cantacuzenus hoped to secure unity without usurpation while he entrusted more distant parts of his empire to other members of his own family. John V and John VI quarrelled and their quarrel once again gave opportunities for foreign powers to trample over the body of Byzantium. Cantacuzenus used his old Ottoman friends in Europe and it was at this time, as a result, that the Ottomans advanced from occasional forays into Europe as allies to permanent settlement. The Turks occupied Gallipoli and would not leave it. John V obtained control of Constantinople in 1354 with the help of the Genoese. Cantacuzenus abdicated and retired to a monastery. The Paleologi were to reign in the city unchallenged for another century but for most of that time as powerless clients of other states.

John V had a long and eventful reign from 1354 to 1391. In the course of it he overcame the pride of his predecessors to the extent of begging for help from the West for the beleaguered empire at almost any price, the empire of the Serbs collapsed and the Ottomans established their state on the mainland of Europe. John V pinned his faith at first on the West. He had come to power with Genoese help and he gave them the valuable islands of Chios and Lesbos. In the long run the Genoese were useless to Byzantium because of the rivalry of Venice and because both cities regarded the empire chiefly as a pawn in their game of commercial imperialism. John also revived the idea of religious reunion between Rome and Constantinople as a step towards western aid. He wrote to the pope in 1355 making the most extravagant offers of submission (supervision of ecclesiastical changes by a papal legate, personal submission of the emperor to the pope, his son to be a hostage at Avignon) in return for quite modest military help. A papal legate did go to Constantinople but naturally made no headway against the opposition of the orthodox church though he did receive the allegiance of the emperor. Ten years later John V sought the assistance of another catholic, King Louis of Hungary, demeaning himself as no previous Byzantine Emperor had ever done by visiting the country of another ruler to seek his aid. The visit was a miserable failure. In 1366 he did receive some help from the West. This was in the shape of an expedition led by the adventurous and ambitious Count Amadeus of Savoy, his cousin, whose army cleared the Turks out of Gallipoli and strengthened the emperor in his own country before demanding jewels as pledges for the payment of his expenses. It may have been partly because of the impression made upon him by this expedition that John V in 1364 took the very remarkable step of journeying to Rome to signify to Pope Urban V his personal acceptance of Catholicism and to seek help. The visit was quite fruitless. On his way back he even got into embarrassing financial difficulties at Venice where the republic still had in its possession jewels which his mother had pledged for a loan in the days of the civil war with Cantacuzenus.

One of the legacies of John's journey to the West was a promise to give the strategically important island of Tenedos to Venice. The Genoese who held it were naturally against this. In 1376 they supported a successful rebellion by the emperor's son, Andronicus IV, thus beginning a war which was both a Byzantine civil war of father against son and an imperialist war between the two Italian maritime republics, known in Italian history as the War of Chioggia (see above, p. 100). The situation was further complicated by the help given to both sides by the Turks. John V recovered control in 1381.

During John V's reign the Ottomans greatly enlarged and consolidated their position in Europe. What this meant in terms of population and methods of occupation is not very clear. It looks as though the Turks did actually transport themselves in large numbers from Asia Minor to Europe, perhaps taking over lands depopulated by the Black Death. There was also clearly a great deal of massacre, deportation and plunder: Europe became a field for the *ghazis* to practise their profession of holy warfare as they had done in Asia. There were many prudent conversions. On the other hand, there may have been many peasants who benefited from the dispossession of their previous feudal lords by the Ottomans and the position of the non-Muslims paying tribute in return for protection was not necessarily worse than that of the Christian taxpayer in a Christian state: the Turks were more tolerant of other religions than Christian crusaders were and this facilitated their advance into Europe. While the social history of the expansion is obscure the inexorable military superiority which made the Ottomans so effective against their divided Christian opponents is very clear. It is also clear that it was greatly assisted by the continual political divisions within Byzantium; the Turks were able to enter Europe because they were repeatedly able to participate in Byzantine civil wars. Orkhan was succeeded by Murad I (1362–89) who assumed the title of Sultan and it was during his reign that the fall of Constantinople itself became an accepted likelihood. His main achievement however was the expansion of Turkish occupation to the west. In the 1360s Murad captured Adrianople and established his court there. The Ottomans were then brought into confrontation with Serbia which in the recent past had been a more formidable state than Byzantium. But the great days of Stephen Dušan were past. In 1371 Murad defeated the Serbs at Černomen on the River Marica. This was the first great victory of the Turks over the Slavs of south-east Europe. It was followed by rapid advance into their territory. In 1387 Murad took the Byzantine city of Thessalonica far to the west. Meanwhile, the Turks had raided far to the north and west in Bulgaria and Serbia up to the Danube. In 1389 Murad's army met the Serbs in the great battle of Kossovo, so famous in Slav legend. Murad himself was killed but the Serbs themselves were overwhelmingly defeated, their nobility were subjected to the Sultan and the fate of the Balkans was sealed. Byzantium was now completely confined and encircled. Indeed, by this time John V had become accustomed to acting as a dependent of the sultan, providing him with military service when required. The subjection had been symbolized by a curious episode in 1373 when John's son, Andronicus IV, had joined a rebellion by one of the sultan's sons. After it had been subdued Murad blinded his rebel son and demanded that John should inflict the same punishment on his and he had at least to pretend to comply. In the competition within the family of Paleologus at the end of John V's reign between the emperor and his sons, the Turkish sultan was, in effect, the arbiter.

Murad I was succeeded by an equally formidable leader, Bajezid I (1389–1405). He completed the subjection of Serbia and in 1394 began to besiege Constantinople itself. It was at this late moment that the European reaction to the Turks produced the first really impressive Latin attempt in the fourteenth century to come to the rescue of Byzantium, the Crusade of Nicopolis.

The idea of the crusade was very far from dead in late medieval Europe. Although of course there were no enterprises comparable with the great invasions of Syria and Palestine which established and sustained the Latin rule in the Holy Land in the two centuries after 1095, the essential conception of the crusader's role was unchanged and was still a very important factor in the European outlook. In 1365 a crusading army attacked Alexandria under the leadership of a papal legate who exhorted the soldiers before they landed with the words 'Chosen knights of Christ, be comforted in the Lord and His Holy Cross; fight manfully in God's war, fearing not your enemy and hoping for victory from God, for today the gates of Paradise are open.' The Muslim control of the Holy Places was an affront and the conversion of non-Christians was a duty. The idea that the slaughter or conversion of unbelievers was particularly meritorious remained a profoundly important assumption of the Latin Christians which distinguished them sharply from Greek Christians and made their attitude to the meeting of cultures rather more like that of the Muslims and even less tolerant. It was to reappear as a more obviously positive force in the Iberian expansion beyond Europe in the sixteenth century. In the later Middle Ages, though the sentiment was widespread, its expression was in abeyance for two reasons. Firstly, because political developments in the Near East, especially the strength of Mamluk Egypt, made the reconquest of the Holy Land a practical impossibility. Secondly, because the restless and expansive nobility of north-west Europe in the early Middle Ages which had provided the eager fighting men of the early crusades, had settled down and it was difficult to mobilize effective crusading armies.

Nevertheless, the crusade still played a large part in European life. The Teutonic knights had transferred their activities from the Levant to Prussia where they carried on continuous crusading activity against the pagan Lithuanians. The Castilians were faced by Granada. The French nobility of Outremer had partly withdrawn to Cyprus which was ruled by the Lusignan dynasty. The Knights Hospitallers seized Rhodes from Byzantium in 1309 and held it throughout this period. The organization of a crusade remained a cardinal point of papal policy and, although the results may seem derisory, a great deal of thought and political effort was devoted to it at the Curia. Finally, there was much crusading literature which helped to keep the idea alive in the minds of the European nobility. On the other hand, there were great obstacles. All the interested parties were in practice ambiguous in their attitude; not only were the Genoese and Venetians more interested in the security of their commerce, the Hospitallers were ultimately more interested in their control of Rhodes and the popes in the preservation of their ecclesiastical absolutism. All the Christian powers in the Levant showed themselves at one time or another willing to ally with Muslims against other Christians. Among the large number of minor crusading enterprises of the fourteenth century a few more successful ventures stand out. In the 1330s serious plans were made by Philip VI of France and Pope Benedict XII. They collapsed because Philip became more interested in the Hundred Years War. In 1344 a coalition of forces from Cyprus, Rhodes, Venice and Genoa, with the blessing of the pope, captured Smyrna from the Turkish Emir of Aydin – but this was really an episode in Levantine politics. The nearest thing to a revival of the crusade on the old pattern, that is an attempt to liberate the Holy Land, took place in 1365. This was the result of the initiative of King Peter I of Cyprus for whom the crusade was a lifelong passion. With papal blessing he toured Europe seeking assistance and managed to gather a substantial army which sailed from Rhodes to attack the Egyptian city of Alexandria in the hope of forcing the Mamluks to bargain over Jerusalem. Alexandria was taken. The crusaders then plundered the city cruelly, destructively and indiscriminately and went home. Any harm done to the Muslim world was compensated by the harm done to Italian commerce. The crusade had never appeared more clearly as a symptom of the destructive aspect of feudal society. This was the last attempt to recover the Holy Land, which became even more obviously irrecoverable when the Christian kingdom of Armenia in, south-east Anatolia succumbed in 1375.

With the conquests of Murad II in Europe and the evident danger to Hungary and central Europe as well as to Constantinople the strategic conception of the crusade changed. The recovery of the Holy Places became an ultimate aim subordinated to the immediate need to check the Turks. There was a new front line in Hungary and the King of Hungary was henceforward the prince with most direct interest in the promotion of crusades. For over half a century from 1382 to 1437 the ruler of Hungary was King Sigismund who for this reason always had a strong personal interest in the crusade and made intermittent efforts throughout his life to interest Europe in it. The man behind the Crusade of Nicopolis however was not Sigismund but Philip the Bold, Duke of Burgundy, who throughout his life had a yearning for crusading projects, not as a matter of life and death but as one of the desirable trappings of a nobleman's life. He was one of the very few princes who could afford to indulge the taste on a large scale. When Philip decided to launch a crusade against the Turks all the resources of his possessions in the Netherlands were mobilized. The crusade and its aftermath probably cost him, or rather his subjects, about half a million francs. This really was the mobilization of superior western European resources on the grand scale to meet the Turkish threat. But the way in which they were used was consistent with the life-style of the French aristocracy of the period, with the half-serious chivalric warfare of the Hundred Years War, not with the grim machinery of conquest directed by their opponent, Bajezid. A substantial army, mainly of French and Burgundian knights, led by Philip's young son, John de Nevers (later Duke John the Fearless) travelled down the Danube in 1396, joined a Hungarian army and penetrated Turkish territory as far as Nicopolis. When the Turkish army approached, they appear to have behaved with foolhardy bravery and tactical carelessness. Many were killed and the leader was one of those captured. His father later paid an enormous ransom for him. The holiday jousting spirit was no way to deal with the Ottoman army. This was the last serious crusade.

The check to Ottoman expansion, which the Crusade of Nicopolis failed to bring about came a few years later, not from Europe but from Asia. In the general history of Asia the most remarkable development of the late fourteenth century – though it was a transitory phenomenon – was the sudden rise of a new empire among the Steppe peoples – a successor to Genghis Khan and Chagatay. Timur began to build his empire from Samarkand in 1369. By the end of the century he controlled the Steppes, Persia, Caucasia and Syria and was influential in Asia Minor, most of which lay by this time within the Ottoman empire. Timur's army was a force before which even that of the Ottomans paled into insignificance. When Bajezid resisted Timur's intervention in Asia Minor, Timur retaliated with a crushing defeat of the Ottoman army at Ankara in 1402. Bajezid himself was captured and according to legend carried around in a cage until he died. The empire of Timur did not in fact last much longer for the conqueror himself died in 1405 and his creation disintegrated quickly. The damage to the Muslim world, which it was widely hoped in the West would follow from a revival of Mongol power, did not in the long run take place. Temporarily however, the encounter with Timur seriously reduced Ottoman power. Ottoman control over the other Turkish emirates in Asia Minor was undermined for a time and competition for the succession between the sons of Bajezid further weakened the empire. It happened also that this period coincided with the rule at Constantinople of an intelligent and effective emperor, Manuel II (1391-1425), who was able to exploit it. The disaster of Nicopolis had been followed by a long and almost fatal siege of Constantinople by Bajezid. Manuel II decided to follow the example of his father by journeying to western Europe in search of help. His journey, which he made in the years 1400 to 1403 and which took him even to England, was largely fruitless but he returned to a much happier situation in his own country. Bajezid's successors, Suleiman (1402-11) and Mehmed I (1413-21), needed Byzantine help to establish themselves in their state. The relationship of the previous generation was therefore reversed for a time: the Ottomans became explicitly dependent on Byzantium and some territories were restored including Thessalonica. In the first two decades of the fifteenth century Byzantium enjoyed the last of its Indian summers.

The Ottoman and Byzantine rulers who faced each other in the next generation, Murad II (1422-51) and John VIII (1425-48), had a different relationship produced by the revival of Ottoman unity and expansion. The Byzantines tried to support a pretender against Murad in the early years but this ruse did not succeed. Murad got control and besieged Constantinople again. Byzantium rather surprisingly tried the experiment of handing over one of its most important and also most threatened possessions, the city of Thessalonika, to Venice which accepted the trust and ruled it from 1423 to 1430. But here too Ottoman strength was too great. Thessalonika was captured, terribly pillaged and many of its people enslaved in 1430. The sphere of Byzantium shrank again. Only in the Morea, ruled by John VIII's brothers, did it flourish. In the face of these disasters John VIII revived again and for the last time the grand but impractical dream which had repeatedly haunted the imagination of both the East and the West in the last two hundred years: the dream of a reunion of the eastern and western churches followed by aid to Byzantium arranged under papal auspices. In the 1430s when John made his approaches the situation in the Latin Church was uniquely favourable to the project of union. In the past a major difference between the two churches had always been that the Latins assumed that union was simply a matter of submission to papal supremacy, while the Greeks saw the only hope in a reconciliation worked out by a general council of both churches. During the period of success of the Council of Basle in the mid 1430s not only was papal authority at a very low ebb, but also the influence of conciliarist theories of the Church held by the protagonists of Basle was at its height. The idea of a general council therefore found very much more easy acceptance than on previous occasions. It was theoretically in line with fashionable western thinking – whereas previously Latins had regarded the idea as simply an impertinent threat to papal supremacy - and moreover Pope Eugenius IV and his opponents at Basle were willing to vie with each other for the honour of being the instruments of reunion. There was therefore some prospect of arriving at an agreement which was not merely a personal arrangement between emperor and pope but involved the Greek Church. After negotiations with both pope and council, the emperor himself finally travelled west to meet the pope at Ferrara and Florence in 1438–9. The delegation included also the Patriarch of Constantinople, representatives of the patriarchs of Alexandria, Antioch, and Jerusalem and some other notable clergy. The outcome of the long discussions was a decree of Union, the provisions of which consisted either of submission by the Greeks to the Latin doctrines or blurring of the differences between them; in particular it asserted the supremacy of Rome. It was signed by all the Byzantine delegates except Mark Eugenicus, Bishop of Ephesus, who stood out against it, but it became clear as soon as the emperor returned to Constantinople that it was a worthless document. The concessions made by the delegates had practically no support among the people and clergy of the Greek Church. Two of the leading supporters of the Union, Bessarion, Bishop of Nicaea, and Isidore, Bishop of Kiev, fled to the West and ended their days as cardinals.

Papal interest in the question did however lead to a revival of crusading activity in the 1440s. The continued pressure of

Turkish armies on the borders of Hungary, where Belgrade was now under siege, produced a reaction led by the Hungarian general John Hunyadi and King Ladislas III of Poland and Hungary. In 1443 these two participated in a crusade organized by a papal legate Cardinal Giuliano Cesarini, which pressed down into Bulgaria and then made a ten-year truce with the sultan. Later in the same year, Cesarini, Ladislas and Hunyadi apparently decided to disregard the truce and advance again. At Varna on the Black Sea coast, the enraged sultan overwhelmed their army killing both Ladislas and Cesarini. Hunyadi was again defeated in 1448 at Kossovo, the site of the great victory over the Serbs in 1387. These were effective checks to Western hopes of rolling back the Turkish frontier in Europe but Murad at the end of his life was willing to accept the existing limits of Turkey. In 1451 however Murad II was succeeded by a sultan with much more ambitious designs, Mehmed II the Conqueror (1457–81). Mehmed decided to take Constantinople itself and started preparations for the siege in 1452. The defenders of the city were poor and reduced in numbers. They got little help from outside except for the Venetians and Genoese, some of whom fought heroically. They depended chiefly on the strength of the city's geographical position and its great wall which had been first built a thousand years earlier. Constantinople had been often besieged, never taken. Now it faced an enormous army and advanced artillery. The Turks overcame the defenders by sheer weight of numbers and arms. On 29 May 1453, they got over the walls, killed the last emperor, Constantine XI, and subjected the city to a dreadful pillage.

The fall of Constantinople was regarded by the whole European world as a momentous event. The historian cannot regard the final collapse of a state which had been so weak for so long as epoch-making: the balance of power was scarcely altered by the catastrophe of 1453. For most of the period covered by this book, Byzantium was one among a number of rival states in the Balkans and the Levant and not pre-eminent. This is an appropriate point however to consider its relation with the orthodox world. The importance of the Byzantine empire and emperor was inseparable from the relationship of the state with the Greek Church. There was nothing parallel with it in the West. It was expressed in a revealing interchange of letters between Prince Basil I of Moscow, a Greek Christian, and the Patriarch of Constantinople at the end of the fourteenth century. The Russian commenting on the impotence of Manuel II said, 'We have a church but no emperor.' The patriarch replied with a rebuke: 'It is not possible for Christians to have a church without an emperor, for the imperial sovereignty and the Church form a single entity and they cannot be separated from each other.' The emperor was unique. This conception of the relationship of Church and state was very different from the dualism of Latin Christendom. It allowed greater power in ecclesiastical matters to the emperor and there was no Greek pope. During Byzantium's last enfeebled centuries the emperor and his capital, whose churches and monasteries were venerated throughout the Orthodox world, derived prestige from their relation to the Greek Church. The Serbian ruler, Stephen Dušan, for example, imitated the imperial court and acknowledged a general superiority of the emperor. But in the end Prince Basil was right – the Church could do without the emperor. In the orthodox tradition, churchmen were more deferential to lay rulers than they were in the West but they had no central authority Hence, the pathetic futility of the various attempts culminating in the Council of Florence to engineer a reunion through the agreement of pope and emperor, and hence the relatively slight effect which the fall of the empire had upon the Church. Throughout this period the orthodox church had the allegiance not only of Greeks but also of the Serbs, the Bulgars, the Wallachians and the Russians, though they had been isolated politically from Byzantium by the Mongol conquest of southern Russia. The advance of the Turks did nothing to shake their preference for the Greek over the Latin Church. The Russians in 1441 imprisoned their Metropolitan Isidore because he was a supporter of the Union and eventually elected a native Metropolitan of their own. In Turkish occupied Europe, in spite of the desecration of many churches and the conversions to Islam, the Church continued to exist under the protection of the infidel state. After the taking of Constantinople, Mehmed

II deliberately sought out the scholar and monk, George Scholarios, who had been a fervent opponent of the Union, and installed him as Patriarch of Constantinople with the intention that he should continue, as far as possible, the working relationship between the ruler of Byzantium and the Church. The Orthodox Church therefore, to a large extent, preserved its amorphous existence in eastern Europe through the agony of the Byzantine empire remaining geographically as extensive as before and equally hostile to the Church of Rome.

It is paradoxical that, in spite of the ecclesiastical gulf, the intellectual influence of Byzantium on Europe was greater during its last period than it had been for long before that. The fourteenth century saw a revival of interest in pagan Greek literature among Byzantines and a new emphasis on the Greek background. It was facilitated by the diffusion of higher education among laymen which distinguished Byzantine from traditional Latin society. At Constantinople learning was much less a preserve of the clergy: the emperors John Cantacuzenus (who wrote a history of his own times in retirement) and Manuel II (who wrote rhetorical works) are examples of cultivated lay statesmen of a type which would be hard to find in the West in that period. Byzantine Hellenism found a receptive audience in the bourgeoisie of the Italian cities and, in addition to the trade links of the Venetians and Genoese, the political interest of the Greeks in Western aid threw the two parties together at a crucial stage in the development of Italian Renaissance thought. Two names should be particularly singled out. Manuel Chrysoloras, who was Manuel II's envoy in the West at the turn of the century, was one of those mainly responsible for stimulating the study of Greek in Italy. In the first half of the fifteenth century one of the chief centres of Byzantine life was the despotate of Morea, which was more sheltered than Constantinople from the constant menace of Turkish attack. In that small state the town of Mistra became a cultural centre. Its most remarkable luminary was George Gemistos Plethon, who revived the study of Plato and constructed a pagan political philosophy based on Plato's *Laws*. As a delegate to the Council of Florence, he

gave an impetus to the study of Plato and Greek in general in
Italy.

The despotate of Morea fell to the sultan soon after Byzantium itself. Mehmed II was curiously influenced by the
Byzantine legacy. His aim was to create a world empire, such
as Byzantium had been, based on the same city. 'In his view,'
said an Italian commentator, 'there should be only one
empire, only one faith and only one sovereign in the whole
world. No place was more deserving than Constantinople
for the creation of this unity in the world. The Conqueror
believed that thanks to this city he could extend his rule over
the whole Christian world.' Mehmed imagined, as he showed
in his preservation of the patriarchate, that he could be the
greatest power in both the Muslim and the Christian worlds.
From the Western point of view, the most remarkable feature
of his reign after 1453 was the long war with Venice in 1463-79.
Up to this time the Venetians still held Euboea and they tried
to establish control over Morea. Eventually they were driven
out of both and concluded a peace which limited them to a
few footholds in Greece and the Aegean. They still held Crete.
At the end of his life (1480-81), Mehmed's soldiers even for a
time established a bridgehead in Italy at Otranto.

The structure of the Ottoman state was fundamentally
different from anything else in Europe. It depended on
administration by officials who, however exalted, were the
personal slaves of the sultan. His rule was enforced by the
Janissary Corps of lifelong professional soldiers again per-
sonally dependent on the sultan. No European ruler had
comparable power over his subjects. In spite of its exotic
character, however, the Ottoman empire had now established
itself as a major European power filling the vacuum which
had been left in the Balkans by the decline of Byzantium.

ii *The Beginnings of European Expansion*

If one can imagine an impartial and omniscient observer
surveying the prospects of the world's peoples in the fourteenth century, it is rather doubtful whether he would have

predicted the triumphant future of Europe. In 1400 Latin Christendom was one, and probably not the largest in total population, of several areas of advanced civilization, comparable in extent with the Muslim, Indian and Chinese worlds, and rather on the defensive geographically. Within a century of course, Vasco da Gama had travelled to India and Columbus to the Caribbean and Europe was decisively launched on the career of discovering the true geographical nature of the world and of subduing rival civilizations. The contracting Europe of 1400 and the expanding Europe of 1500 are significantly connected. Medieval Europe in the twelfth and thirteenth centuries had shown strong expansive tendencies towards the East; not only the crusades in the Levant but also the penetration of Asia by Italian merchants which led to Marco Polo's travels in China and the appointment of a Catholic Bishop of Peking in the early fourteenth century. But in the course of that century, Asia was closed to the Italians. The break-up of the Mongol empire made transcontinental journeys more difficult and European merchants were effectively confined to ports like Caffa, Constantinople, Smyrna and Alexandria, on the edge of Asia. At the end of the century the Ottomans presented a new formidable obstacle and were spreading into Europe. Though Italian trade with Asia was not prevented and remained of the greatest importance long after the discoveries of the sea routes, it was hindered and limited. Italians were less encouraged to go east and therefore potentially more interested in going west. If Asia had been more open it is less likely that an adventurous Genoan like Columbus would have been shipwrecked on the coast of Portugal. This is not just a matter of one man. The Italian contribution to the Iberian take-off into the world was crucial. The closing of Asia did tend to turn Europe's face from east to west and therefore towards the sea routes of the Atlantic in which there might otherwise have been less interest.

By its geographical location, maritime background and trading connections Ming China was arguably much better equipped than Europe to open up the countries around the Indian Ocean to extensive trade, to establish contacts with the coast of Africa and in general to discover the world. In 1400

the Chinese were probably more advanced than Europeans
in the construction of manageable ships and in techniques of
navigation. There was a long tradition of Chinese trade not
only with India but also with southern Arabia and parts of the
African coastline. Moreover, it happened that in the late
fourteenth century, on the eve of the Portuguese enterprises
the imperial government instituted an ambitious programme
of trading voyages. A fleet of sixty-two large ships carrying
30,000 men was sent in 1405 to the East Indies and south
India. This was succeeded by other voyages of a similar kind;
a few years later their range was extended as far as Aden and the
Somali coast of Africa. At the very time when the Portuguese
were beginning to be interested in the west African coastline
therefore the Chinese were reinforcing old contacts in the
East in a much more impressive manner. The last of these
expeditions to the African coast went in 1431. The policy of
sending them was then abruptly and decisively ended. The
voyages had probably had several motives: the military and
diplomatic aim of impressing other countries with a display of
Chinese power, the improvement of the navy, profitable trade,
and perhaps also the satisfaction of scientific curiosity. They
were promoted and financed by the imperial court. The reason
for their abandonment appears to have been a conflict within
the imperial administration. The expeditions were favoured by
the eunuchs of the court and the early ones had been commanded by a prominent member of that class. Eunuch power
was regarded as a danger by the scholar gentlemen of the
imperial bureaucracy who controlled state policy. Against the
policy of the expeditions it was urged that the promotion of
trade was an inferior and improper activity for the emperor's
government and that the defences of the land frontier of the
empire needed money which was being wasted on unnecessary
demonstrations of power in the far south. China therefore
turned away from maritime exploration and expansion and
left the field free for the west Europeans. The check to Chinese
expansion was not a matter of technical or administrative
competence – in these fields they were in the lead – but of
social and political structure.

The centralized control of Chinese voyages of discovery

and their semi-scientific nature contrasts very clearly with conditions in Europe and goes far to explain why it was Europe that effectively explored the world. In the very long perspective of world history the reasons for European superiority in exploration and conquest are to be found in certain essential characteristics of European society: the wide distribution of power and wealth which led to fierce competitiveness between kings, between nobles and between merchants; the individual wealth and economic enterprise fostered by the European cities; the crusading spirit of Latin Christianity. These were characteristics which already existed before the period covered by this book, products of the evolution of Europe in the high medieval period from the tenth to the thirteenth centuries. It is one of the paradoxes of European history however that the impulse towards overseas expansion came at a period of overall contraction both in the European economy and in the geographical extent of Latin Christendom. The Portuguese exploration of Africa, which was to lead directly to the discovery of the route to India around the Cape of Good Hope, started with the taking of Ceuta in 1415 when the European economy appears to have been entering its period of greatest global contraction. This raises the problem of explaining not the general conditions of European superiority in maritime and commercial enterprise but the particular circumstances which led to the beginnings of expansion at that time.

An important place in this explanation must be given to the economic conditions of that part of Europe. Broadly speaking the Portuguese exploration of the African coast was motivated by the search for three things: crusading success against the Muslim world, gold and slaves. North Africa was a crucial source of gold for the late medieval world in which precious metals were very scarce. Mediterranean Europe had a favourable balance of trade with the Maghreb, the coastlands of north-west Africa. European cloth and wheat were exported there, principally by the merchants of Genoa and Catalonia and the rest of the Iberian peninsula. The caravan routes of the Sahara brought Sudanese gold to the African coast which was exchanged for European products. In this way African gold irrigated the European economy at a time when it was badly needed and helped to maintain the unfavourable trade balance of Europe with the Asiatic world. The relationship with North Africa was old-established and well known. One of the motives of the Portuguese was to break into it and acquire a particularly advantageous position by getting closer to the source of the gold. African slaves were also a well known import into Europe, particularly into Iberia and labour was very scarce in the early fifteenth century.

The first explorers who are known to have ventured into the Atlantic were the Genoese brothers Vivaldi who set off to find 'India' beyond the Straits of Gibraltar in 1291 and disappeared. Another Genoese built a fort on one of the Canaries probably in the early fourteenth century. In 1341 a joint Florentine-Genoese expedition patronized by the King of Portugal sailed to the Canaries. In the 1340s Catalan and Majorcan expeditions went to the Canaries and brought back some of the inhabitants. In 1346 the Catalonian expedition of Jaime Ferrer went down the African coast explicitly in search of gold. These attempts of the Mediterranean maritime powers up to 1350 to break into the South Atlantic world failed. Little is known about the movement but one of the reasons why it failed may have been the unsuitability of their ships. This raises the important question of the technical background to the discoveries. It was essential that the explorers should have technical equipment of two kinds: firstly an adequate system of navigation, secondly suitable ships.

For the first requirement the Portuguese were initially dependent on the systems of navigation which had been developed in the Mediterranean. The sailors of the Mediterranean had by this time good charts of the area they frequented and they had the magnetic compass. The 'portolans', as their maps were called, were fairly accurate charts of coastlines covered with networks of lines joining ports and prominent landmarks. With one of these charts, a compass and a little simple trigonometry, the sailor could steer a course between two ports. By the end of the fourteenth century the Italian and Catalan maps covered the Mediterranean, some of the west coast of Europe and the African coast down to Cape Bojador, the genuinely known world. The most advanced school of map makers was to be found among the Jews of Majorca who also drew on information from the Arab world. It is known that the great patron of the explorers Prince Henry employed the most expert cartographers and navigators he could find including the Jews of Majorca. The early Portuguese pioneers used this system of navigation but at some stage they advanced beyond it to the beginning of astronomical navigation using quadrant and astrolabe to determine latitude by the pole star. At what point the Portuguese in their advance into the unknown began to make use of this highly abstract method of determining their position – an important intellectual advance – is uncertain. It was probably towards the middle of the fifteenth century.

In the design of ships however the Mediterranean had less to contribute. The well developed trade routes of Mediterranean commerce were served by galleys, big long ships with shallow draught, driven by oarsmen. Admirable in their own sphere they were at a severe disadvantage in the Atlantic. North-west Europe had developed a quite different kind of boat to deal with the Atlantic gales: the 'cog', a short, rounded boat powered by sails and given great manoeuvrability by a variable number of sails and a fixed rudder. The great technical strength of Iberia as a take-off point for the exploration of the seas was that it had the benefit of both the Mediterranean and the Atlantic experience. The maritime development of both Atlantic Castile and Portugal was advanced by the late fourteenth century; one indication of that is the part played by their fleets in the Hundred Years War. Lisbon was both an important point on the Genoese, Venetian and Catalan route to the Low Countries and also the centre of a native trading community. The Portuguese developed the ship which made the discoveries possible, the caravel, a long ship with both square and triangular sails and a fixed rudder.

The patron to whom the inception of the Portuguese voyages of discovery was due was a familiar type of late medieval adventurer. Henry the Navigator was the third son of King John I of Portugal. Like his grandfather, John of

Gaunt, he was a prince in search of a suitable sphere of activity. His enterprise in Africa began with the attack on and capture of the Moorish city of Ceuta near Tangier in 1415. From that time Henry devoted himself to the linked activities of crusading and economic expansion, sending many voyages down the African coast, partly because he failed several times to expand the foothold at Ceuta into a larger conquest of Morocco. There is no evidence however that he had any great intellectual interest in exploration or that he was interested in the propagation of trade except as a source of money for his own enterprises. Everything suggests that he was above all a dedicated crusader who hoped to achieve immortality by making contact with the legendary Christian Prester John and encircling the Muslim world. Henry was made governor of the province of Algarve in southern Portugal and the port of Lagos in that region became the centre of exploring activity. Until 1434 his ships were confined to the coastline north of Cape Bojador. In that year they managed the difficult sailing feat of using the winds both to pass the cape and to return. By 1444 they had reached Cape Verde. By the time of Henry's death in 1460 they were pressing down past Sierra Leone. By this time also the first settlement for trade with the interior had been established at Arguin. A more permanent 'factory' was established in 1483 at Mina in what is now Ghana. Before the death of Henry part of his dreams had certainly been realized. Gold was being bought on the African coast and returned to Portugal. The first cargo of black slaves was landed at Lagos in 1444. Arguin as described by the Venetian Cadamosto, who commanded an expedition down the coast for Henry in 1455, was already a pattern of future European trading settlements. Those who took part in the contract with Henry had houses on the island and exchanged cloths, silver, silk and wheat with Arab visitors in return for slaves and gold. At the same time the economic potentialities of the islands in the Atlantic were being developed. Madeira was rediscovered by two squires of Henry in 1420. By the middle of the century cane sugar was being produced there on a large scale and was beginning to pass into European commerce. The Canaries had been occupied in 1402 by two French noblemen supported by the King of Castile. Henry the Navigator tried to take them by force in 1425 and initiated a long series of disputes with Castile over the right to them, but Castile was the effective occupier. Henry's men rediscovered the Azores in 1427 and began to occupy them effectively. By the end of his life the Portuguese along the African coast and in the Azores and Madeira had produced for the first time outside the Mediterranean the pattern of commercial imperialism which the European nations were to apply throughout the world.

It was into this Portuguese complex of discovery and trade that Christopher Columbus was accidentally initiated later in the century. In 1476 he joined the Genoese colony at Lisbon. He became involved in the Madeira sugar business and also seems to have made a voyage to the factory at Mina. His conviction that it would be possible to sail westwards to Asia however depended on influences from the intellectual world of the Renaissance. How Columbus acquired his ideas is not known, or at least is very uncertain, but the general background from which they came is fairly evident. Before the fifteenth century, although it was known that the world was a sphere, no interest was taken by practical map makers and little by scholastic scientists in the problem of plotting geographical points accurately in relation to latitude and longitude. This had been done in antiquity notably in the second-century *Geography* of Ptolemy. This was a Greek book. It was first translated into Latin and thus made available to the European world by a Florentine pupil of Manuel Chrysoloras, Jacopo d'Angelo, in 1409. With the information given by Ptolemy it was possible to draw a map of Europe, the Near East and south Asia which is recognizable in its general outlines. The importance of Ptolemy however is not the precise geographical information which his book contained but the encouragement which it gave to people to imagine the known world stretched across a globe with co-ordinates of latitude and longitude related to the size and shape of a sphere: in other words to see the world in perspective. This was an intellectual revolution which originally had nothing whatever to do with the endeavours of practical chart makers, who went on making empirical portolans, or of explorers. It was an entirely bookish influence from the world of the Florentine humanists and was popularized during the fifteenth century by intellectuals like Eneas Sylvius. It happened that in the case of Columbus a passionate interest in scientific speculations about the size of the world was joined with a practical experience of Portuguese maritime enterprise.

Columbus's amalgamation of science and technique, like Leonardo's, took place later in the fifteenth century. Before 1450 the foundations of expansion were laid by practical men seeking traditional objectives. As in the contemporary invention of printing, the remarkable thing about the discoveries of the early fifteenth century is their unspectacular origins.

CHAPTER VII

THE FIFTEENTH-CENTURY CRISES OF THE MONARCHIES

Medieval monarchy was subject to endemic conflict and rebellion because it depended on a balance of power between the prince and the nobility which could easily be upset by personal failings. Therefore the internal history of all the regions of Europe where kingship on a large scale flourished – France, England, Spain and eastern Europe – had been far from tranquil in the fourteenth century. In the fifteenth century, however, in all these regions monarchies went through crises which seemed to be of a more profound character than earlier disturbances: the prolonged sickness of the French monarchy during the English invasion, the collapse of royal authority in the early part of the Wars of the Roses in England, the impotence of the Spanish monarchies in the reigns of Henry IV and John II, the disintegration of Luxemburg-Habsburg power in central Europe. Too little is known as yet about the structure of these crises for the historian to be able to judge how far they had similar origins. They involved dynastic problems and wars. They also involved structural weaknesses in states. One reason why this was a bad period for government in general was that increasingly obsolete systems of taxation and authority survived from the medieval state and were ineffective in a period of declining landed wealth; but the characters and policies of individual princes were very important too. The interrelationship is complex. The phenomenon of the crisis of monarchy is however fairly plain. It is equally clear that in all the main regions traditionally dominated by strong monarchs there was a striking recovery of power in the later part of the century.

i *France: the end of the Hundred Years War*

In 1380 at the end of the reign of the great King Charles V
the French monarchy was once again unquestionably the most
powerful state in Europe, its territories reunited after the
lacerations of the earlier phases of the Hundred Years War,
its financial system remarkably flexible and productive, its
army large and efficient, its nobility on the whole submissive
to the royal will. The next eighty years were neatly divided
between the reigns of only two Valois kings, Charles's son
and grandson, Charles VI (1380–1422) and VII (1422–61). It
was however to be a period of very great importance and of
the most violent upheavals in the history of the French crown.
During those eighty years France as a political unity came
nearer to extinction than at any other time since its creation
by Philip Augustus (1180–1223). From the disasters it emerged
more powerful than ever before and more recognizably the
monarchy of the *Ancien Régime*.

The Hundred Years War between England and France
may be divided for convenience into two major phases. The
first drew to a close soon after 1380 largely because neither
the English nor the French kings had the ambition or tenacity
to prolong it. The second began with the invasions of the
English King Henry V in 1415 and after. After 1380 warfare
with England which had dominated the previous three reigns
now played a much smaller part in French history for some
thirty years.

Charles VI was eleven when his father died. Since he was
too young to rule, the government of France in his early years
was in effect carried on by councillors, many of whom had
the prestige and the skill derived from long association with
the government of his father but were nevertheless referred
to as the *Marmousets* (little fellows) in contrast with the great
lords. The great lords were above all the boy king's uncles,
Philip the Bold Duke of Burgundy, Louis Duke of Anjou and
John Duke of Berry. Inevitably the grander aspects of French
policy were to a large extent controlled by them; they were all

very great magnates and two of them had strong political
interests outside France. Burgundy was keen to assert French
power over the Low Countries. Down to 1385 when the Peace
of Tournai finally assured his control over the county of
Flanders he diverted French royal power as far as possible to
this objective. Anjou had interests in Italy. The last two decades
of the fourteenth century are a strange period in French
politics because, although the ambitions of the crown itself
were in a sense very limited, the influence of the court stretched
over Europe. The politics of Germany were affected by the
ambitions of Philip the Bold, the politics of Italy by those of
Anjou (with his claims to Naples and ambition to win a
kingdom by the support of Pope Clement VII). To them
were added later the king's brother Louis Duke of Orleans
who in 1387 was married to Valentina the daughter of Gian
galeazzo Visconti of Milan and thus became another actor on
the Italian stage.

In 1388 the king, now twenty years old, took over the
direction of government from his uncles and ruled with the
help of his councillors. Down to 1392 the control of the
Marmousets at the heart of government persisted. Royal
ordinances strengthened the position of the administrators
by introducing the principle that the *parlement* was to be self-
perpetuating and that the *Grand Conseil* was to choose the
lesser members of the bureaucracy. Charles VI appeared to
be growing into a prodigal, pleasure-loving king devoted to
the ceremonial and luxury of the wealthiest court in Europe.
Festivities of the court were remembered, notably that which
celebrated the coronation of Isabella of Bavaria, to whom he
had been married to further the German plans of his uncle of
Burgundy, or an occasion when he visited the castle of the
Count of Foix in the south and was greeted by the local
nobility dressed as cowherds, driving animals which carried
silver bells. The elegant pictures of court life in the manuscript
of the *Très Riches Heures* were actually painted for the king's
uncle the Duke of Berry about 1416. The royal court of
Charles VI's youth reads like an attempt to realize that dream-
world. It came to an end, as a result of a gradual but very

complete disintegration of political life which began in the early 1390s.

The first signs of mental weakness in the king appeared in 1392. They were connected by contemporaries with the endless excesses of his life at court and also with a political crisis involving the Constable of France, Olivier de Clisson, successor to Du Guesclin, to whom the king was devoted and who was one of the props of the *Marmouset* régime. The Duke of Brittany, an enemy of Clisson, tried to arrange his assassination. This agitated Charles. On a hunting expedition near Le Mans, the king, overheated by his armour in the summer sun, was surprised by someone seizing his horse and by a sudden clash of arms. He had a fit of madness which thereafter became a repeated and increasingly frequent occurrence. As time went on he was less and less able to rule his kingdom. The inability of the king to rule left as usual a vacuum which could only be filled by the leading members of the royal family. The *Marmousets* were quickly driven from power. They were not loved by the great nobility. The people who now mattered were the queen, the king's brother Orleans and his uncle Burgundy. Queen Isabella was not fitted for this role. She was a self-indulgent woman, sometimes suspected of infidelity and certainly not politically faithful to her husband. Louis Duke of Orleans had been endowed with immense estates in the heart of France but his scale of life and Italian ambitions absorbed all his revenues and more. Philip the Good, Duke of Burgundy, was of course a very considerable power in his own right, but was also interested in the court chiefly as an instrument to further his own interests. In the period up to 1407 Orleans was on the whole the dominant figure.

After the failure of plans for the invasion of England in 1386–7, the court had entirely abandoned the active anti-English strategy of Charles V in favour of a much more confused support of the German and Italian ambitions of Burgundy and Orleans. In 1396 the betrothal of the king's daughter, Isabella, to Richard II of England and a ceremonial meeting of the two kings after the conclusion of a long truce signalized that relations between the two courts were better than they had been at any time since the beginning of the

Hundred Years War. On the other hand, French intervention was active beyond the Alps. Orleans's interest in Italy led to Charles VI becoming titular lord of Genoa in 1396. The politics of the later part of the Schism and Benedict XIII's adventures in Italy (see above, p. 182) led also to French involvement in Italy at the turn of the century.

The power of Orleans at court provoked a reaction against him by his uncle Philip the Bold, who for a time won the support of the queen. The king was forced in 1402 to pacify them by giving them equal power over the levying of *aides*. They not only vied for control of the spoils of the court but also supported opposite policies abroad. Orleans was for support of the Avignon Pope Benedict XIII to further his own aims in Italy; Burgundy for withdrawal of obedience to ease his position in Germany. In 1402-3, Orleans favoured the resumption of war with England, while Burgundy opposed it because he was sensitive to the need of his Flemish subjects to trade with England. Orleans began to turn his attention even to undermining the position of his uncle in the Low Countries using his great wealth to acquire the homage of the Duke of Guelders and the lordship of Luxemburg. In 1404 Philip the Bold died. This made Orleans even more overweening. In 1404-5 his plundering of the court reached its height; in that year he drew in French money £150,000 from royal *aides* levied in his own appanage and £251,000 in grants from the royal funds, approximately equivalent to £60,000 of English money, something like half the total income of the King of England. He was suspected of the intention of seizing Normandy in addition to the vast estates he already held of the crown. The death of Philip the Bold also brought on to the scene, however, his successor as Duke of Burgundy, John Fearless, a more dangerous opponent. In 1405 Burgundy refused to have the *aides* procured by Orleans levied on his lands and brought an army to menace Paris so that Orleans and the queen were forced to flee. The first signs of civil war were appearing. Between 1405-7 there were periods of intense rivalry and periods of co-operation in small-scale fighting with the English.

In November 1407 came the blow which clearly initiated

the long period of disruption of French political life. Orleans was assassinated by a gang of ruffians in the pay of John the Fearless who soon afterwards accepted and boasted of his responsibility for the deed. The crime was not generally unpopular for Orleans had been rightly associated in the public mind with heavy taxation to produce money which he squandered. Burgundy engaged a theologian, Jean Petit, to compose an apology for his action on the ground that Orleans had been a tyrant. But the crime had the effect of dividing the nobility irreparably and bringing France into a state of civil war. The new Duke Charles of Orleans was supported by the great dukes of Berry, Bourbon and Brittany and by his father-in-law Bernard Count of Armagnac in the south, a powerful personality whose leadership led to the group being called the 'Armagnacs'. Burgundy was supported mostly in the north and east where his territories lay. It came to war in 1411, both sides turning to the English for support, a presage of the horrors that were to come. Burgundy was able to take control of Paris with the help of a contingent supplied by the English king. The following year the Armagnacs won English support by offering a still larger bribe: the old enlarged duchy of Aquitaine, free of French overlordship. A reconciliation between Armagnacs and Burgundians came only just in time to forestall a serious English invasion.

French politics were now in a state of division and disorder, similar in some ways to that which prevailed after the battle of Poitiers and, as in 1357, the national disaster led to a crisis in which a meeting of Estates General produced an explosion in the overheated atmosphere of Paris. The Estates General were summoned to Paris in January 1413 to grant taxes to pay for resistance to an English invasion. Resentment against the years of disordered corruption burst out. They presented lengthy denunciations of the malpractices of the crown's administrators, especially financial officers. Demands for a thorough reform of the administration and dismissal of the guilty were accepted by the queen and the court. But the proceedings of the Estates inflamed smouldering resentments in the city of Paris. The lead was taken by the guilds of butchers and skinners and particularly a skinner called

Caboche. They had links with the Duke of Burgundy. In April and May there were daily risings and demonstrations in the city threatening the court which was compelled to produce a document usually known as the *Ordonnance Cabochienne*. This listed a long series of measures designed to reform in detail many sectors of the royal administration by imposing checks on the appointment and action of officials. Like most such reform programmes produced by insurrection in medieval states its effect was very short-lived but it was no doubt a justifiable indictment of the last twenty years of bad government. Its promulgation was followed by a reign of terror in the city which lasted through the summer of 1413.

The Armagnac party gathered troops in Normandy to rescue the king and court from their virtual imprisonment in Paris by the *Cabochiens*. They were able to come to an agreement with Burgundy and in August recovered control of Paris and executed some of the leading rebels. But, after this, conflict between the two noble factions broke out again. Burgundy fled from Paris leaving the young Orleans supreme. The *Ordonnance Cabochienne* was revoked. The country remained on the edge of civil war until peace was restored between the two parties at the beginning of 1415.

It was in this unhappy state that the French monarchy faced its greatest enemy of all, Henry V of England. For thirty years, 1385–1415, though there had been frequent minor clashes in Gascony, at Calais and at sea, there had been no large-scale conflict between France and England. The revival of English invasion of France on a large scale in 1415 was in essence a new expression of the English magnates' conception of France as an arena for the indulgence of their love of fighting and plunder. They were returning with enthusiasm to the ravaging of the fair land which their fore-fathers had enjoyed in the previous century. In their new King Henry V (1413–22) they had an ideal leader, brilliant, inflexible and austere, to set against the hopeless disarray of the French political system. Henry also pursued a radically different policy from that of his predecessors. After the Agincourt campaign his aim was not simply to raid the country but actually to conquer it piecemeal, establish settled government and even to introduce English colonists. The coincidence of English aggression and French disunity was now to lead to a period of catastrophe which exceeded even the disasters of the reign of John II.

Henry's great successes were made possible by Burgundy whose hatred of the Armagnac party was great enough to drive him into the hands of the English. Henry's first invasion was preceded by a secret agreement with Burgundy in 1414 by which Burgundy agreed to help him and to do homage to him. He then picked a quarrel with the French court and invaded in the following year. After taking Harfleur at the mouth of the Seine he set out across country to Calais to return home. At this point the suspicion between the two parties in the French nobility led to catastrophe. The Armagnacs refused Burgundy's offer of help because they distrusted him; he therefore forbade his followers to help. The French army which met Henry V at Agincourt was badly placed tactically, knee-deep in mud, but also lacked leadership. The result was a massacre of the French nobility. Orleans himself was captured and was to languish in English captivity, a sad, exiled poet, for twenty-six years. The catastrophe did nothing to restore unity. The lead at court was still more firmly taken by the Count of Armagnac who became Constable. Burgundy hovered near Paris with an army. In 1416 he renewed his understanding with Henry V, agreeing now to help him secretly and to recognize his claim to the throne of France openly when he had successfully enforced it. Henry V also had the support of the other most powerful European sovereign, Sigismund King of the Romans.

The success of Henry V's real invasion when it came in 1417, therefore, was less the result of his brilliance than of the crippling of French resistance – half the nobility were either helping Henry or hindering Charles VI's court. A new arrangement of forces arose. Burgundy, in alliance with the queen, tried to set up a regency government for the mad king at Tours while the Armagnacs at Paris held the king himself and were also supported by the Dauphin, the future Charles VII, who was now fourteen years old. While the English were beginning the conquest of Normandy by taking

Caen, the Burgundians were menacing Paris. In the following year Burgundy and the queen took control of Paris and massacred many of their Armagnac opponents. In 1418 and 1419 the English were systematically occupying the whole of Normandy. Part of the process was a terrible six-month siege of Rouen to the point of starvation.

The Dauphin abandoned his father and mother to Burgundy at Paris and set up a rival court with his financial headquarters at Bourges and his *parlement* at Poitiers, drawing on his resources of support in the centre and south of the country to balance the power of Burgundy in the north. Burgundy was manoeuvring for position to make the maximum use of his links with the English but his policy was still vacillating and inconclusive. He was negotiating with both sides. In the autumn of 1419 he veered over to the Dauphin's side and a meeting was arranged between them to take place at Montereau on the Yonne about fifty miles south-east of Paris. Burgundy was persuaded to meet the Dauphin in an enclosure erected on the bridge over the river. He came with ten men and was let into the enclosure where the Dauphin was waiting with a small group of his followers. As soon as they entered, the enclosure was shut and a few minutes later the duke was killed by a blow from an axe, probably delivered by one of the Dauphin's followers, Tanguy du Chastel. The 'Bridge of Montereau' is one of the great disasters of French history. Responsibility for the deed was always denied – it was said to have been the accidental result of a scuffle. Whatever the truth about that, there is no doubt that it completed the fatal division of the French nobility into two bitterly opposed camps, it was 'the hole by which the English passed into France'.

John the Fearless's son, Philip the Good, the new Duke of Burgundy, naturally determined to avenge the murder of his father, rapidly made an agreement with Henry V accepting the English claims in France. This in turn led quickly to the Treaty of Troyes in 1420 between the old King Charles VI, controlled of course by Burgundy, and Henry V, which embodied in effect a capitulation to English claims. Charles accepted the substance of Henry's claim to the throne of

France, by recognizing him as his heir – he was already married to his daughter Catherine – and disinheriting the Dauphin. By the end of 1420 Henry was in Paris with Charles VI meeting an assembly of the Estates General which voted money for him to continue his war. The Dauphin made some efforts to recover control of the capital but he was unsuccessful and withdrew again south of the Loire, leaving Burgundy and the English in control of a great part of northern France. In August 1422 Henry V died of dysentery and was followed to the grave two months later by the old, mad King of France, Charles VI.

The Duke of Burgundy, undeterred by the death of Henry V, accepted his baby son, Henry VI, as King of France. For the next fifteen years France was divided between three régimes. The Regent of France, Henry V's brother, the Duke of Bedford, controlled the greater part of the north, the Ile de France, Normandy, Picardy and Champagne. Bedford's government was, for the most part, simply a continuation of the previous French monarchy, the same institutions very largely staffed by Frenchmen. The *parlement* of Paris under the English régime, for instance, continued to cause resentment by its interference in Burgundian territories as it had done before. Normandy, the heart of the English conquest, was kept partially separate with its own council and Bedford preferred to reside at Rouen. Though greedy and hard, Bedford genuinely tried to run the French monarchy so that it could eventually be taken over by Henry VI and was by no means subservient to the English council at Westminster. He found no lack of French officials ready to support him, many of whom did very well out of the English administration. There were however permanent English garrisons, many English nobles acquired lands and the whole régime was geared for the conquest of the rest of France, using as far as possible taxes voted by the French estates. The second power was the Duke of Burgundy, holding an enormous area in the north and east and in practice exercising a great deal of authority in Champagne and Picardy, which were partly governed by Burgundian officials.

Apart from Gascony the south was controlled by Charles

VII, *le Roi de Bourges*. Though he controlled the most territory and was supported by the largest number of nobles, the early part of Charles's reign was extraordinarily inauspicious. He was nearly killed in an accident just before his father's death and was widely believed for a time to be dead. During the first years English power was still expanding. There seemed to be a real danger that they would break through, across the Loire, and overrun the south. Charles's one effort in 1424 to oppose this positively with a large army was disastrous. It led to his defeat at the battle of Verneuil which was a minor Agincourt. The English then occupied Maine. In 1428 they were threatening Orleans which was the gateway to the south.

With such a training in political misfortune it is perhaps not surprising that Charles VII appears to have been somewhat apathetic and that he seemed to fall rather passively under the sway of successive groups of courtiers. The old Armagnac councillors were replaced by his mother-in-law, the Duchess of Anjou. She was interested in safeguarding the Anjou lands and therefore engineered an understanding with the neighbouring Duke of Brittany. This brought into the circle his brother, Arthur Count of Richemont, who became Constable and remained an important figure at the court. Another man who gained some ascendancy over the king was an unscrupulous adventurer called Georges de la Trémouille. The Count of Foix was an ineffective lieutenant-general of Languedoc. While the life of the court was confused and corrupt the country was disordered and very imperfectly controlled. Taxes were voted by estates but not successfully collected. The general tendency to anarchy was particularly exemplified in Poitou where Richemont and la Trémouille waged private wars for several years.

The decisive change in the fortunes of the French monarchy is rightly associated with the name of Joan of Arc. About the visionary power of her personality and her superhuman gifts of leadership there can be no doubt – she is a unique figure. It is more difficult to decide how far, through her social background, she effectively represented and then appealed to the political sentiment of the non-noble French. Joan was from a peasant family of Domrémy in eastern Champagne, a village where the peasantry had suffered acutely, through flight and loss of animals, from the lack of order and had very good reasons for regarding the English invasion as an affliction. Disorder appears to have been fairly common in English France as it was in the south and frequently to have taken the form of anti-English action. As a chronicler said there were many 'desperate people, lost children, who abandoned their fields and their houses, not to inhabit the strongholds and castles of the French but to lurk like wolves in the depths of the forests'. The period which we are now reaching was also, apart from the war, the low point in the fortunes of landowning seigniorial society when manpower was at its scarcest and the peasantry at their strongest. In the peasants' revolt which took place in Normandy in the 1430s it is difficult to separate the social and political backgrounds. Joan represented a class which was stronger than it had ever been before and as in the time of the *Jacquerie* had every reason to feel loathing for *seigneurs*. Many of them may genuinely have seen the Valois King as their only hope. Joan's effective career lasted for a very short time. Saints told her in visions that she must save France. At the beginning of 1429 she decided on her course of action. By April she had got to the court at Chinon and won over several soldiers and courtiers. In May she raised the siege of Orleans and in the next month the army which she had inspired defeated the English at Patay. In July she was able to take Charles VII to be anointed in the cathedral at Reims in the heart of Champagne and this did much to improve his prestige in the eyes of his subjects. Her confident policy was to drive straight on to recapture Paris and install the king in his proper seat. This policy was only half-heartedly pursued and was a failure. In 1430 Joan was captured by the Burgundians and the rest of her short life until the following year saw only the long torture of her imprisonment, interrogation and execution.

After the burst of activity inspired by Joan, Charles VII and the court returned to their old ways. The rivalry of Richemont and La Trémouille continued. No spectacular progress was made for some years. The next and in some ways the decisive, step in French recovery owed little to the efforts of Charles. It was the decision of Burgundy to change sides. The English invasion had long lost its momentum and he wanted peace. After a conference at Arras in 1435 Charles gave generous terms in the addition of territory to secure Philip the Good's recognition of him as king. The Regent Bedford died in the same year.

Even after this the reconquest was a fairly slow process. English policy was very uncertain and divided but the English nobility had a big stake in France and they resisted the loss of their empire tenaciously. Charles's forces first entered Paris in 1436, but it took a long time to recover possession of the lands around. It was not until 1444 that Charles was able to make a truce with the English which restricted them to Normandy and Gascony. Normandy was conquered in 1449–50. By this time the balance of military power and inner political strength had shifted decisively to the French side. In 1450–3 Charles was able to accomplish something which many of his predecessors had failed to do – to take over Gascony which, in spite of its bitter resistance and strong attachment to English links, was now ruled directly by the French crown for the first time.

The turbulence of the court continued to be a feature of French politics. A plot to gain control of the court led by two disgruntled major nobles, the Dukes of Bourbon and Alençon, was discovered in 1437. The most serious conspiracy, similarly inspired, was that which led to the disturbances known as the *Praguerie* (so called because of resemblance to insurrections in Bohemia) in 1440. This time the plotters aimed to put the young Dauphin Louis on the throne. Louis tried again in 1446 and after this was packed off to the Dauphiné, never to see his father again. In spite of these and other disturbances it was in the years after 1442, when his dominating mother-in-law, the Duchess of Anjou, died and he began to surround himself with a legendary collection of mistresses, that Charles took firmer hold of the court and acquired the devoted group of councillors which led to his being nick-named *le bien servi*, 'the well served'.

The later years of the war, 1435–44, like the period following the Treaty of Brétigny, were marked by chaotic brigandage in many parts of France as the regular garrisons and retinues of the English and Burgundians declined. The *écorcheurs* as they were called were troop leaders who lived by plundering and there is much evidence of the misery which they caused. Prolonged occupation and warfare had naturally caused many social difficulties, collapse of authority, conflicting claims to lands, sheer physical destruction. All these required a long process of social convalescence. The French monarchy, however, rose from the ashes with a surprising access of strength. It is remarkable how much the threads of development which can be discerned in the reign of Charles V were taken up nearly a century later in that of his grandson. Charles VII created a new army which was divided into two parts. Firstly the *Grande Ordonnance* of 1445 established a standing army of cavalry – lancers and horse archers – which was to be regularly lodged in garrisons. Secondly it was laid down in 1448 that there should be a reserve infantry army of *francs archers*, theoretically one man for 50 households. This was a military organization which was to serve the monarchy for a long time.

More important for the political structure of the kingdom was the fact that Charles strengthened his financial independence and reduced the power of assemblies. The *tailles* (direct taxes) and *aides* (taxes on sales), abolished at the end of Charles V's reign, had in fact been revived a few years later and collected intermittently and they remained the basis of the royal taxation system, though much reduced by concessions to nobles and of course by the effects of war. The outstanding development of Charles VII's reign was that he began to collect these taxes regularly without parliamentary consent. *Aides* were levied in this way from 1436 and the *taille* after 1439. Thus the French monarchy acquired an enviable freedom to use types of taxation whose yield would expand with economic growth which gave it a very strong position among the European powers. The larger assemblies of estates declined into insignificance: those of Languedoil were unimportant after 1440, those of Languedoc met regularly but were not very troublesome. Small provincial estates continued to exist; the tendency however was for parliamentary assemblies to be fragmented into smaller geographical units. This is slightly surprising in view of contrary developments in other European states. The explanation is probably to be found partly in the size of France and its many provincial divisions which made it difficult to generate a sense of political community in the whole country, partly in the position of the nobility whose exemption from taxation made them uninterested in common political resistance in alliance with the townsfolk. Charles VII was troubled more by the difficulty of persuading estates to assemble than by parliamentary opposition.

At the death of Charles VII France remained of course a country with powerful noble families ruling semi-independent territories, not only Brittany and Burgundy, both virtually separate powers, but also Orleans, Anjou, Bourbon and Alençon. Still the monarchy had become once again the most powerful in Europe. The Dauphin who was to succeed him in 1461 as Louis XI was well qualified to develop this inheritance. Since 1446 he had ruled the Dauphiné with extraordinary success, imposing his will on the local nobility and pursuing his own very positive policies. He was an autocratic, treacherous, physically unhealthy man, contemptuous of the nobility. Louis's powerful and unattractive personality aroused a coalition of magnates against the crown which demonstrated the potential instability still inherent in the French political structure. He succeeded in the first years of his reign in alienating a group of powerful men: the Count of Dunois a bastard member of the Orleans family, the Angevin Duke John of Calabria who felt his interest in Naples was being betrayed by the king, Louis's own brother Charles Duke of Berry, a weak man who made a good figurehead for the movement, the Duke of Bourbon, Francis II, Duke of Brittany, and the young son of the Duke of Burgundy, Charles the Bold, Count of Charolais. The movement which they created, and which caused a civil war in 1465, the League of the Public Weal, aimed to bring the court to heel and to reduce its power. They were not very well co-ordinated and their success was largely due to the energetic intervention of Charles the Bold who threw in the weight of Burgundy, but the survival of Louis XI's system of government was in the balance for several months and the indecisive battle at Montlhéry nearly caused the fall of Paris. At the peace which was concluded at Conflans in the same year, Louis had to make concessions. His brother was given the Duchy of Normandy as an appanage. Charles the Bold recovered the Somme towns which Louis had bought back from the Duke of Burgundy in 1463 under the provisions of the Treaty of Arras.

For a decade from 1467 to 1477, Louis was forced to witness the progress of Charles the Bold in his plan to convert the Burgundian inheritance into a kingdom. But the diversion of Burgundian interest towards the Rhineland left Louis freer to suppress his enemies in France. Brittany, Bourbon and Anjou were reduced to a more subservient position. The death of Charles the Bold in battle in 1477 was an unforeseen blessing which completed the recovery of the French monarchy. The Duke of Burgundy had been an exceptional danger to the French crown because he was both a peer of France with an acknowledged role in French politics and a prince commanding power on a kingly scale. That danger was now removed. Louis had to fight Charles's heiress Mary and her husband Maximilian of Habsburg, but the agreement which was eventually concluded at Arras in 1482, restored to France the Duchy of Burgundy, Picardy and the Somme towns.

ii *Castile and Aragon*

At the end of the fourteenth century there were still four kingdoms and four royal houses in the Iberian peninsula, the kingdoms of Castile, Aragon, Navarre and Portugal. The most momentous political development of the fifteenth century in Iberia was the union of the two major kingdoms, Castile and Aragon, by the marriage of Ferdinand and Isabella in 1469 which created modern Spain. This event had to some extent been prepared for by the earlier political history of Iberia. The histories of the two royal houses had become deeply interwoven. In 1410 the royal house of Aragon became extinct in the male line on the death of Martin I who had ruled over both Aragon and Sicily. In Castile the dynasty of

Trastamara was by now well established. Henry of Trastamara whose ambitions caused the major upheavals in Iberia in the fourteenth century was long dead and the kingdom was in the hands of his grandson John II (1406–54). In their search for a suitable king after the death of Martin I, the nobles of Aragon eventually decided in the Compromise of Caspe upon Ferdinand of Antequera, the uncle of the King of Castile and the daughter of an Aragonese princess. Ferdinand I of Aragon as he now became, had been naturally a very great and powerful magnate in Castile and in fact regent during the minority of the young Henry II. From 1412 kings of the Trastamara family ruled in both Castile and Aragon.

The attention of the rulers of Aragon was divided as always between the opportunities open to them in the Mediterranean and on the mainland of Iberia. Ferdinand of Antequera was succeeded in 1416 by two brothers, Alfonso V who became king and a younger brother, John. Alfonso V's interests were quite decidedly turned eastwards. He was determined to build upon his control of Sicily by adding Naples after the death of Joanna II. His intervention in Naples in the 1420s was not successful. But after Joanna's death in 1435 (see above, p. 192) he eventually succeeded in conquering the kingdom and he never returned to Aragon although he remained king until his death in 1458. A deputation from the Cortes of Aragon which attended him in Italy in 1452 complained that war, depopulation and economic decline required the presence of the king. Alfonso preferred to leave Aragon in the hands of his wife and put his Italian interests, which he no doubt thought were more vulnerable, first. He became primarily an Italian prince and was succeeded in Naples after his death by his son Ferrante I. However, the interests of his long-lived brother who survived him to reign for twenty years as John II of Aragon (1458–79) were firmly tied to the politics of Iberia and this was a fact of great importance.

Alfonso V's aim had been to interest John in Spanish affairs in order to leave himself a free hand in Naples. He had therefore arranged a marriage between John and the heiress of the kingdom of Navarre, Blanche. The hope was presumably that John would be satisfied with the sphere of activity open to him as consort of Navarre. John however was an ambitious and treacherous man and even in his brother's lifetime showed much interest in the politics of Aragon and also in the weakly governed kingdom of Castile. On the death of his wife in 1441 he determined to force himself on the Navarrese as king, against their wish to be ruled by his and Blanche's son Charles of Viana. John married as his second wife a prominent Castilian noblewomen Joanna Enriquez, by whom he had a son Ferdirand, thus deepening his interest in Castile and further alienating the nobility of Navarre, concerned, like other aristocracies, to maintain the effective independence of their country. After Alfonso V died and he became John II of Aragon, he continued to have great difficulties with his stubbornly independent Navarrese relations in law, who found some support also among the nobility of Catalonia. These difficulties encouraged him to turn for help to Louis XI of France, who was glad to have an excuse for intervention and expansion in Iberia. In 1462 he made the Treaty of Olite with Louis XI who promised to help him enforce his rule in Navarre. Later in the same year he had to make a further agreement with Louis XI who promised to help in putting down opposition in Catalonia this time, in return for the cession of the border provinces of Cerdagne and Roussillon. This proposed diminution of the territory of Catalonia still further inflamed the hostility of the nobility. John II was unable even with French help to subdue them but Louis XI nevertheless took Cerdagne and Roussillon. For the next few years John was unable to control or recover the confidence of the nobility of Catalonia who offered the kingdom in succession to various other possible rulers: to Henry IV of Castile, to a Portuguese prince, to the Duke of Anjou who invaded in 1467. But eventually, in spite of the active opposition of Louis XI, to whom a united Iberia was an extremely unattractive proposition, events did move towards a rapprochement between Aragon and Castile and ultimately to the momentous marriage alliance.

Castile was in theory ruled in the first half of the fifteenth century by another John II (1406–54), but he was an ineffective king. The early years were a minority. After he came of age in

1419 the most powerful individual in the kingdom was in fact the Constable, a great noble called Alvaro de Luna. This phase came to an end in 1447 when John II married, as his second wife and under the influence of Alvaro who hoped to weaken Aragonese influence, Isabella of Portugal. Isabella dominated the court and brought about the downfall of Alvaro. John was succeeded in 1454 by his son by his first wife, Henry IV, nicknamed 'the Impotent' because of his supposed weakness and certainly, even more than his father, a political failure. Henry IV had a daughter called Joanna who was rumoured to be in fact the bastard child of a prominent courtier, Beltran de la Cueva, and therefore called *la Beltraneja*. The factions in the court and the strong noble opposition which developed in the country at large seized on this rumour to justify a movement in favour of the succession of Henry IV's young half-brother and half-sister, Alfonso and Isabella, the children of John II by his second wife. The opposition to Henry IV and to Joanna's succession was led by the very powerful Pacheco family which supported John II of Aragon. In 1464 they staged a curious ceremony at Avila, in which an effigy of the king was tried and stripped of royal insignia. The rebels captured Isabella after a battle with the king in 1467. Alfonso died in the following year and the dispute now turned on the question of Isabella's claim to succeed instead of Joanna and her choice of husband. Isabella in 1469 accepted the hand of Ferdinand, son and heir of John II of Aragon. For the next five years the issue remained uncertain. Many of the nobility were hostile to the idea of a strong united Spanish monarchy and Henry IV remained attached rather indecisively to the claim of his daughter. When he died Isabella was immediately crowned. She had to face a long period of violent opposition in Castile supported by King Alfonso of Portugal who was betrothed to *La Beltraneja* and claimed the throne for her. But this was ended by 1478. When John II of Aragon died in 1479, he was succeeded by Ferdinand and thereafter the husband and wife, the 'Catholic Kings', ruled the whole of Iberia except for Portugal, Navarre and Granada.

Spain as it was under the rule of Ferdinand and Isabella,

was in one important respect very much changed from the Spain of the fourteenth century. The precocious economic development of Barcelona had been severely checked; Catalonia was in fact the most spectacular commercial casualty in the economic contraction of the fifteenth century. The symptoms of serious disease first appeared in 1381 when there was a large number of bankruptcies among the bankers and merchants of Barcelona. In the first half of the fifteenth century Barcelona's trade declined sharply: it has been estimated that the shipping activity at the port declined by 75 per cent between 1432 and 1454. The reasons for this are not clear. Barcelona in many ways resembled the Italian cities; why did she not continue to enjoy the same prosperity? The most likely explanation seems to be that the industrial backing for trade, the textile industry of Barcelona had contracted and was too narrow for a great international commercial system. Catalonia suffered a severe relative loss of wealth. In the united Spain of the years after 1469, Castile with its different social and political traditions was to be predominant.

The marriage of Ferdinand and Isabella involved no unification of Castile and Aragon which remained quite separate kingdoms. Nevertheless, the joining of the two crowns solved some of the political problems which had made the internal history of the two states extremely turbulent in the previous generation because that turbulence had resulted partly from Aragonese intervention in Castile. The Catholic kings also made institutional changes which helped to strengthen the monarchy. In 1476 Isabella established a militia based on troops supplied by boroughs – the *Hermandad* – which was a counter-balance to noble power. The land-owning military orders of Santiago, Alcantara and Calatrava were taken over by the crown, Ferdinand becoming Master of each one. Isabella herself was an exceptionally austere, forceful and decisive ruler who imposed her will and worked through an effective council, very different from the ineffective kings of the previous half-century. But though the internal stability and strong monarchy of Castile from the 1470s were in dramatic contrast with the chaos of the previous period there was no underlying social change. The landed power of the great nobility such as the Guzmáns, dukes of Medina Sidonia, was largely untouched. In Castile as in eastern Europe society was dominated by an alliance between the crown and the great nobility.

iii *Germany and the Empire*

When the Emperor Charles IV died in 1378, he had been faced for two years by a threat to royal authority from certain of the German towns. In 1376, fourteen Swabian towns led by Ulm established a league whose purpose was to resist attempts by the emperor to tax them and to use them as pledges for loans from the princes, a practice which could easily lead to their loss of juridical independence. The towns defeated the most prominent Swabian prince, Count Eberhard of Württemberg, in battle at Reutlingen (1377) and went on to increase their power by alliances with the towns of Franconia and Bavaria. The Swabian Town League of 1376 ushered in a long period in which the most notable feature of the history of central Europe was the political instability caused by the weakness of princely power and by conflict between classes. The town movement of 1376–8 had affinities with the contemporary eruptions of class conflict in other parts of Europe, caused by the social tensions of the generation following the Black Death – this was the age of the *Ciompi*, the *Mailiotins* and the Peasants' Revolt. In most of Europe for most of the time, social tensions of this kind were contained by princely authority: the structure of government, even though weaker itself, was strong enough to hold. In Germany, however, social conflict which became prominent at this period, persisted as a dominant factor in politics for at least half a century.

In central Europe, particularly southern and western Germany, political organization was at all times relatively weak. Although the big dynastic blocks of the Luxemburg, Wittelsbach and Habsburg families in one sense dominated German politics they were curiously enfeebled at this period by the custom, which had a particularly strong influence in German politics in the late fourteenth and early fifteenth centuries, of dividing princely inheritances between members of the family instead of following the rule of primogeniture. This custom was particularly the downfall of the Wittelsbach family. Even such a small state as the Rhine Palatinate was divided between four sons of Rupert III on his death in 1410 and Bavaria was divided between a number of other branches of the Wittelsbach family. The Habsburg lands were divided into three in 1395. While the Luxemburg Wenceslas, son of Charles IV, succeeded to Bohemia and the German crown in 1378, his brother Sigismund succeeded in Brandenburg, two of his cousins in Moravia and his uncle held Luxemburg. The Luxemburg partition was not so serious because the units were large. The Wittelsbach family, however, was made impotent by the partition of its inheritance for much of the fifteenth century. And in general even the greater princely families were much weaker in the face of other class interests than they would have been if primogeniture had prevailed.

In 1378 Germany was entering a period of which one of the striking characteristics was the relative weakness of princes and the relative political prominence of other social classes: the towns, the peasantry, the nobility. In some cases these classes worked within the framework of princely power; in others, of which the Swabian Town League is an example, they threatened it with alternative kinds of political organization. The history of central Europe for the next half-century contained a number of movements – the town leagues, the peasant movements of the Swiss confederation and Appenzell, the leagues of knights, the revolutionary field armies of the Hussite left wing – which were opposed and effectively opposed to princely government. It was in this part of Europe that the structural weaknesses of political organization at this period appeared most clearly. This general feature of political life overshadows all the events of dynastic and imperial history.

The character of the interaction between princely government and class interests may be illustrated from the history of the Habsburgs. Between 1379 and 1386 the Habsburg lands were divided between two rulers, Albert III (Austria and Styria) and Leopold III (Tirol, Carinthia and the Swiss areas). Leopold III, who was an aggressive ruler anxious to extend his power, found himself faced by an alliance between the Swiss cantons and the imperial towns of southern Germany. Both the Swiss and the Swabian towns were in a sense permanent rebels against princely and noble authority. In 1384 the town of Basle over which Leopold was trying to extend his authority, joined the Town League, followed in 1385 by Zürich, Lucerne, Zug and Bern which were towns but also members of the Swiss Confederation. The war which broke out in 1386 took on the character of a struggle between the Swiss and the nobility of southern Germany for Leopold assembled a large army containing contingents of the Swabian nobility. Advancing into the mountains the army was attacked by the Swiss at Sempach, as it passed through the narrow road between the mountains and Lake Lucerne and overwhelmingly defeated. Many knights and Duke Leopold himself were killed.

On Leopold's death the Habsburg inheritance was reunited from 1386 to 1395 then divided again after Albert III's death in 1395, between his son and the four sons of Leopold. The details of the family history in the succeeding years are too complicated to set down here but one important development emerged from them: the propensity of the princely family to divide its inheritance and to quarrel about the division gave much more influence to the nobility and gentry organized in parliamentary estates. When the ruler of Austria was succeeded in 1406 by a child (Albert V), the estates of Austria (made up of representatives of nobility, towns, knights and Church) met and settled his succession and the regency without reference to the other branches of the family: their concern was to maintain the integrity and independence of the 'land' of Austria in which they lived. Already in 1402 the Habsburg dukes had tried to cope with disorder in their lands by allowing the appointment of judges who represented the nobility and the city of Vienna and were to have powers to enforce judgements. In 1406 Duke William (one of the sons of Leopold III) recognized a league of knights and nobles, called the 'Society of the Buckle with the Star,' as an organization with power to maintain law and regulate feuds among the nobility. The succeeding years saw a series of conflicts about succession between members of the family and interference by the estates.

Meanwhile another social threat to the Habsburgs developed in the north-east of present-day Switzerland, the region of Appenzell. In 1401 the peasantry of Appenzell revolted against the lordship of the great abbey of St Gallen. They were supported by the Swiss so successfully that in 1404 the Abbot was forced to make peace with them. He sought the assistance of one of the Habsburg dukes, Frederick IV, but the men of Appenzell, now under the leadership of a renegade Count Rudolf of Werdenburg who led them into battle in peasant's clothes, defeated a Habsburg force in the Rhine Valley in 1405. They then established a 'League above the Lake' including St Gallen and other towns and districts south and east of Lake Constance. In 1406 they swept over the Vorarlberg into the Inn Valley, making easy progress because, as a chronicler said, 'the peasants all wanted to be Appenzeller'. The success of the movement was facilitated by the divisions in the Habsburg house. The nobility of the region joined in two noble leagues, the League of the Elephant and the League of the Falcon, to protect themselves against the peasantry and princes alike. The duke had to join one of the leagues. The Appenzell area was not restored to order for several years.

This general failure of political authority is most easily observed in south and south-west Germany because there it had always been weakest. But it occurred to a lesser extent in other areas, in Bavaria and east Prussia for example. Partly as a result of it the spectre of social upheaval was more menacing in central Europe than elsewhere, it hung over society and was of course alarmingly embodied in the Hussite movement which threatened all the surrounding countries. Princely weakness also had an effect on conventional political structure. It was at this period, the late fourteenth and early fifteenth centuries, that the power of the parliamentary estates – to grant taxation, to control government expenditure, to appoint the princes' councillors and to regulate the succession in the princely house – became really deeply entrenched in the German states.

Meanwhile the imperial power declined still further.

Wenceslas reigned in Bohemia from 1378 to 1419 and until 1400 was universally accepted as King of Germany. But he was a poor successor to his father, a drunkard and a weak man. The difficult problems presented by disorder in western Germany, the Great Schism and the rivalry of his own relations, especially his brother Sigismund, were too much for him. In the 1380s Wenceslas tried seriously to intervene in the conflicts between towns and princes in the west. In 1383 with the agreement of many of the princes, he tried to use the old royal right to impose a *Landfriede*, a general peace, in an area of the empire. Wenceslas put forward the idea of a division of the empire into four parts within each of which a *Landfriede* should be organized. But the conflicts of interest between the towns (many of which were claiming the right to extend their jurisdiction over nearby country areas), the nobility, and those princes most interested in south-west Germany (the Counts of Württemberg and Habsburg Dukes) were too great. In 1389 at Eger he proclaimed a general peace of the empire (a *Reichslandfriede*) for six years which many accepted at the time but which did not have a lasting effect. The town-noble conflict however was dying down. The 1390s saw the development of a movement in the west for the replacement of Wenceslas, promoted chiefly by his enemies the Wittelsbachs, but also finding wider support among the Electors and the Rhineland princes who had little love for Luxemburg power and little respect for Wenceslas himself. In 1399 the archbishops of Mainz and Cologne and the Count Palatine (a Wittelsbach, Rupert) formed a league to defend the powers of Electors and they soon found enough support for the election of Rupert as king.

For ten years after this there were two rival kings. Rupert was an energetic and attractive character. He made a disastrous journey to Italy in 1401 (see p. 287). In 1403 he secured recognition by the Roman Pope Boniface IX. But his dangerous energy provoked the opposition of the man who had originally been the chief promoter of his candidature, Archbishop John of Mainz, who represented the intense West-German suspicion of effective royal power. When Rupert died in 1410 he also was rather isolated.

Wenceslas's incapability to rule the kingdom of Germany was generally accepted. A complicated series of manoeuvres in the years 1410–11 led to the election of Wenceslas's brother, Sigismund. Although he agreed to share the position with Wenceslas (who died in 1419) Sigismund was in effect king from that time until he was crowned Emperor in 1433 and emperor until his death in 1437. Sigismund's relation with Germany was a curious one. His personality was commanding; he was a man of grand conceptions and restless energy. He was therefore not very easy to challenge. On the other hand comparatively little of his attention was actually given to German affairs. He was King of Hungary. After 1419 he claimed to be King of Bohemia though it was not until the last two years of his life that he was able to make the claim good. The problems of defending Hungary against the Turks were enough to draw his attention for most of the time far away from Germany. His territorial interests in Germany itself were not very extensive especially as in 1411 he handed Brandenburg over to his ally Frederick, Burggrave of Nuremberg the founder of the Hohenzollern family.

Sigismund did make some efforts towards a political strengthening of the German monarchy, shrewdly realizing that it might be to the interest of the crown to work with the imperial towns and independent nobility in the south-west rather than with the princes against them. This was the area where the town leagues had first developed. A knightly 'Society of St George's Shield' which originated in Swabia at the beginning of the fifteenth century was to be an important political organization for a long time. Sigismund put forward in 1415 the idea of a town league under his leadership. In 1422 he issued a general privilege for the German knighthood allowing them to unite in leagues and later encouraged negotiations between the Swabian towns and knights. He also tried hard at times to act as an arbitrator. Nothing much came of all this except that the idea of a natural identity of interests between the emperor and his second rank subjects (knights and towns as opposed to princes) was somewhat promoted. German politics remained in varying degrees chaotic. At the councils of Constance and Basle, Sigismund

played a central role in European affairs and the Bohemian
question was of interest to much of Germany, but his most
permanent and dominant interest was Hungary and his
marginal relationship with German affairs is in very marked
contrast with the attitude of his fourteenth-century predecessors. The idea that the emperor should be the decisive agent
of reform, unification and peace in Germany nevertheless
remained alive. The 'Reformation of Sigismund' (*Reformatio
Sigismundi*), an influential tract composed by an unknown
author at Basle in 1439, could still couple the general reformation of the church, on lines of conservative moral reform, with
the reformation of the empire under the leadership of the
emperor. The author wanted a division of the empire into
four areas for arbitration in disputes rather in the way which
had earlier been suggested by Wenceslas. The hope of an
advance of this kind remained a strand in German thought to
be taken up seriously by the emperors Maximilian and
Charles V much later. The *Reichstag* was a fairly frequent
feature of German politics in the mid-fifteenth century and the
– extremely ineffective – sense of national unity was given some
life by the consciousness of external threats, the Hussites, the
Turks pressing Hungary and Austria, the Burgundian expansion in the Rhineland.

The withdrawal of the imperial ruler to the periphery of
German political life proceeded still further in the next
generation. On Sigismund's death without a male heir the
provisions of the Luxemburg-Habsburg succession treaty of
1364 (see above, p. 57) came into effect. Sigismund's successor was Duke Albert of Austria, known as King Albert II of
Germany. From his succession the development of the
Habsburg family as the dominant political force in central
Europe, a major feature of the European scene in the Renaissance period, was ultimately to follow. The Luxemburg and
Habsburg inheritances were united. And with his election in
1438 began the unbroken Habsburg occupation of the German
or imperial throne until the nineteenth century. But the
beginnings were very inauspicious. The Habsburg lands
were still split between several branches of the family. Albert
was accepted in Austria and as the successor of the Luxem-

burgs in Hungary and he was elected King of Germany. He could not enforce his rule in Bohemia in the face of the national pride born of the Hussite movement. He died young in 1439. His successor was a son born after his death, Ladislas surnamed Posthumus. The claims of succession were strong enough for Ladislas to be generally accepted in Austria, Bohemia and Hungary, but a child could not rule and the effective power in all these kingdoms – an interesting illustration of the uniformity of political evolution in the states of east-central Europe – fell to nobles acting as leaders of their class. In Bohemia, George of Podiebrady became regent, in Hungary John Hunyadi, in Austria the lead was taken by Ulrich von Cilli and Ulrich Eizing. Ladislas died at the age of eighteen in 1457.

Throughout Ladislas's short life the senior male Habsburg was a remote cousin Frederick and it was paradoxically from this obscure and inactive princeling that the imperial Habsburg line was to descend. Frederick was accepted as king in Germany in 1440 and made a rapid trip to Italy in 1452, without pretence of military power, to be crowned emperor. But, while possessing these grandiose titles in the outside world, within the Habsburg inheritance itself he had only a limited and insecure footing disputed alike by his relations and by the estates of the *Länder*. During the remainder of his long life (to 1493) however he was able to a large extent to restore the unity and to extend the power of the Habsburg inheritance. The claims to Bohemia and Hungary which had offered the possibility of an empire of the Danube basin, were in effect lost and only to be revived in the next century. But as a result of the natural extinction of the other lines of the family, the German Habsburg lands were completely reunited in the hands of Frederick and his son the future Emperor Maximilian, before Frederick's death in 1493.

Frederick III's attitude to the empire was extraordinarily inactive and detached. He made no visit to Germany outside his own dominions between 1444 and 1471. The tendency for German politics to disintegrate into a series of local conflicts between states with virtually no reference to a central royal authority reached its extreme point. In Germany as a whole the most interesting political development of the later fifteenth century is the emergence of more unified territorial states, such as Brandenburg and Saxony, in which the power of the prince was balanced against the weight of the estates of nobles and towns. Throughout the first half of the century conditions favoured the assertion of authority by the estates. This tendency is well exemplified in the history of the Habsburg lands. Other examples abound elsewhere. In 1430, the estates of Upper Bavaria set up a committee of arbitrators chosen from the nobility and towns to judge cases where the duke was alleged to have infringed their privileges. In Saxony in 1445 the estates assembled independently of any princely summons in order to decide their attitude to a partition proposed between members of the ruling Wettin family. Everywhere princes were feeble and nobles and towns disrespectful. In 1450 the power of the princes like the power of the emperor was at its nadir. In the second half of the century the direction of political evolution changed, circumstances were much more favourable to the princes and powerful rulers such as Albert Achilles of Brandenburg (1471–86) restored princely control.

CHAPTER VIII

PRINCES AND TOWNS IN
THE NETHERLANDS AND ITALY

i *Valois Burgundy*

In most parts of Europe the predominant form of political structure was the monarchy based primarily on rural society. In two regions, the Netherlands-Rhineland area and northern Italy, cities were more important. The fifteenth century was a period in which economic circumstances favoured the cities. Those regions therefore had a political and cultural prominence in that century which they did not have either before or after and which enhances their interest for the historian.

The ambition of the French monarchy in the earlier fourteenth century to extend its control over the county of Flanders eventually led to the marriage of Philip the Bold, brother of Charles V, with Margaret of Flanders and Philip's establishment of his authority in the county against the resistance of some of the towns in the years 1381 to 1385. By 1385 Philip was effectively both Duke of Burgundy and Count of Flanders. This triumph of French expansion, however, was to lead to something which had not been intended by its promoters. Philip was the first of a line of four Valois dukes who, in effect, established a new dynasty which eventually became quite autonomous and independent of the French crown. The territories over which they ruled eventually covered a large part of the lands stretching between the French and German worlds from Lake Geneva to the mouth of the Rhine. Thus, for a time the conception of a 'middle kingdom' was actualized. Valois Burgundy was a temporary phenomenon in the map of Europe, but for various reasons it is an important piece of European history. In the long run it established a united Netherlands which passed to the Habsburg family and became an important factor in Renaissance Europe and after. In the Valois period itself the combination of ducal ambition and city wealth made Burgundy a major force in European politics and in some respects a microcosm of European society.

The Valois dukes pursued, intermittently and with varying degrees of intensity but still consistently, the aim of enlarging their territories. There was nothing surprising about this, it was the purpose of every normal noble family large or small, but in their case the two original possessions, Burgundy and Flanders, were so substantial that they provided the basis from which developed a state with the dimensions of a large kingdom. From one point of view, therefore, the history of Valois Burgundy is the story of those efforts of dynastic expansion. The dukes had to meet the resistance of two kinds of opponents: firstly, the rulers of neighbouring territories which they coveted and secondly the 'estates' of those lands, the parliamentary representatives of nobility and towns who very much disliked the prospect of their country being swallowed up in a larger political unit and often opposed it fiercely, sometimes with success.

The first major territory on which Philip the Bold cast envious eyes was the duchy of Brabant, ruled by a conveniently childless duchess, Joan of the German Wittelsbach family. As soon as he was securely established in Flanders, Philip set about strengthening his ties by a marriage alliance with the Wittelsbach family in order to ensure that Brabant would come to him after her death. But although Joan was willing to fall in with this plan, her subjects, as was often the case in late medieval Europe, were more concerned about the integrity and independence of their homeland. The most that they were willing to accept was a compromise scheme by which the duchy was to be inherited not by Philip or his oldest son, but by his second son, Anthony, with the important city of Antwerp detached from Flanders and added to it. This was what actually happened when the duchess died in 1406. When Philip the Bold died in 1404, therefore, his oldest son, John the Fearless, took over approximately the same collection of territories as Philip had ruled since 1384.

John the Fearless (1404–19) continued his father's policy of friendship with the Wittelsbach family designed to strengthen

his position in the rest of the Netherlands. This did not enable
him to lay his hands on Brabant when Duke Anthony was
killed at Agincourt (1415). The estates of the duchy would not
deliver it to him and insisted on appointing a regency council
to act as the government during the minority of Anthony's
son. John the Fearless was deeply embroiled in the politics
of France during the extremely troubled later years of the
reign of Charles VI, which saw the successful English invasion
which John did much to promote. His main enlargement of
the inheritance was at the expense of France by the acquisition
of towns in the Somme Valley.

It was during the early part of the reign of John's son,
Philip the Good (1419–67) that Burgundy went through the
decisive transformation from an enlarged French appanage
to an independent major power. During these years, Philip
was involved in the Hundred Years War between England
and France and his disaffection from the French king was the
chief factor favouring English success. But most of his ambitions were concentrated on the fruitful policy of expansion
which he followed in the Netherlands. The situation there
when he succeeded, was that Brabant was ruled by his nephew,
Duke John (son of Anthony). The counties of Hainault and
Holland had been inherited by a lady called Jacqueline who
was married to John of Brabant. A curious succession of events
played into Philip the Good's hands and enabled him to
seize all the lands of this couple. John of Brabant was an
improvident and unintelligent ruler. Among other mistakes
he alienated his wife to such a point that she left him and in
1422 married, with dubious legality, Humphrey Duke of
Gloucester, brother of Henry V of England and as such
attended with the aura of the military invincibility which in
those days was attributed to the family of Lancaster. Jacqueline
and Humphrey took an English army to Hainault. Philip the
Good invaded and also challenged Humphrey to decide the
matter by single combat according to the laws of chivalry.
The combat never took place; Humphrey lost interest in
Jacqueline and her inheritance and withdrew; Jacqueline's
husband meanwhile died. Philip therefore had a good chance
of seizing her lands. She fled to Holland. Philip spent a large

part of the years 1425 to 1428 in the difficult task of subduing the complex water-divided country of Holland and Zeeland, an enterprise which foreshadowed the attempt of Spain to hold down the Dutch rebels at the end of the sixteenth century. Philip was successful and Jacqueline accepted defeat. In Brabant the independent line of dukes died out in 1431. The other major acquisition of Philip was the duchy of Luxemburg, another Wittelsbach territory which had been ruled by Anthony of Brabant by right of his wife, and which by a complex process of inheritance and conquest finally came to Philip the Good in 1451. The great period of expansion however was the first dozen years of his reign. By 1432 Philip had succeeded in uniting in his hands the various hitherto fiercely independent states which covered the mouth of the Rhine, a great part of what we should call the Low Countries.

The Burgundian state was a remarkable creation. Not only did it unite lands with long traditions of separateness, it also united a variety of urban communities which were not very well disposed to seigniorial rulers anyway, and also had their own rivalries. It was, therefore, a complex and unstable compound. The dukes made considerable efforts to unify it. At the centre the government was essentially a seigniorially directed organization to serve the ends of the duke. Like other great lords, he had a council, consisting of officials, expert advisers and friends, which was loosely attached to his household and helped him to manage his affairs. His most important official was his chancellor, who was in effect the architect of ducal policy. Philip the Bold and John the Fearless probably conceived of themselves primarily as French princes, involved in the internal politics of France, and therefore kept their court and household in France, generally in Paris in the time of Philip the Bold. The Flemish towns requested that John the Fearless should live in Flanders, but he did not do so. In Philip the Good's reign, however, partly because of the estrangement from France, partly because the centre of gravity had shifted with the acquisition of more territory outside France, the ducal court did spend most of its time at Dijon, Brussels, Bruges and other places in the Burgundian territory. It also became in every respect a very grand affair. The ostentation and ceremonial of the court were unsurpassed in Europe, possibly unequalled. The elaborateness of the administration was also outstanding, as is shown perhaps most strikingly by the sophisticated memoranda produced by ducal officials which have survived. The wish of the Burgundian court to take the lead in the seigniorial world of Europe is shown perhaps most clearly in its crusading plans. The conception even of the Crusade of Nicopolis in 1396 (see above, p. 223) was surpassed by the plans drawn up after the fall of Constantinople in 1454–5. The duke himself was to command the expedition, and plans were made for a large army, the household staff and a vast equipment of shipping and artillery to accompany him. The plans were revived again in 1463. They came to nothing, but they were serious and far beyond what any other European prince could contemplate.

Below the court level the administration inevitably bifurcated because the territories were divided into two geographical groups, the Netherlands and the two Burgundies. For each of these two groups, however, the dukes established a central administration. Philip the Bold set up a council chamber (*chambre du conseil*) and an accounting chamber (*chambre des comptes*) at Lille for the northern territories and a similar organization at Dijon for the southern. Philip the Good had four provincial centres of this kind, at Dijon, Ghent, Brussels and the Hague. He undertook the ambitious enterprise of introducing a single, common coinage for the Netherlands in 1433. He also made some attempt to organize the parliamentary life of his dominions in a more centralized way. Valois Burgundy covered an area where parliamentary institutions, meetings of assemblies of nobles, gentry, towns and churchmen to treat with the prince, were very richly developed. Every political unit, not only Brabant or Burgundy, but Namur or Limburg, had its 'estates'. Flanders was of course peculiar or outstanding in this respect in having the special organization of the 'Four Members' (Ypres, Ghent, Bruges and the Franc) whose representatives met much more frequently than did the parliaments of other states, monthly rather than annually. This fragmented and intensely active political life was obviously a considerable obstacle to ducal

authority. While in France in the mid-fifteenth century the
estates were falling into decay and disuse, in Burgundy,
perhaps because of the much greater prominence of the towns,
they were undiminished in importance. The cause of these
contrasting developments is not very clear. It is clear however that, unlike his contemporary, Charles VII, under
whom the French estates general practically ceased to function,
Philip the Good attempted to build up estates general representative of all his dominions, as a unifying force. The policy
went back to the early years of the reign and became more
marked at the end.

From the point of view of political structure, the great
interest of Valois Burgundy is the confrontation of seigniorial
and urban politics. Here was a ruler following a seigniorial
policy at its most ambitious, the founder of the most presti-
gious chivalric order in Europe, the Order of the Golden
Fleece (founded by Philip the Good in 1430), whose wealth
and power depended chiefly on an advanced urban society
and who was often harassed and affronted by opposition of the
mobs of his cities. The commercial centres of the Netherlands
were, financially, easily the most valuable part of the duke's
dominions. Even in the time of Philip the Bold and John the
Fearless, when the profits of control of the French court were
still appreciable, the revenues of Flanders were the most
valuable of the three main sources of income available to the
dukes (Burgundy, Flanders, the French court). By the time
of Philip the Good, of course, the various provinces of the
Netherlands far outweighed Burgundy in importance. Flanders
and Brabant included some of the most important old-established industrial and commercial towns in Europe; Zeeland
and Holland were a region of new industries and trade. But
this valuable commercial empire was not an easy thing to
manage as one entity. In many ways a large commercial state,
though more profitable as a source of taxation, was more
difficult for a ruler to handle than a large agrarian state.
Merchants had little sympathy with the political aims of
conventional seigniorial rulers and on a different level they
had little sympathy with each other because their commercial
interests conflicted. There was a sharp conflict of interests for

instance, between Antwerp, the growing centre of international trade, and Bruges the declining centre of the Flemish cloth industry. Some of the dilemmas of the Burgundian government were stated very perceptively at a moment of crisis, 1436, in a memorandum for the duke written by one of his leading councillors, Hue de Lannoy, who was at that time his governor in Holland.

'You must have appreciated, during the siege of Calais, what harm was done by lack of finance, and it is to be feared that the war has only just begun. If you need to raise finance in Brabant, Holland and other lands of yours, it can only be with the consent and good will of the people, especially when they see that you are at war [with England] and that the Flemish seem likely to rebel against you at any moment. If the truth be told, you have no territory whose populace is not hard pressed financially; nor are your domains, which are mortgaged, sold or saddled with debts, able to help you.

Again, you have seen how agitated your Flemish subjects are; some of them, indeed, are in armed rebellion. Strange and bitter things have been said about yourself, your government and your leading councillors; and it is very likely that, having got as far as talking in this way, they will soon go further than mere talk. Moreover, if you pacify them by kindness and by accepting their demands, other towns, which have similar aspirations, will rebel in the hopes of getting similar treatment. On the other hand, if you punish and repress them, it is to be feared that they will make disastrous alliances with your enemies. If by chance they start pillaging and robbing, it is possible that every wicked person will start plundering the rich. Covetousness exists among the well-off; you can imagine how much worse it is among the populace. In this matter, there is much cause for anxiety.

I note that, according to reports, the English are planning to keep a large number of ships at sea in order to effect a commercial blockade of your land of Flanders. This is a grave danger, for much harm would result if that country were deprived for any length of time of its cloth industry and commerce. And you can appreciate how much it would cost to send a fleet to sea to protect this commerce and resist the enemy. Moreover, if Holland and Zeeland continue their trade with the English, and they will probably want to do this, the Flemish, finding themselves without commerce, without their cloth industry, and involved in war on sea and land, will probably make an alliance with the English, your enemies, which could be very much to your prejudice and dishonour.'

In this report, De Lannoy pointed out one of the difficulties in political control of commercial towns in the mid–fifteenth century. As counts of Flanders, the Valois dukes naturally had from the first to be sensitive to the commercial interests of the Flemings. In the first two decades of the fifteenth century, they had to follow a policy of peace with England even though the French court was for war, because the lifeline between England and Flanders through Calais, carrying English wool, was still vital to the Flemish cloth industry. Later in the century the problem changed its character. As the Flemish cloth industry declined the Flemings were now at times more anxious to fight the competition of English cloth. But this did not please the traders and shipmasters of Antwerp, Holland and Zeeland. In the circumstances of depressed commerce in the mid-fifteenth century, rivalries between merchants were acute and politically important – hence for example, the war between Holland and the Hanse in 1438–41, about the control of traffic through the Sund into and out of the Baltic.

De Lannoy also pointed to the danger of outright rebellion by the towns which was a constant danger threatening the dukes and often a reality. The main offenders were Bruges and Ghent, the chief towns of Flanders, which had strong traditions of independence. In most cases, city opposition to the duke was connected with internal divisions between governing magistrates who were willing to co-operate with him and radical groups who were hostile to the magistrates and to ducal control and ducal taxation. Philip the Bold began his reign by subduing the Flemish towns and did not have much trouble with them later. John the Fearless, early in his reign, imposed magistrates and taxation systems of his own choice on Bruges and Ghent without rousing them to serious action against him. But in 1411, the exigencies of his war against the Armagnacs in France aroused both the cities. The trouble arose from the perennial danger of using troops from the Flemish towns in the ducal army. In general the pattern of provision for war followed by the dukes was the natural one: the nobility of Burgundy and the rural Netherlands provided the troops while the cities provided the money. On some occasions, however, infantry was supplied by the cities. In 1411 they were exceptionally undisciplined and went home when they felt like it. When the contingent from Bruges reached home they refused to go inside the town until certain radical demands had been made: the abolition of some taxes and restoration of some privileges of the craft guilds. John the Fearless was forced to agree to some of their demands and the government of Bruges became less submissive to the duke and more permissive to the craft guilds. A new period of troubles came in the 1430s. There were riots by the weavers in Ghent in 1432. The worst troubles began in 1436, in the conjunction of circumstances described in De Lannoy's memorandum. There had been a conflict with England, an embargo on English wool aimed at reducing its price in the interest of the Flemish textile industry, an unsuccessful attack on the English stronghold town of Calais. The return of the city troops set off risings at both Ghent and Bruges. At Bruges, the town militia took charge of the city and arrested a number of magistrates. After prolonged troubles Philip decided in the following year to teach them a lesson. When he entered the town in force the citizens counter-attacked to such good effect that the duke had to flee leaving many of his men dead. Next year a humiliating pacification involving a fine, scapegoats and destruction of fortifications was imposed upon the town. The most impressive confrontation between the duke and a town, however, was still to come. It arose from an attempt by Philip to impose upon Ghent a more lucrative taxation system. When it was refused he imposed various constitutional sanctions on the town. This eventually led to the establishment of a more radical town government which in 1452 turned to the offensive, replacing the normal magistrates with elected captains, executing some pro-ducal citizens and eventually trying to conduct a military offensive outside the city. The Ghenters failed in their siege of the nearby town of Oudenarde but the ducal army also failed at first to conquer them. It was not until 1453 that Philip defeated the Ghenters in a pitched battle at Gavre.

Although the Flemish cities did not have the industrial pre-eminence in Europe that they had had in the early fourteenth century, it is evident from the political history of Valois Burgundy that they still had outstanding economic power and a strong sense of independence. The dukes had to compromise with them particularly in the economic climate of the first half of the fifteenth century, when the opportunities for tapping rural wealth were so limited. It was during this period also, that the Flemish cities made their most famous contribution to European civilization in the development of realistic painting. This revolution in painting has of course much in common with the contemporary revolution in Florence. It is remarkable that the innovations associated with Donatello and Masaccio at Florence (see below, p. 309) and those associated with Jan van Eyck and others in Flanders both took place within the two decades 1410–30, apparently independently of each other. In both cases, painting made a sudden leap forward in spatial realism and realism in the characterization of individual people. This is more than a technical evolution in painting. It is a change in the artist's consciousness. In Florence the intellectual connections and implications of the change are prominent, while in Flanders they are not; but they both took place in an urban milieu and if we knew more about the obscure background of the Flemish painters we might find more in common between them.

The aesthetic tradition from which both the Florentine and the Flemish innovations stemmed was the realistic style of painting which had been developed by Giotto and his school in Tuscany in the early fourteenth century. Some of the technical achievements of this school were adopted by painters in northern Europe in the course of the fourteenth century, especially the construction of scenes with a limited half-developed perspective which gave a limited spatial realism and the realistic painting of human faces. These traits were incorporated into the works of the painters who produced illuminated manuscripts and altar pieces for the rich courts of Europe at Milan, Turin, Avignon and Prague, at Paris and at the courts of great French dukes of the late fourteenth century, John Duke of Berry and Philip the Bold. Courtly art was infused with something of the spirit of earlier Italian invention in much the same way as the courtly literary art of Geoffrey Chaucer was infused with the realistic techniques of Dante and Boccaccio when he wrote the Canterbury Tales. This style of art has come to be known as 'International Gothic'. Its most famous surviving manifestation – and a very good one – is the *Très Riches Heures*, the manuscript painted for the Duke of Berry by the Limbourg brothers about 1416. Its elegant, elongated, richly-clothed figures set against fantastic backgrounds of castles and landscapes painted with precise and realistic detail are well known.

The origins of the new form of art are essentially Burgundian because, like the Burgundian state, they involved both the court and the cities; the court as the richest centre of patronage and the towns as sources of technical skill and inventiveness. All the dukes were great patrons and could pay for the best. Philip the Bold's chief contribution was the Carthusian convent, which he built at Champmol outside Dijon. Two leading Netherlandish artists were employed to embellish it and both produced works in which the realistic representation of human figures suggests that they were trying to break out of the conventional elegance of International Gothic: Melchior Broederlam, a painter of Ypres, and Claus Sluter, a sculptor of Haarlem. This was around 1400. The artist who made the decisive leap forward in the next phase has never been identified certainly, but the probability is that he was Robert Campin (*c.* 1378–1444) a painter of Tournai, who was associated only with the Flemish town world, not with the court, and was in fact a member of a radical city

council at Tournai in the period 1425–7. Campin's world as
it appears, for instance in the 'Madonna of the Firescreen' in
the National Gallery, or the 'Annunciation' in New York, is
quite different from the world of the *Très Riches Heures*. It is
an everyday world of ordinary people, though sometimes
exhibiting highly dramatic emotions. His rooms and landscapes
are realistic in a new way, partly because of better perspective,
more strikingly because he has grasped the notion that the
spatial unity of a scene depends on the uniform direction and
character of the light throughout it.

If the painter of Tournai was indeed the author of the
works associated with him, he was a very great innovator and
the central genius of medieval Flemish civilization. His ideas
were carried forward by a younger contemporary, Jan van
Eyck of Maastricht (d. 1440) and a pupil, Roger van der
Weyden (*c.* 1400–64), both of whom had more links with the
court. Van Eyck is, of course, the most famous of the Flemish
painters and his work best symbolizes the aspects of Burgundian civilization. He was appreciated and regularly employed
by Philip the Good who sent him to Portugal to paint a
portrait of the future duchess, Isabel. It does not survive
but there are several other portraits by van Eyck which reveal
him as a great interpreter of human character. He was also
patronized by the townsmen of the Flemish cities: his grandest
work, the altarpiece in the cathedral of Ghent, was paid for
by a citizen of that great city. His best known picture 'The
Marriage of Giovanni Arnolfini and Giovanna Cenami', was
painted for Arnolfini who was an Italian merchant from
Lucca, established like many other Italians at Bruges. Another
very famous painting 'The Madonna of Chancellor Rolin'
also contains a portrait of an individual, Nicolas Rolin, who
was Philip the Good's Chancellor and the most powerful
person in the Burgundian administration for about thirty
years from the 1420s to the 1450s.

The Burgundian state which had been created by Philip
the Bold and Philip the Good was destroyed by the last and
most forceful of the four dukes, Charles the Bold (1467–77),
Philip the Good had been a proud, determined but also self-
indulgent and amiable ruler. The substantial additions which

he made were partly the result of luck, partly the working out of the implications of treaties and marriages made by Philip the Bold with results which had been partly intended. He insisted on his rights but did not envisage new ones. Charles the Bold, on the other hand, was an austere, extremely energetic man with a consuming ambition to turn his inheritance into a larger and more powerful kingdom. One of his chief aims indeed was to persuade the weak Habsburg Emperor Frederick to grant him the title of king within the Holy Roman Empire, but although there was a meeting between them at Trier on the Rhine in 1473, they did not reach agreement about it.

Charles's efforts were mainly directed towards the deliberate expansion of his territories. His first step in this direction, and a very considerable one, had been taken in 1465 before his father died. As Count of Charolais, Charles was already a more positive force in Burgundian policy than his aged father. It was he who took the initiative in throwing Burgundian power into the war of the Public Weal on the side of the noble rebels against Louis XI, who took the army to the outskirts of Paris and fought the battle of Montlhéry and who recovered the Somme towns from the French king. Most of Charles the Bold's expansive efforts however were turned not against France, but eastwards towards the Rhineland. His first campaign was directed in 1467 against Liège. This was in part a continuation of an old Burgundian struggle. Liège was an independent state ruled over by a bishop. Lying between Brabant and Luxemburg it was an obvious object of Burgundian covetousness. The city itself was a large and independent commune after the Netherlandish pattern which resented the power of the bishop and feared the power of the dukes. As early as 1406–8, John the Fearless helped the bishop to crush a revolt of the city. Philip the Good was at war with them in 1430. In 1465 at the time of the war of the Public Weal, when the bishop was again a Burgundian ally, the Liègeois made a treaty with Louis XI. This affront was still unrequited when Charles the Bold became duke in 1467. He began his reign inauspiciously with a visit to Ghent from which he was forced to flee by a rioting mob, but he turned his attention to a very thorough subjugation of Liège. At the end of his second campaign against the city in 1468 it was sacked by his army and, although the bishop continued to be the official ruler, Liège fell effectively under Burgundian domination and its strivings for independence were completely suppressed. This seemed a convincing finish to the long struggle of the Valois dukes against city politicians in the Netherlands.

Charles the Bold's eyes were then turned towards outward expansion. Apart from his acquisition of the northern Netherlands his plans for expansion were mainly concerned with the area between Burgundy and the Rhine, a country of even more extreme political fragmentation than the Netherlands and also one in which towns and cities, some of them large – Cologne, Trier, Nancy, Strasburg, Basle – were influential. In 1469 he acquired by mortgage control of parts of Alsace from the Habsburg Duke Sigismund. This was an area in which the Burgundians had not previously been interested. It brought him into contact and conflict with the Swabian and Swiss towns and the Swiss confederation itself. They formed the League of Constance against him in 1474. In 1475 Charles occupied the Duchy of Lorraine. This was the farthest extension of Burgundian territory. It was no longer two separated sections but covered the whole area from southern Burgundy to the Zuider Zee in a continuous belt. But Charles could not hold it. He had already been checked in 1475 when he tried to intervene on the side of the Archbishop of Cologne against the towns of that area and failed in the siege of Neuss. He was checked again in 1475 when he tried to stop a Swiss invasion of northern Savoy and his armies were defeated at Grandson and Murten. Finally, in 1477 he was faced by an alliance of the Duke of Lorraine, the city of Strasburg and the Swiss in Lorraine and he was defeated and killed at Nancy.

This was the end of Valois Burgundy. Charles had no son. His daughter eventually married Maximilian and the bulk of his dominions fell to the Habsburgs. A considerable part of the French territories were recovered by Louis XI of France. The legacy of the united Netherlands, the creation of the Valois dukes, remained. For those who are interested in the structure of fifteenth-century Europe, however, the greatest interest in the Burgundian story from beginning to end is the relationship between the prince and the towns. In the Netherlands the Valois dukes had been able, with some difficulty, to subdue the towns largely because of the inherited constitutional structure – the towns could not break out of the princely framework of duchies and counties in which they were enclosed. The frequent revolts against the dukes were a more or less feeble continuation of the efforts to do this in the fourteenth century. They ruled over a princely state in which the elements of characteristically urban civilization were prominent. Within the Burgundian lands, Charles the Bold appears as one of the great princely consolidators of the late fifteenth century, a statesman of the same species as Louis XI, Ferdinand and Isabella, Henry VII of England. Apart from the accident of his death without a male heir there is no reason why the Burgundian state, which had become one of the half-dozen most important political units in Europe, should not have continued to develop along those lines. When he moved outside the Burgundian lands into the Rhineland, however, Charles entered an area in which the towns had never been subordinated to an effective political framework and in which they had a long tradition of vigorous action in defence of their rights. Such powerful towns as Strasburg and Basle, in alliance with the Swiss Confederation which was another anti-seigniorial force with a different social basis, were too much for the Duke of Burgundy; they destroyed him and preserved their brand of political freedom.

ii *Italian Politics*

The beginning of the Great Schism in 1378 was a stage in the emergence of Italy from the domination of northern European armies. This was not due to the brilliance of Italian commanders or troops but to the relative decline of the northern powers. Between the beginning of the Great Schism and the French invasion of 1494, the Italian states were left to themselves to a much larger extent than they had been in the previous century. Foreign administrators and armies no longer controlled the papal state. German intervention in the peninsula was almost negligible. Foreign condottieri like Hawkwood fairly soon became extinct. The isolation was far from complete. A major new force from outside emerged in the fifteenth century when Alfonso V of Aragon conquered Naples. There was an almost constant possibility of French invasion connected with French interests in Genoa, Milan or Naples and French armies controlled Genoa for long periods. But Alfonso V quickly became absorbed in the Italian world. French armies did not dominate Italy as they had at times in the early fourteenth century. This is the Italian Golden Age. Italian society was at its most independent and inventive in thought and in art. On the political plane the Italian powers played their part in a concert of Italy which was relatively self-contained.

In the story of this concert of powers there are two developments which perhaps deserve to be given special prominence. Firstly, there was a continuous expansion of the larger powers at the expense of the smaller. The political map of northern Italy was much simpler in 1454 than in 1378. Politics consisted increasingly of the relations between the major states: Milan, Venice, Genoa, and Florence. Secondly, for most of the period, there was one power which tended to dominate the others: Milan. The tendency of Milan to expand into the rest of northern and central Italy determined many of the reactions of other powers during this period. Milan was a despotism, ruled by members of the Visconti family. Its opponents were often led by the republic of Florence. Florentines saw this relationship as a duel between the principles of tyranny and liberty enshrined in the two states. This conception has an important role in the history of political ideas. It would be dangerous to use it as a key to the history of Italian politics. Other states certainly did not always see Florence as the champion of liberty and she was quite capable of suppressing other free communes when expediency demanded it. Nevertheless, it is broadly true that during this period, Milan was commonly the aggressor. The expansive tendencies dictated by the ambitions of her rulers gave her policy basic aims which were generally different from those of the republics of Genoa,

Venice and Florence and the papacy, none of which was very
well adapted by its internal constitution for the pursuit of an
aggressive foreign policy. The politics of the peninsula tended
therefore to be dominated by Milanese initiatives.

Between the thirteenth and the fifteenth centuries the
Visconti family produced a series of rulers of outstanding
capacity. One of these, Giangaleazzo, emerged as the dominant
figure in Italian politics at the end of the fourteenth century.
Up to 1378 the Visconti dominions were divided between
two brothers, Galeazzo ruling the western portion, Bernabò
the more important eastern territories. In 1378 Giangaleazzo
succeeded his father. Bernabò was a powerful, ambitious,
self-centred and self-indulgent man, strikingly endowed with
those characteristics even by the standards of Italian despots,
but his nephew was a man with even more political skill.
One of the main problems which haunted the Visconti like
other Italian despots, was the problem of succession. They
were not legitimate rulers, bound like the royal houses of
Europe to moderately clear rules of succession which were
accepted by their subjects, nor in cases like Milan (a collection
of communes) could their states be regarded as having a
natural unbreakable unity; yet they were anxious like other
fathers that their inheritances should descend intact to their
children. Bernabò had five legitimate and more than two dozen
illegitimate sons. He was particularly anxious that his nephew
Giangaleazzo should not disinherit his descendants and he
therefore persuaded him to marry his daughter Caterina.
Giangaleazzo found a very clear and decisive way out of the
difficulty. In May 1389 he invited Bernabò to meet him near
Milan. He seized and imprisoned him, instituted judicial
proceedings against him on the ground that he had ruled
Milan without obtaining the proper authority of the imperial
vicariate from the emperor, and poisoned him. Giangaleazzo
had little difficulty in gaining control of the whole of the
Visconti inheritance. He had himself taken the precaution of
obtaining the imperial vicariate earlier. He is often referred to
as the Count of Virtù, a title which he assumed because his
first wife, Isabella de Valois, had been Countess of Vertus.
Ten years later he persuaded the emperor, Wenceslas, to grant

him the title of duke which was certainly appropriate to his power.

Having established himself securely in Milan, Giangaleazzo embarked on the most ambitious plans which the Visconti had yet pursued for extending their dominions. Giangaleazzo's stance was to pose as the leader and defender of Italy against the barbarian intruders who disturbed its peace. There was something to be said for this view of Italy's needs and of his role. Though he was certainly not unwilling to use foreign help and played a long diplomatic game to secure French support, his armies were Italian and he constantly patronized great Italian generals, notably Jacopo dal Verme and Facino Cane, while his enemies made rather more use of foreigners. It was certainly true that Italy had suffered greatly in the recent past from the depredations of French and English mercenaries. His real purpose however was to absorb other Italian states into his own. To this end he began very early to build up support for himself in the communes of Tuscany and farther south. His first chance however came in the north. Between Milan and Venice were the two smaller states of Verona, ruled by the della Scala family, and Padua, ruled by the Carrara. Aggressive action by the Carrara in the hinterland behind Venice alarmed that city and gave Giangaleazzo the opportunity to intervene. He took Verona in 1387; Antonio della Scala the last of the Scaligeri fled and the independent state came to an end. Giangaleazzo then made an agreement with Venice for the partition of Padua. Padua was suppressed (1388) and divided and as a result, the territories of Milan and Venice for the first time met. Francesco Novello Carrara, the former lord of Padua, however, remained alive and active.

Meanwhile, Giangaleazzo had been preparing the ground by intervention in central Italy and negotiation with France. The marriage of his daughter, Valentina, to the King of France's brother, Louis, future Duke of Orleans, in 1387 was a coup. Two years earlier, he had formed a league for the defence of Italy against the foreigners and intervened in Gubbio and Bologna. Florence, the largest power in central Italy apart from the pope, was alarmed and was the natural leader of resistance to Visconti moves to the south. As the danger became clearer, Florence took action by collecting as many friends as she could and by hiring a variety of military commanders. The first war came in the years 1390 to 1392, and the Florentine league was on the whole successful. Verona rebelled against its new lord. Hawkwood, fighting for Florence, penetrated into Milanese territory but was held back by the efforts of Giangaleazzo's general, Jacopo dal Verme who also halted a French invasion from the West. Francesco Carrara was restored to Padua.

After the war Giangaleazzo turned his attention to the Riviera, Pisa and Genoa. Pisa under her tyrant Pietro Gambacorta had been an ally of Florence against Milan. In 1392 a rebellion replaced its ruler by another tyrant, who supported Giangaleazzo with the dangerous power of cutting Florence off from the sea. The chronically weak political constitution of Genoa had been further undermined by the War of Chioggia (see above, p. 100). The city was torn between factions led by the two great families of Adorno and Fieschi, who appealed respectively to Milan and France for help. Giangaleazzo, belying his claim to work for an Italian Italy, negotiated for French intervention on his side. Apart from Genoa, the bait was the offer to the Duke of Orleans of a new kingdom of 'Adria' in central Italy, constructed out of the north-eastern parts of the papal state, a revival of the offer which Pope Clement VII had made to the Duke of Anjou earlier, but this time designed to give support to Milan instead of the papacy. An Orleanist expedition went to Italy in 1394 and established French domination of the Riviera. But the French king accepted the lordship of Genoa for himself, thwarting Giangaleazzo's plans to acquire it with French help. The kingdom of Adria came to nothing. The French alliance did not ultimately help him much and French support veered round to Florence. The next major conflict was the War of Mantua in 1397–8. Giangaleazzo's general, Jacopo dal Verme, entered the independent Gonzaga state of Mantua but was repulsed. The war ended indecisively.

In the last years of the century, Giangaleazzo was increasing his penetration into central Italy with the evident intention of surrounding Florence and eventually making Tuscany part of his empire. In 1399 he obtained the lordship of Perugia, Assisi and Siena to the south. In 1400 he supported another *coup d'état* in a Tuscan city: this time Paolo Guinigi obtained the lordship of Lucca, very close to Florence. Florence was intensely conscious of the tightening ring. She paid for an expedition by Rupert of the Palatinate the new King of Germany. He attacked the Milanese city of Brescia but was defeated ignominiously. This was the last German attempt at military intervention in Italy for a century. The allied forces were defeated at Casalecchio near Bologna. Then, crowning disaster, Bologna, the gateway to the south, overthrew its tyrant and recognized Giangaleazzo. Florence was awaiting the final duel when Giangaleazzo died suddenly in 1402.

His death not only ended for the time being the Visconti hope of engulfing Italy but also shattered the Visconti dominion in Lombardy itself, revealing the still fragile nature of the despotic structure. Giangaleazzo left two sons, Giovanni and Filippo Maria, aged fourteen and ten, and a widow, Caterina. He had made no effective arrangements for a regency, leaving the care of the inheritance chiefly in the hands of his favourite adviser and man of business, Francesco Barbavara. The Visconti state was quickly rent by both local upheavals and intense feuds at the centre. A rising at Milan itself replaced the old government with that of a new group including Visconti relations of other lines of the family. Barbavara was chased out. At the beginning of 1404, Caterina suddenly showed her own Visconti blood by arranging for the assassination of some of the usurpers and the return of Barbavara, to whom she was attached. But Giangaleazzo's precocious sons, now a little older, hated their father's old confidant and plotted against him and their own mother. In 1405 Caterina herself was driven from Milan and killed. While this was happening at Milan the extremities of the state were falling away. Francesco Carrara not only recovered Padua but took Verona as well. His success aroused the anxieties of Venice which decided that the balance of power in Lombardy was shifting too far against Milan and in 1405 took over Padua herself. Pisa had been bequeathed to a bastard son of Giangaleazzo. Florence determined in the aftermath of Milanese collapse to remove once and for all this threat to her lines of communication. In 1405 she bought the city from him for 80,000 florins, paying at the same time a larger sum to the French who were the chief military power on the Italian Riviera and might otherwise have impeded the deal. The port of Leghorn, which was essential to Florence, remained in French hands. When the citizens of Pisa themselves objected to being sold the Florentines starved them into surrender. In the end, therefore, the career of Giangaleazzo led to significant expansions of the territories of the two great republics of Venice and Florence as well as to the temporary disintegration of Milan from which several subject cities in Lombardy had freed themselves.

The period between 1402 and 1414 witnessed the rise and fall of another splendid rocket in the Italian sky, the career of Ladislas of Naples who threatened to swallow up Italy from the south as Giangaleazzo had done from the north (see above, p. 184). When he died the Florentines, who stood half way between, could reckon that they had been saved by miracles twice in a dozen years. Meanwhile, the Visconti state was being slowly reconstructed. At the time of Caterina's death in 1405 there were two jealous and inexperienced boys as heirs of the duchy and a group of very powerful and experienced condottieri dividing the spoils. The leading ones were Facino Cane and Pandolfo Malatesta. Cane's power was concentrated in the West, towards Savoy, Malatesta's in the east, where he became lord of Bergamo and Brescia. Facino Cane in the end did most to restore unity to the Milanese inheritance. For several years while the very young Giovanni Maria Visconti maintained tenuously the Visconti hold over Milan, the power of the rival condottieri ebbed and flowed over his father's dominions. Jacopo dal Verme, Giangaleazzo's chief general, defeated Cane in 1407 and forced him back into the west, but Cane recovered. In 1409 a league was formed to resist him. Giovanni Maria called on the help of the French forces based on Genoa. The French responded enthusiastically but Cane did better, advancing himself on Genoa and inspiring the Genoese to throw out the French occupiers. He was then able to move on Milan himself and Giovanni Maria had no alternative but to accept him as the real power in the Visconti lands, appointing him governor of Milan. Facino Cane then set himself to the task of piecemeal rebuilding of the Visconti inheritance on behalf of the young lord. This process was incomplete when Giovanni Maria and Facino Cane both died within a few hours of each other in 1412 – the latter from disease, the former by the hand of an assassin inspired by the belief that Visconti power would collapse again after the death of the great condottiere. It did not. Filippo Maria, now twenty years old, quickly seized his brother's power and was to retain it for thirty-five years.

Filippo Maria was to be the dominant Italian politician of his generation as his father Giangaleazzo had been of his. In some ways he was curiously ill-fitted for the role: nervous, physically weak, intensely superstitious. He made up for these disadvantages by a fanatical, absolutely overriding devotion to the acquisition of power and an extraordinary skill in politics which had been, of course, trained and tested in the hardest school since childhood. He once told the pope, according to a biographer, that 'he cared less for his body than for his soul, but he put his government before the health of body and soul'. Filippo Maria began characteristically by marrying the widow of Facino Cane, who was twice his age, to make sure of her husband's possessions. He then took up Cane's work in the reconstruction of Visconti power. He was assisted in this by a great Savoyard condottiere, Carmagnola. During the years between 1412 and 1420 the work was laboriously and success-fully done: Lombardy was brought once again under Milanese domination and even Genoa was recovered.

By the beginning of the 1420s there were clearly three chief states in northern Italy: Milan, Venice and Florence. Two of these were states ruled by city republics. From a European point of view, one of the most remarkable features of the early fifteenth century is the rise of the two principal republican city states to the level of great powers. The rise of Venice as a land power was quite sudden. The decisive period was the first decade of the century and the decisive factor the menace of Milan. This led directly to the acquisition of Padua and Verona. On the other side, alliance with Ladislas of Naples against King Sigismund of Hungary, whose expansion also threatened Venice, led to the acquisition of more territory on the Adriatic coast. By 1420 therefore Venice had, in addition to its widely dispersed commercial empire in the eastern Mediterranean, a land empire comparable in size with that of Milan. The republican institutions of the subject cities were left largely undisturbed as far as internal government was concerned but it was none the less an empire, with a Venetian *Capitano* and *podestà* in each city. The doge Tommaso Mocenigo (1414–23), famous for his pride in Venice's commercial greatness, was succeeded by Francesco Foscari (1423–57) who advocated a policy of active defence of Venetian security on the mainland against those who thought that a mercantile republic should pursue a policy of splendid isolation.

At Florence, the years between 1382, when the troubles connected with the *Ciompi* rebellion of 1378 were finally at an end, and 1433, when the troubles leading to the acquisition of power by Cosimo de Medici began, were in some ways the golden age of republicanism. That half-century was less disturbed by constitutional upheavals than the previous century. This may have been partly because the government of the city was in reality more narrowly oligarchical, and therefore more stable, than it had been before. Giangaleazzo Visconti is reported to have said on one occasion 'under the name of Archguelfs a few Florentine citizens keep their compatriots under and oppress this republic'. The degree of oligarchy is difficult to measure because it was determined by informal contacts just as much as by the written rules of the constitution. Certain individual citizens were very prominent during this period such as Maso degli Albizzi and his son, Rinaldo. Members of the oligarchy wished that the Florentine constitution could be made more similar to the Venetian, which seemed an ideal arrangement for ensuring the perpetual rule of leading families. They did much to strengthen their hold by exiling the most dangerous individual opponents and by modifying the constitution to exclude popular elements from power. In 1387, five years after the restoration of the oligarchy, they attacked the Alberti, the richest family in

Florence, which had allied itself with the rebellious elements in 1378. The Alberti were in the same position as the Medici were to be later – outstandingly rich merchants whose individual influence outshone that of the oligarchy – but unlike the Medici they were successfully banished. The lists of citizens eligible for election to offices were revised and a commission appointed to choose from them a smaller list of specially eligible men from which some of the elections were to be made. The representation of the lesser guilds was reduced to two out of the nine priors. In 1421, it was decreed that none could be eligible for office unless he or his ancestors had paid taxes uninterruptedly for thirty years. Meanwhile, like Venice though not nearly so spectacularly, Florence had increased her land empire partly by reaction to the intervention of other powers in that part of Italy. The Angevin intervention led her to purchase the city of Arezzo for the modest sum of 4000 florins. Visconti's intervention had led to the purchase of Pisa. In 1421 Florence bought from Genoa the adjoining port of Leghorn. The rulers of the city could congratulate themselves on the fact that they had at last made it possible for Florence to become a seapower like Venice. Arrangements were quickly made to exploit this possibility. Before many years had passed, Florence too was sending galleys to Alexandria in the east and Bruges in the west.

The great powers of the peninsula were about to confront each other in war. The period from 1419 to 1423 was a period of mounting suspicion of the intentions of Filippo Maria Visconti. In 1419 Filippo Maria proposed to Florence a treaty laying down spheres of influence which Florence accepted, knowing that it was a cover for aggression which must follow soon. In 1423 he was intervening in Romagna within the Florentine sphere of influence. The ruling Florentines reluctantly accepted the fact that they must sooner or later fight Filippo Maria and they took the usual step of appointing a small *balìa* (committee) of ten men to conduct the war and engaging the brothers Pandolfo and Carlo Malatesta to lead their mercenary armies. The war which followed was extremely expensive and, on the whole, inglorious for Florence. Filippo Maria's troops advanced into the Romagna. The

Florentine mercenaries were defeated in one of the two main battles of the war at Zagonara in 1424. Carlo Malatesta, who was taken prisoner then went over to Milan and was followed in the next year by another great mercenary captain, Piccinino. The war was marked on both sides by perhaps an unusual amount of defection and treason by condottieri. Florence was desperate in anticipation of a new Milanese invasion of Tuscany. In her fear she made an effort to rouse Venice to a joint effort to resist the Visconti tyrant, sending to Venice an impressive delegation of leading citizens who spent some months in diplomatic effort. The moment was propitious; Venice felt strong but worried about Filippo Maria's aggressions, the condottiere Carmagnola left Milanese service and offered himself to Venice. An alliance was made between the two republics. Venice was to supply most of the troops, under Carmagnola's command, while Florence was to supply most of the money. The rest of the war was glorious for Venice and expensive for Florence. Milan was finally defeated decisively by Carmagnola at the battle of Maclodio in 1427 and peace was made at Ferrara in the following year. Filippo Maria lost territory to Savoy and Brescia and Bergamo to Venice – a further big expansion of the Venetian empire. He promised again not to intervene in Tuscany.

The relation of Pisa to Giangaleazzo Visconti, which led to its seizure by Florence, was repeated in the relation of Lucca to Filippo Maria. Lucca, an ancient commercial republic in the Arno valley between Florence and Pisa, was ruled by a tyrant Paolo Guinigi, whose aim had been to pursue as neutral a policy as he could. In 1429 Florence accused him of owing her 14,000 florins under the terms of the league against Milan and of befriending Filippo Maria. When he paid the debt and denied the treason the Florentines found other ways of putting pressure on him. A condottiere stationed on the frontier in Florentine pay ravaged Lucchese territory, probably at the instigation of certain Florentine politicians. This stirred up a conflict and aroused the widespread feeling in Florence that it was time to conquer Lucca or, at least, teach her a lesson for being well disposed to Filippo Maria. A serious attack was launched in 1430, which turned into an extraordinary exhibition of ineptitude, confusion and intrigue, demonstrating that republics were wiser to buy out their enemies than to wage war on them. The command in the field was entrusted to Rinaldo degli Albizzi, a very prominent member of the Florentine oligarchy. He quarrelled with the leaders at home. Filippo Brunelleschi, the architect, evolved a scheme to breach the walls of Lucca by deflecting the river Serchio but it is said that, after much money had been spent on it, only the Florentine camp was flooded. Accusations of corruption forced Rinaldo to return to Florence to defend himself. Under the stress of the Florentine invasion some of the Lucchese decided that it would indeed be best to turn to Milan. Filippo Maria was glad to give help at second hand. He sent his condottiere, Francesco Sforza, who quickly forced the Florentines to retire in 1430, entered Lucca himself and sent Guinigi off to prison in Milan. Florence tried to buy off Sforza. Then she suggested that he might help in capturing the other free Tuscan republic Siena. This plot quickly reached the ears of the Sienese who, in their turn, appealed to Milan for help. The Florentine leaders had thus succeeded in reducing their own strength and provoking another wave of Milanese influence in Tuscany.

Florence was successful once again in 1431 in obtaining an alliance with Venice against Milan but the Venetians were rather unsuccessful in their military operations which were entrusted as before to Carmagnola. A Venetian fleet on the Po was lost and Carmagnola made no impression on the forces or territory of Filippo Maria. It became the opinion of some in Venice that he was guilty of a treacherous agreement with Milan; he was lured to the city and executed in 1432. This was a rather unusual example of an outstanding condottiere effectively called to account by his masters. The Italian condottieri of this period could hardly be regarded in general as an obvious improvement on their alien predecessors of the fourteenth century. Perhaps they plundered less but they were devoted, naturally enough, to provoking and prolonging wars from which they profited and fleecing the powers which employed them. They constituted a whole sector of Italian society which preyed on the wealth of the cities. Increasingly their most successful generals like Carmagnola or Sforza had become independent powers in the international scene. Venice, with its prodigious commercial wealth, was the only Italian state which really had resources equal to the cost of fifteenth-century warfare. Towards the middle of the century Venice adopted the policy of maintaining condottiere armies at half strength in time of peace, a large step towards an adequate standing army.

The war between Milan and the Veneto-Florentine alliance was ended by peace at Ferrara in 1433. The Venetian constitution could stand such conflicts but the Florentine had been badly shaken. The duel with Filippo Maria from 1423 onwards had forced upon Florence a revision of the old taxation system, which had been questioned at the time of the *Ciompi* rebellion but had survived the stresses of the intervening years. Direct taxation had a particular political importance because it touched the interests of the wealthy and politically active immediately through their property. From 1425 onwards it gradually came to be accepted by the oligarchy that some more equitable form of direct taxation was necessary in order to reconcile the population in general to providing more money for the war against Filippo Maria. In 1427 Rinaldo degli Albizzi managed to win over his colleagues to a tax based on a new assessment of property, the *Catasto*. The new system taxed all income and moveable wealth as well as landed property, it made the tax payments of the rich much larger and it became the basis of later direct taxation in Florence. The financial difficulties continued to be acute. In 1434 it was said that credits in the state debt were changing hands at a fifth of their face value and it was hard to find cash to pay the mercenaries. Still the introduction of the *Catasto* is a testimony to the political resilience of the city state, its ability to mobilize resources to meet even the enormous demands of the wars now being fought with big and expensive mercenary armies.

The war against Lucca added political stresses of another kind and brought to the fore a conflict between the oligarchy and one outstanding citizen, Cosimo de' Medici. The Medici had by this time come to occupy the place held by the Alberti at the end of the fourteenth century. They were the chief bankers of the post-Schism papacy and this helped them to become the wealthiest family in Florence. They also had a tradition of sympathy with the lesser guilds. The Medici were an old Florentine family but the founder of their family fortunes at this level was Giovanni di Bicci de' Medici who died in 1429. His son, Cosimo, was critical of the policy pursued in the war with Lucca and appears to have risen into political prominence because of that role. He took a large part in the peace negotiations. The chief promoter of the war, Rinaldo degli Albizzi, therefore decided to dispose of him by imposing exile. In the autumn of 1433 a hostile group of priors imprisoned Cosimo and banished him. He went to live comfortably at Venice. But Rinaldo was not ruthless enough in stamping out opposition. Only a few Medici supporters were exiled. When the war against Milan started again it seemed once more to be inefficiently managed. Rinaldo allowed a government favourable to Cosimo to get office in the autumn of 1434. Rinaldo and his friends then made preparations for a *coup d'état*. Their handling of it however turned out to be strangely and disastrously half-hearted. On the crucial day Rinaldo seems to have been persuaded to abandon his purpose by Pope Eugenius IV who was at the time a refugee in Florence and who had a close business relationship with Cosimo. So Cosimo returned, exiled his enemies more whole-heartedly and became the most powerful man in Florence until the day of his death in 1464. 1434 therefore was in a sense the year in which the Medici rule in Florence began. Even contemporaries suggested that Cosimo was virtually ruler of the city. As Pope Pius II said, 'Nothing was denied to Cosimo. He was the judge of peace and war and the arbiter of the laws, regarded not as a citizen but as lord of his country. In his house the councils of the republic were held and the magistrates designated by him. Of kingship he lacked only the name and the pomp.'

It would be a great mistake however to suppose that Florence ceased in 1434 to be a republic; on the contrary, its citizens long considered themselves just as characteristically republican as they had been before. Cosimo was a private citizen and most of the time worked behind the scenes as the leader of an influential group, not as a ruler. A Milanese envoy caught the distinction when he wrote to his tyrant master in 1458, at a time when Cosimo held no public office, 'write secretly to Cosimo your desire and you will always get it . . . Popular governments are different from others and Cosimo cannot continually be at the palace and do as he used to.' Cosimo's power was based on the fact that he was widely supported and financially influential. He also manipulated the constitution in various ways to strengthen his position. He virtually abolished the system of random choice of magistrates which had made the control of elections difficult: thus Medici supporters generally got elected. The system of imposing heavy taxation on the wealthy which started with the *Catasto* of 1427, was elaborated by Cosimo and he seems to have used crippling tax assessments as a weapon against his enemies. He extended the system of government through appointed councils which had been used earlier only for special emergencies but were now appointed for long periods to carry on large sectors of the normal government of the city. Under Cosimo, therefore, Florence was undoubtedly changed in the direction of princely government. Cosimo himself survived only because of his enormous political skill. Both as a statesman and as a patron of arts and letters, he was the greatest of his family. He led a large party. In the earlier part of his rule the most important Florentine politician apart from himself was Neri Capponi who survived from the old oligarchy and was often critical of Cosimo. There were occasional periods when Cosimo's influence was seriously endangered by the election of men who disagreed with him. But though he ruled by handling the republican institutions just as much as by changing them, his long period of power virtually established the Medici. In 1464 his son, Piero, succeeded to his position, though he had to face a severe crisis in 1466 in which opponents of Medici rule were overawed only by armed force. In 1469 Piero's son Lorenzo the Magnificent succeeded.

During the crisis of Cosimo's exile in 1434, Milan again attacked in the Romagna and Piccinino defeated a Florentine army at Imola. This reopened the struggle against Milan's expansion which was to last intermittently down to 1445.

At the same time, Florence had become host to Pope Eugenius IV who was engaged in a struggle with Alfonso V of Naples. For a time there were two parallel and connected wars in Italy between the pope and Alfonso in Naples, between Florence (sympathetic to the pope) and Milan (sympathetic to Alfonso) in central Italy. In 1435 Neri Capponi went to Venice to revive the alliance against Milan which was to be continued for ten years with an army commanded by Francesco Sforza. Piccinino and Sforza were now the two leading condottieri in Italy and Sforza also ruled a section of the papal state given to him by the pope. They were to be ranged on opposing sides. As an immediate result Milanese forces were defeated at Assisi. Florence then tried to cause Filippo Maria trouble by sending help to Genoa which was in rebellion against his lordship. In retaliation Filippo Maria sent a really dangerous force under Piccinino to Pistoia, very near Florence itself. In 1437 a Florentine army commanded by Sforza compelled Piccinino to withdraw from Tuscany. Florence then returned to the old attack on Lucca but Sforza would not persist in it and was eventually won over to Milan by an extremely flattering offer by Filippo Maria to betroth his daughter and heiress, Bianca, to him. This left Florence very exposed and Cosimo had to journey to Venice to use his personal influence to patch up another agreement between the two republics. The Venetians were not enthusiastic.

The alliance sprang into life again however in 1439, when Piccinino acting as Filippo Maria's agent, resumed the old Visconti policy of encouraging factions favourable to Milan in the cities of Romagna and in Bologna. Once more a joint army under Sforza was engaged. Sforza spent most of his time on the frontier between Milan and Venice. Piccinino however, devoted himself chiefly to Romagna and Tuscany and this led to one of the battles of which Florentine tradition was later most proud – it was the subject of a lost painting by Leonardo da Vinci for the city's *Palazzo*. In 1440 Piccinino was threatening Florence itself. He had been within a few miles of the city. An army commanded by a Florentine, Neri Capponi, brought him to a battle at Anghiari in the upper Tiber valley and decisively defeated him. This phase of the

war dragged on however until 1441, when Sforza again changed
sides because of Bianca Sforza and this time married her,
getting the lordship of Cremona as well. In the peace which
followed, both Venice and Florence emerged with enlarged
territories. The most striking beneficiary was Francesco
Sforza who had been able to adopt the rule of arbiter and had
taken a significant step in his ascent from the role of condottiere to that of prince. The last phase in the wars with
Filippo Maria followed in 1442–4. This time the war started
with an attack by Alfonso of Naples on Sforza's possessions
in the Campagna and the two sides were built up around this
quarrel. By the end of the year, Italy was divided again into
roughly the two groups which had existed in the previous
conflicts. Alfonso turned to Filippo Maria and got him to send
Piccinino down into Romagna again and also won the support
of the pope. On the other side Sforza, whose central Italian
properties were threatened by Alfonso, naturally lined up with
Florence and Venice. The war was fought out largely in
Romagna and the March of Ancona, mostly in a series of duels
between Sforza and Piccinino and it was brought to a close by
Sforza's victories in 1444 at Montelauro and Montolmo which
made him master of the March and by the death of Piccinino
in the same year.

After 1444 Filippo Maria's days of greatness and activity
were coming to an end. He had failed in his attempt to carry
the inherited Visconti tradition further. His inheritance had
been diminished instead of increased. Sforza was the rising
star. He now bestrode Italy. The years after 1444 saw a
realignment of the Italian powers. Sforza's allegiance remained
uncertain. He changed sides to join Milan although in 1446
Filippo Maria had tried to deprive him of Cremona. The death
of Filippo Maria in 1447 threw the Italian political world into
confusion. Like Giangaleazzo, Filippo Maria had made no
proper arrangements for the succession in his dominions.
Unlike Giangaleazzo he left no sons. Sforza was his son-in-
law, but of inferior blood and with no other connections in
Lombardy. The most formidable alternative candidate was
Alfonso V of Naples though his claim was based on an un-
proven report that Filippo Maria had designated him as his

successor. The immediate result of the death of the last
Visconti was that the lands of the inheritance were plunged
again into chaos as after the death of Giangaleazzo. At Milan
itself a serious attempt was made to revive a communal form
of government by the establishment of the Ambrosian Republic with a council of nine hundred and a government of
Captains and Defenders of Liberty. Outside Milan parts of
the Visconti state fell away as they had done after 1402. The
enemies of Milan naturally took the opportunity to strengthen
themselves at her expense. Venice advanced from the east.
Charles, Duke of Orleans, another pretender as the son of
Valentina Visconti, Filippo Maria's sister, advanced from the
west. Alfonso of Naples was a long way away but he moved up
into the papal states and in 1448 to Siena which supported him.
The Ambrosian republic was naturally in danger of extinction
and was driven to call on Sforza to save it from its multitude
of enemies. Sforza however was, of course, chiefly concerned
to establish his own claim to the succession.

Superiority of military power and skill made it inevitable
that Sforza should eventually vindicate his claim to Milan.
Sforza's life is the greatest personal success story of the fifteenth
century. He was the son of a condottiere's concubine and
resented by his father-in-law for that reason. Filippo Maria
once wrote, 'better to be obedient to a lord or a natural king
than to be in danger of subjection to a community or government in which there are shoemakers and tailors and every sort
of man, or to captains of whom one does not know who their
fathers were'. But he was already a very powerful lord when
he married Bianca. The change in alignment of powers which
was produced by this upheaval chiefly affected Florence. The
traditional Florentine stance as leader of the resistance to
Milanese expansion, preferably in alliance with the other great
republic of Venice, which had been the logical position for
Florence for the past half-century or more, now became
obsolete. Venice tried to shore up the Ambrosian republic
against Sforza, but when he finally entered Milan and was
accepted as duke in the spring of 1450 he was supported by
Florence which exhibited no unrealistic republican sympathies.
There were no doubt various reasons for the Florentine change

of front. The most pressing was probably the fear of Alfonso of Naples, who, when he interfered in central Italy, threatened Florence and forced her into the arms of his most effective opponent. With the relative decline of Milan, Venice had become the most impressive power in Lombardy. Cosimo de'Medici played a considerable part in the Florentine shift to a pro-Milanese position and was thought to have been influenced by a long background of dealings with Sforza including the lending of large sums of money which he did not wish to imperil. Cosimo certainly threw his weight at Florence decisively behind support for Sforza, but it was easy enough to frame a defence of that policy in terms of Florentine self-interest. In 1452–3 Florence did find herself apparently threatened by Venice as she had been threatened in the past by Milan, through Venetian intervention in Bologna, while Alfonso still hovered in southern Tuscany in alliance with Siena. From this danger Florence was saved by Sforza's army, subsidized by Florentine money, which decisively defeated Alfonso and drove him out of Tuscany. Cosimo's policy was therefore vindicated.

In 1454 Sforza and Venice came to terms at the peace of Lodi. Later in the year Venice and Florence made a league for twenty-five years which was later joined by the other Italian states. This general pacification of 1454 neatly divides the political history of Italy in the first half of the century from the history of the second half. For forty years, until the French invasion of 1494, there was to be a more peaceful concert of powers. The real reason for the change was the extinction of the Visconti family whose appetite for aggression had dominated Italian politics since the mid-fourteenth century. After 1454 no Italian power had such an instinct. Other causes of discord remained. The chief were the two problems of the lordship of Genoa and the Neapolitan succession, both of which could potentially lead to French intervention. In 1456 Genoa, attacked by Naples again accepted French overlordship. In 1459, after the death of Alfonso, war again broke out in Naples between the Aragonese claimant, Ferrante, and the French, John of Calabria, this time effectively supported by King Charles VII.

French intervention came to nothing. But deeply rooted now in a variety of ancient claims – to Naples, to Genoa, to Milan – the French menace was still there and it was eventually to lead, through the invasion of 1494, to the destruction of Italian political liberty. For the time being however the Italians had achieved both self-sufficiency and stability.

iii *The Ideas of the Italian Renaissance*

The most remarkable cultural development of fifteenth-century Europe took place in the Italian cities and courts. To some extent Italian culture both in the great commercial cities and in smaller places was unified and distinct from the rest of Europe. Writers and painters moved fairly easily between employment in, for instance, the urban centres of Florence, Padua, Venice and the courts of the pope, the King of Naples, the Visconti, the Gonzaga of Mantua. These were all centres of patronage at one time or another in the fifteenth century. But one community, the city of Florence, overwhelmingly surpassed the others in the originality and importance of its contribution and for various reasons the most remarkable innovations with which we are concerned would have been inconceivable except in the milieu of the city. The Renaissance, as these innovations are often summarily called, was a product of the life of the Italian cities. Something has been said in an earlier chapter about the characteristics of the Italian city in the fourteenth century. There was no internal transformation of a decisive kind in the next hundred years. The mercantile system and the lay intelligentsia of this period grew naturally out of those of the age of Dante and Petrarch and, apart from the progressive accumulation of wealth and sophistication, were not radically different from them. As a result of the operation of economic and political forces, however, the place of these cities in the world, their position in relation to the other European states and to the Church, had changed a great deal. In the age of the councils, Florence, Venice and Milan had a command over wealth and political power which made them at least equal and often superior to the pope. They had become major European powers instead of appendages to the feudal world. Of course, it is impossible to establish a direct causal connection between this change in the economic and political balance of power and the cultural manifestations. It provided the money for patronage. But more important than the simple capacity to pay for culture was the fact that the self-confidence of the bourgeois communities was built up to the point where they could assert their own scale of values. The balance of European society had changed.

The first impulse towards the development of humanist ideas beyond the stage which they had reached in the work of Petrarch came from a particularly fruitful meeting of minds at Florence around the turn of the century. The development of humanist enthusiasm at Florence owed most to the initiative of one remarkable disciple of Petrarch, Coluccio Salutati. Salutati, who was a professional notary and rhetorician, was Chancellor of Florence, that is head of the civil service, from 1375 to 1406. He was a very distinguished exponent of his profession: his letters were famous in the world of Italian diplomacy and he conducted the effective Florentine propaganda campaigns both against the papacy in the War of the Eight Saints and against Giangaleazzo Visconti at the end of the century. He was also a passionate cultivator of Latin literature and himself the author of a number of works in which he imitated the style of his models. Salutati was not a man of great originality but he was ideally placed to promote humanist ideals because of his position in Florentine society. Other people had the same idea. Boccaccio, the author of the *Decameron* was also an enthusiastic Latinist and collected a library which remained available to Florentines after he died in 1375. By 1400 there was an influential little group of humanists in Florence which included both professionals and amateur enthusiasts from the bourgeoisie. Into this milieu came the remarkable figure of Manuel Chrysoloras, Byzantine hellenist, friend and envoy of the Emperor Manuel II, who was invited to Florence on Salutati's initiative to teach Greek at the university, an otherwise undistinguished institution maintained by the commune. A knowledge of Greek was a rare accomplishment in the West. Chrysoloras stimulated an interest in it during his stay in the city from 1397 to 1400 and encouraged translations. But his most important role was not so much as a teacher of the language but as a guide to the whole world of classical antiquity: literature, philosophy, architecture and art.

It has often been emphasized that the medieval world had its renaissances and its classicists, it knew nearly all the Latin authors and it translated most of Aristotle after a fashion. Was the Italian Renaissance so different? The answer is that, unlike their predecessors, the Italian humanists wanted the whole of classical antiquity and what they supposed to be its life style, not just fragments of its thought to fit into an alien structure. Such wholehearted historical nostalgia is bound to be very unrealistic but it has been an important ingredient in our civilization and it begins in the circle of Salutati and Chrysoloras at Florence about 1400. Some of the enthusiasts began to say that the ancient writers were better than the moderns even though they were pagan and to regard the politics of the ancient city state and the art of Roman buildings and Greek sculptures as inherently superior to the contemporary styles.

The humanists were often professional writers and Latinists. Another way which they had of making a living was by teaching. One of the features of the early Renaissance which most clearly expressed the sharp break with the past was the elaboration of a new educational ideal based on Roman rhetorical education. The plan was first elaborated in a treatise written by Pier Paolo Vergerio for a member of the Carrara family, the tyrants of Padua, in 1400–2.

'We come now to the consideration of the various subjects which might rightly be included under the name of "Liberal Studies". Amongst these I accord the first place to History, on grounds both of its attractiveness and of its utility, qualities which appeal equally to the scholar and to the statesman. Next in importance ranks Moral Philosophy which indeed is, in a peculiar sense, a "Liberal Art", in that its purpose is to teach man the secret of true freedom.

History, then, gives us the concrete examples of the precepts inculcated by Philosophy. The one shows what men should do, the other what men have said and done in the past, and what practical lessons we may draw therefrom for the present day. I would indicate as the third main branch of study, Eloquence, which indeed holds a place of distinction amongst the refined arts. By philosophy we learn the essential truth of things, which by eloquence we so exhibit in orderly adornment as to bring conviction to differing minds.'

This is a long way from the education of the universities, in which history had no part. It is an education conceived on the Roman model for the man of affairs, the city gentleman. Though it was the revival of an ancient ideal it fitted the requirements and inclinations of the bourgeoisie of the Italian cities, well-to-do men who had also to speak in the assemblies of their councils and manage the state, and it was widely adopted by them.

The paganizing tendencies of the humanists were already recognizable to some people in 1400. Their severest critic was a Dominican evangelist called Giovanni Dominici who belonged to the observant wing of the order and eventually became a cardinal of Gregory XII. Dominici, a highly successful preacher in Florence, denounced the humanists' devotion to pagan authors and pointed out that it was incompatible with Christian beliefs. He was perfectly correct. The humanists were not, like the university students of Aristotle, trying to fit the ancient texts into a Christian structure. They wanted Cicero's world for its own sake. It is characteristic of Italy in the fifteenth century that it held the extremes; the most rigorous sections of the religious orders and the most libertine men of letters existed in the same cities and were often supported by the same patrons. The explanation of humanist enthusiasm is not however to be found in reaction against the system of ecclesiastical authority. On the contrary, part of the reason for the easy growth of the movement is to be found in the comparative weakness of ecclesiastical institutions and particularly of the papacy at this period. Within the cities themselves, though religion was often fervent, ecclesiastical authority had always been weak. Now the papacy had lost much of the European basis of its power. During the first half of the fifteenth century the papal court was for long periods a poor relation of the cities and tended to accept the fashions of contemporary society. The papal court, particularly under John XXIII and Eugenius IV, to a lesser extent under other popes, was a great employer of expert humanists as letter-writers and officials and therefore a centre of classical enthusiasm. It was characteristic of the Renaissance popes that they had closer links with the lay intelligentsia, who were their friends and advisers, than with the rigorists of the religious orders. Intolerance depends as much on the strength of institutions as on the strength of feeling. In the tolerant world of Italy at this period humanists clearly had a comfortable relationship with ecclesiastical authority and could develop an alternative world of ideas without very much feeling of constraint.

They also required positive patronage. The papal court was one of the main providers of this. But the original and normal background of humanist activity was provided by the urban bourgeoisie. If one patron were to be singled out as a positive creator of Renaissance taste, it would be Cosimo de' Medici. Cosimo was not only a merchant of exceptional, perhaps unparalleled wealth, and the virtual ruler of Florence; he was also an informed amateur with a positive interest in classical literature and art. The first of the Renaissance churches, San Lorenzo, was the parish church of the Medici family and a whole cluster of important men, exponents of both literature and the fine arts – Niccolò Niccoli, Brunelleschi, Donatello, Michelozzo, Ficino – owed a part of their livelihood to Cosimo who thus had a positive influence in directing effort towards neo-classical architecture and the study of Plato. No other individual patron is comparable, but in a general way the direction of the movement was determined by the preferences of the bourgeoisie of the cities.

The enthusiasms of the Salutati-Chrysoloras circle bore their fruit a generation later in the 1430s and 1440s when Florence was the source of a considerable output of both literature and art in the new style. Certain individuals provided a continuity from the circle of 1400 through to this period, notably Niccolò Niccoli (d. 1437), a passionate collector of manuscripts and classical antiquities, Leonardo Bruni (d. 1444), the most prolific historian and translator of this period, and Poggio (d. 1459), a gifted imitator of classical styles. These had all been disciples of Salutati and Chrysoloras around 1400. The best way to describe the character of the Florentine Renaissance of this period is to look at the various aspects of it through the whole of the half-century from 1400 to 1450.

The most complete achievement of the early Renaissance thinkers was the construction of a political and social philosophy appropriate to the secular city. It is not surprising that the most rapid advance should have been made in this direction. What Renaissance Italy most obviously had in common with the ancient world was the city state. This was a genuine similarity which made borrowing easy. The crucial breakthrough came at the beginning of the century when Salutati and his young pupil, Leonardo Bruni, began to argue that republicanism was inherently superior to the rule of one man and that the Florentine constitution was the inheritor of the social virtues of the Roman Republic. This line of argument was a significant break with medieval traditions. The prestige of monarchy and of the Roman Empire was so high in the medieval world that even republican Florentines had tried to emphasize the city's alleged connection with Julius Caesar. Now it was argued that the empire had been degenerate and that the really valuable part of the Roman tradition was the liberty and morality of the city before that time. Bruni wrote a *Panegyric of the City of Florence*, based on an ancient model in which he praised the unique virtue of the Florentine political system in terms derived from Rome and Athens. It has been argued that this intellectual innovation was a product of Florentine propaganda against Milan during the last, desperate duel with Giangaleazzo Visconti. There is certainly some truth in this. Florence traditionally posed as the champion of liberty against tyranny: now under the stress of war the further step was taken of making an intellectual defence of a free constitution. Throughout the period of wars with Giangaleazzo and Filippo Maria the commune presented itself as the defender of liberty against tyranny. But once evolved the new theory was in many ways applicable to cities governed by princes as well as to republics: the essential novelty was that it was a political theory of the secular city based on the utilitarian value of the city to its inhabitants not on its relation to a Christian metaphysic or to the destiny of a world empire.

A further impulse to Florentine political thought was given by the international upheavals of the 1430s, when the city was again embattled, and it was in fact during this period that the theories were elaborated and became general assumptions. A Florentine amateur humanist called Matteo Palmieri wrote a book *On Civil Life* which was almost entirely based on Cicero and discussed the proper arrangement of the government of a city. None of the political theorists of this period got beyond the adaptation of ideas taken from Cicero or Aristotle, and in that sense they were derivative, but they had made a decisive break from the political thought of the scholastics. Some of the other kinds of writing associated with the new classical attitude to the city, however, were more original. Bruni, who like his master, Salutati, became Chancellor of Florence, also established a new way of writing history. This also was based on ancient models but here originality could not be avoided because he was writing the history of his own times. Bruni's *History of the Florentine People* was completed about 1440. It covered the subject from the beginning to the wars against Giangaleazzo and it established a new manner of writing history as the evolving political story of a state. This was different from the year-by-year approach of medieval chroniclers or the collection of heroic exploits in Froissart. It is the beginning of the style of history writing which was to persist for centuries. Bruni also changed the conception of the distant past still more fundamentally by treating history, especially in his early sections on the ancient world, as an account of the vicissitudes of civilization. The city and the Roman empire were evaluated by him with reference to the cultural achievements of their citizens, not with reference to any supernatural purpose. The interest in antiquity of course naturally promoted historical investigation. The early Renaissance took a large and fairly sudden step forward towards a more realistic perspective of world history. Another development connected with the theory of the city was the fashion for writing imaginary dialogues between citizens discussing philosophical and political questions. This again was, of course, a literary form imitated from classical authors. The most famous example of it was an Italian dialogue *On the Family* composed *circa* 1433–45, by Leon Battista Alberti. Alberti, still betrer known as the theorist of painting and architecture, was the cleverest of the humanists of this period, a member of a great Florentine merchant family who was employed in the papal court. This dialogue is an imaginary discussion between members of his family in which they exchange views on how to manage their lives in relation to the family, business, personal success, good and ill fortune and politics. Here is the bourgeois world as a self-sufficient way of life.

The connection between humanism and art is more obscure than the connection between humanism and politics. Here again however it is clear that the background was in some ways appropriate. Florence had a very long and distinguished tradition of painting before 1400. One of the main characteristics of that tradition had been the pursuit of spatial and emotional realism, especially in the work of Giotto at the beginning of the fourteenth century. In the latter part of the century however there was a withdrawal from that particular quest and a renewed emphasis on pattern, ornamentation and religious symbolism. At the beginning of the fifteenth century in Italy as in the Netherlands the conventions of the 'International Gothic' prevailed. But the authority of Giotto was still respected and nowhere in Europe was there a greater reservoir of technical skill. During the first half of the fifteenth century the painters and sculptors made revolutionary advances in the two associated fields of spatial and dramatic realism. The most spectacular innovation was the invention of strict perspective drawing by Filippo Brunelleschi about 1420. This simple mathematical device, the basis of the artists' approach to space for centuries afterwards, enabled a scene to be drawn with the objects in the same relationship to each other as they appeared to have been in to the observer's eye. The device was quickly taken up and exploited by such great painters as Masaccio (d. 1428) and Piero della Francesca (1415–92) whose works lost all the spatial unreality of medieval painting. The inspiration for Brunelleschi's invention is unknown but there is a similarity between the conceptual revolution associated with him and the revolution in cartography (see above, p. 237) which began in the same circles with the translation of Ptolemy's *Geography* by a pupil of Chrysoloras. Both involved a clearer grasp of spatial relationships. Both were in a sense improvements of perspective. The clearest connection between art and humanism is to be seen however in sculpture. The humanists were familiar with antique sculpture which they included in their general enthusiasm for all classical things and which some of them collected. The imitation of ancient works of art was the main factor in the innovations made by the great sculptor Donatello (1386–1466). Donatello studied ancient statuary and friezes, he discussed them with humanists and he was patronized by Cosimo de' Medici who probably encouraged his classicizing tendencies.

Donatello and Brunelleschi are the first artists to be treated as giants by their contemporaries because of their artistic genius. Though artists were traditionally accorded more individual respect in the Italian cities than in northern Europe – Giotto was mentioned by Dante in the *Divine Comedy* – this was a change in attitude, encouraged again by the models of antiquity. The first modern treatise on art, Alberti's book *On Painting*, which was written in the 1430s and was a monument to the collaboration of writers and painters because it adduced classical authority for the innovations that had been made by working artists in Florence, was also the first book to present the artist as an inspiration to society rather than a technician. 'The painter Zeuxis began to give his works away, because, as he said, they could not be bought for any price. He did not believe any price could be found to satisfy the man who, in modelling or painting living things, appeared almost like another god among mortals. The merits of painting therefore, are such that when those who are versed in it see their works admired they consider themselves to be almost like a god . . . Painting was so honoured in the old days by our ancestors that while nearly all other makers of things were regarded as workmen, the painter alone was not included among them.' 'The artist ought to take particular care of his morals, especially of good manners and courtesy by which he may get both the benevolence of others, which is a protection against poverty, and rewards, the best assistance to the perfecting of his art. I want the painter to be as far as possible learned in all the liberal arts but I especially desire competence in geometry.' Clearly this was another change in attitudes which could happen much more easily in the individualistic environment of a city than in the hierarchical world of a court. Alberti also himself symbolized the transformation of values by practising the mechanical art of architecture as well as writing learned humanist treatises. The new architectural style imitated from Roman buildings was invented by Brunelleschi and exemplified by him in the rebuilding of the church of San Lorenzo at Florence, which started in 1418, and in other buildings. Alberti, who designed buildings both at Rome and at Florence, developed a general theory of classical architecture in a book written about 1450. In his eyes, and no doubt those of many contemporaries, the purpose of architecture could not be described in merely aesthetic terms. His imagination took in the planning of whole towns, the creation of an environment in which a certain kind of cultivated urban life could be lived. For the devotees of contemporary art and literature a remarkably complete body of connected social and cultural ideals had been created by the middle of the century.

Florence though the most original was not the only centre of humanist activity, which was very widely spread because of the prevalence in Italy of the rhetorical tradition. The Venetian bourgeoisie were also keen patrons and practitioners of humanism and profited from their closer contacts with the Greek world. At the university of Pavia and the Milanese court, Filippo Maria Visconti was a keen patron of Latinists and Greek translators. The kingdom of Naples was in many respects a different world but Alfonso V patronized one of the greatest humanists, Lorenzo Valla. Valla worked for Alfonso during his period of enmity with Pope Eugenius and wrote his famous denunciation of the Donation of Constantine as a forgery in the cause of anti-papal propaganda. Everything suggests however that he was a willing propagandist. Valla was the humanist who came closest to exploiting the potentially anti-Christian implications of his studies instead of ignoring them. Apart from exposing his own anti-clericalism, Valla was a serious critic of scholasticism. He attacked both Aristotle's ideas, and – being a very good Greek scholar himself – the misuse of Aristotle by medieval thinkers who could not translate him properly. In the hands of a scholar with a preference for a simplified ethical Christianity – which was certainly the inclination of many Ciceronians of this period – this historical-linguistic approach could be extremely destructive. On the whole, however, humanists expressed themselves in Ciceronian terms without raising issues which would have produced a clash with ecclesiastical authority.

The Council of Florence, which had so little effect on the history of the eastern or western churches, had a profound effect on the history of Italian thought. It brought not only to the West but to Florence itself distinguished representatives of the neo-Hellenic renaissance at Byzantium including Gemistos Plethon, the interpreter of Plato, and therefore intensified the sporadic intercourse between classical enthusiasts in East and West which had developed since the days of Chrysoloras. It whetted the appetites of the enthusiasts at Florence and the papal court for more knowledge of Greek. Eventually it helped to satisfy that taste because the closer contacts led to the flight of Byzantine scholars to the West, bringing with them a direct knowledge of Greek philosophy which was as yet unparalleled. The most notable of them was Bessarion, who came to Italy in 1442 and became a cardinal. Bessarion, like other Greeks, was an admirer of Plato. No one in the West had his comprehensive knowledge of Plato. The West had never had a corpus of translations of Plato like the medieval translations of Aristotle on which the learning of the universities was based and even in 1440 humanist efforts had not translated all of them. Philosophers still tended to fight shy of Plato as a dangerous thinker. Bessarion revealed Plato's thought much more fully to the Latin-reading world. But a decisive impulse was given to this line of development – and it is perhaps his most important claim to fame – by Cosimo. Cosimo was enthralled by the Greek intellectuals at the council of 1439 and conceived the idea that the Platonic and neo-platonic writings contained keys to celestial wisdom which he must not miss. Years later he picked out a promising young scholar, Marsilio Ficino, whom he set to work to translate the works of Plato and other mystical and neoplatonic writings. Cosimo thought he was buying precious and arcane wisdom. He wrote to Ficino from his country estate in 1462, 'Come to me, Marsilio, immediately. Bring with you my book of Plato *On the Highest Good*, which I think you must by now have translated from Greek into Latin as you promised. I desire nothing more keenly than to know what road leads most easily to felicity.' The dying millionaire's self-indulgent quest for the secrets of heaven has a modern ring. It also had profound consequences. Between 1463 and 1482 Ficino translated the whole of Plato and laid the foundations for the enthusiasm for platonic and neoplatonic ideas which was characteristic of Florence and Rome in the days of Lorenzo the Magnificent and after. Though the new neoplatonism was in some respects a shallow philosophy it fascinated great artists and theologians and was to be the most powerful intellectual force in the high Renaissance period.

When Cosimo wrote to Ficino the see of St Peter was occupied by a pope, Pius II, formerly Aeneas Sylvius (1458–64), who had been a professional humanist. But this remarkable justification of the humanist tradition had already been in some respects surpassed in the pontificate of Nicholas V (1447–55). Nicholas was not a practising humanist but he was a fanatical devotee of humanist literature. In the previous century and a half there had been pious popes and avaricious, absolutist popes, popes devoted to theology and popes devoted to canon law. Nicholas V was a new phenomenon, a man steeped in the new humanist culture which had grown up at Florence in the papal court in the last generation and in which, as Tommaso Parentucelli, an obscure secretary of illustrious cardinals, he had formed his tastes. He devoted his pontificate more than anything else to making papal Rome into a humanist city which would realize the ideas of a literary movement. He hoped to do this both by rebuilding the city as a place fit for new Romans and by assembling an unparalleled library of classical literature. During his short pontificate he began a comprehensive rebuilding of Rome on an enormous scale, reconstructing at the same time the walls, St Peter's, the Vatican palace, Castel S. Angelo, the Capitol and several churches. Naturally the execution of his plans was only begun but the design was vast. On the literary side Nicholas seized on one aspect of the general humanist approach to literature, the fashion of making Greek literature available in Latin translations, and aimed to build up a comprehensive library. For this purpose he tried to attract as many as possible of the leading Italian humanists of the day and the Greek refugees from Byzantium to work at the papal court, offering large rewards. In this way he became responsible for Lorenzo Valla's first translation of Thucydides and for a number of other works. As with the architecture the result was not finally a great monument but then Nicholas reigned only for eight years and the design had been incomparable in its scope. It is ironical that the large sums collected from the pilgrims visiting Rome for the jubilee of 1450 were devoted to purposes so curiously irrelevant not only to the ostensible aims of the medieval papacy but also to its ordinary political interests. The papacy had been captured by the cultural ideals of the Italian cities.

MAPS

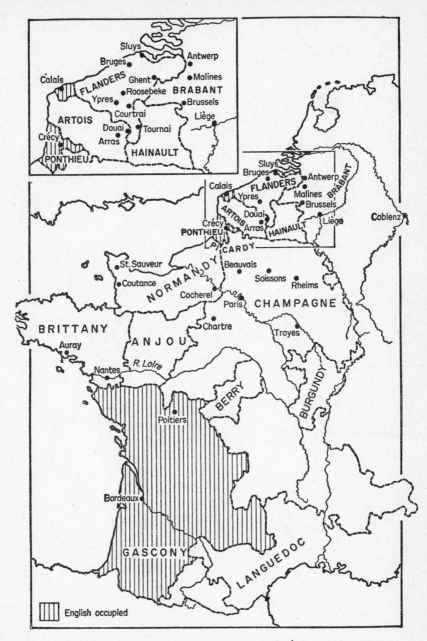

Inset map labels:
Sluys, Antwerp, Bruges, Calais, FLANDERS, Ghent, Malines, Roosebeke, BRABANT, Ypres, Brussels, ARTOIS, Courtrai, Liège, Crécy, Douai, Tournai, Arras, PONTHIEU, HAINAULT

Main map labels:
Sluys, Bruges, Antwerp, Calais, FLANDERS, Ypres, Malines, Brussels, Douai, Crécy, ARTOIS, Arras, HAINAULT, Liège, Coblenz, PONTHIEU, PICARDY, St.Sauveur, Beauvais, Coutance, NORMANDY, Soissons, Rheims, Cocherel, Paris, CHAMPAGNE, BRITTANY, ANJOU, Chartre, Troyes, Auray, Nantes, R. Loire, BERRY, BURGUNDY, Poitiers, Bordeaux, GASCONY, LANGUEDOC

|||| English occupied

FRANCE AFTER THE TREATY OF BRÉTIGNY 1361

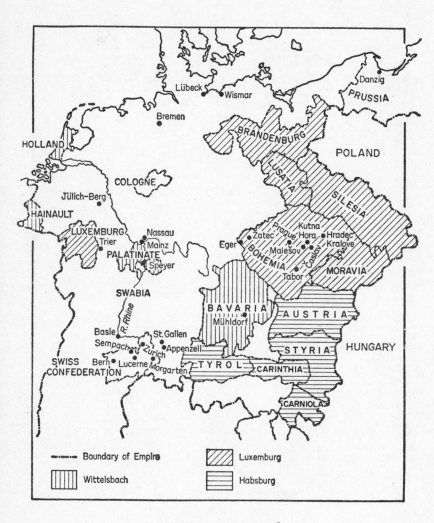

GERMANY IN 1378

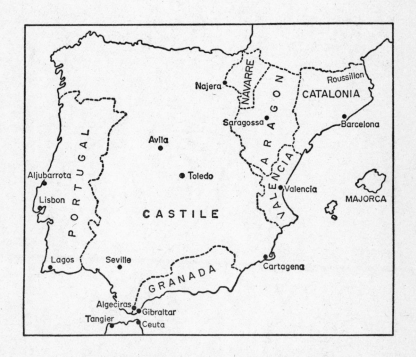

THE KINGDOMS OF LATE MEDIEVAL IBERIA

ITALY ABOUT 1340

THE LEVANT ABOUT 1360

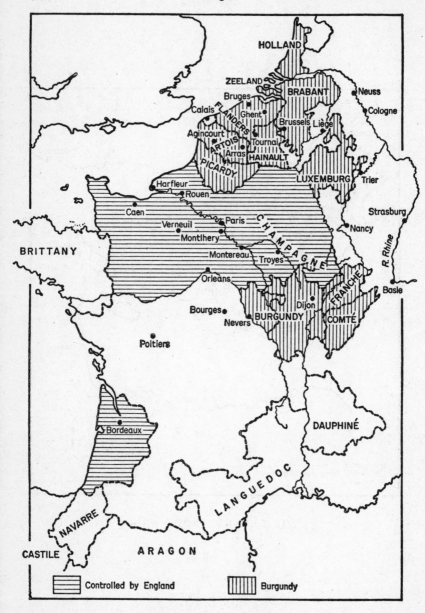

FRANCE ABOUT 1430

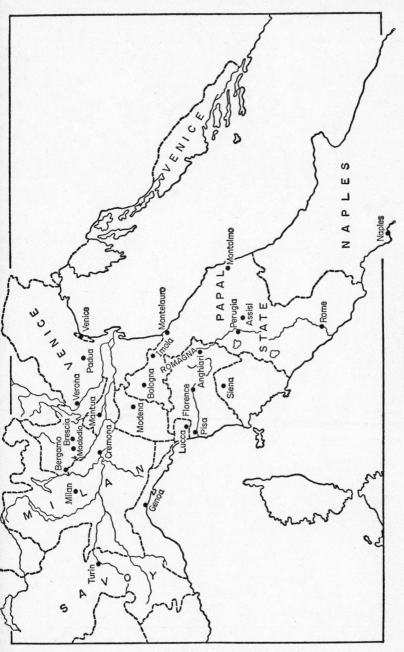

ITALY IN 1454

TABLES

THE POPES

John XXII (1316–34)
Benedict XII (1334–42)
Clement VI (1342–52)
Innocent VI (1352–62)
Urban V (1362–70)
Gregory XI (1370–78)

Nicholas V (1328–30) (anti-Pope)

ROME
Urban VI (1378–89)
Boniface IX (1389–1404)
Innocent VII (1404–6)
Gregory XII (1406–15)

Martin V (1417–31)
Eugenius IV (1431–47)
Nicholas V (1447–55)
Calixtus III (1455–8)
Pius II (1458–64)

AVIGNON
Clement VII (1378–94)
Benedict XIII (1394–1417)

PISA
Alexander V (1409–10)
John XXIII (1410–15)

BASLE
Felix V (1439–49)

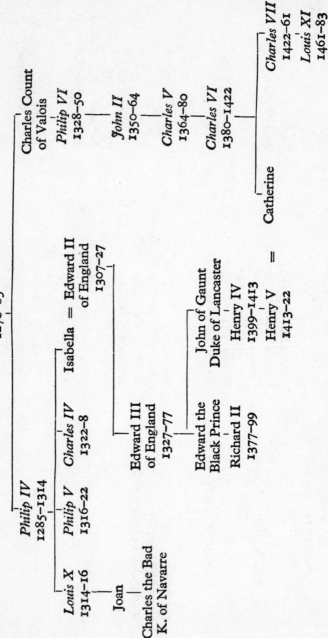

THE KINGS OF FRANCE AND ENGLAND

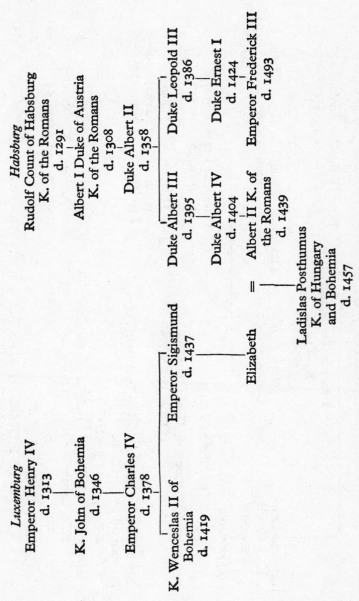

THE LUXEMBURG AND HABSBURG FAMILIES

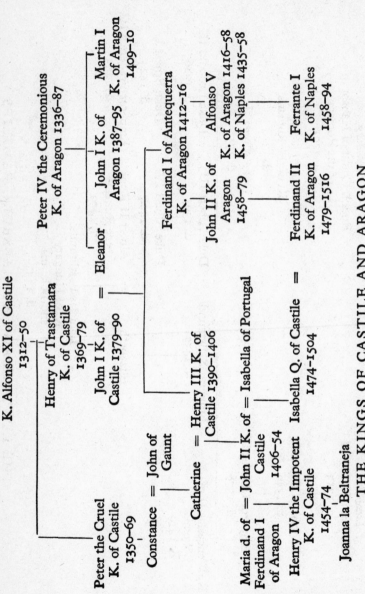

THE KINGS OF CASTILE AND ARAGON

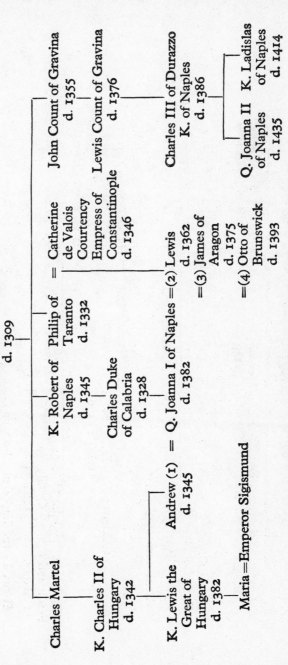

THE ANGEVINS OF NAPLES AND HUNGARY

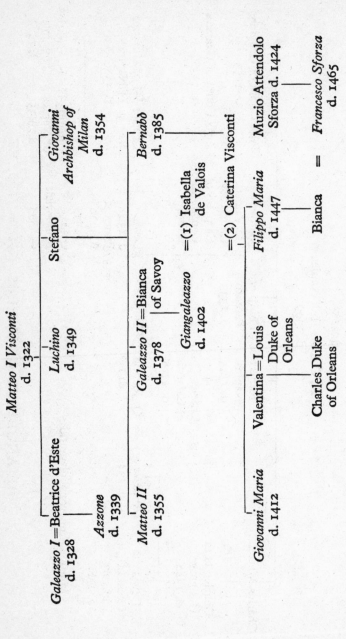

THE RULERS OF MILAN

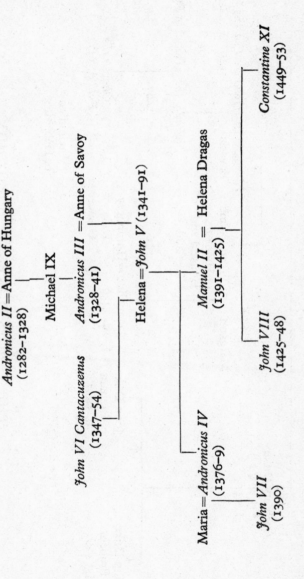

Andronicus II = Anne of Hungary
(1282–1328)

Michael IX

Andronicus III = Anne of Savoy
(1328–41)

John VI Cantacuzenus
(1347–54)

Helena = John V (1341–91)

Manuel II = Helena Dragas
(1391–1425)

Maria = Andronicus IV
(1376–9)

John VII
(1390)

John VIII
(1425–48)

Constantine XI
(1449–53)

THE BYZANTINE EMPERORS

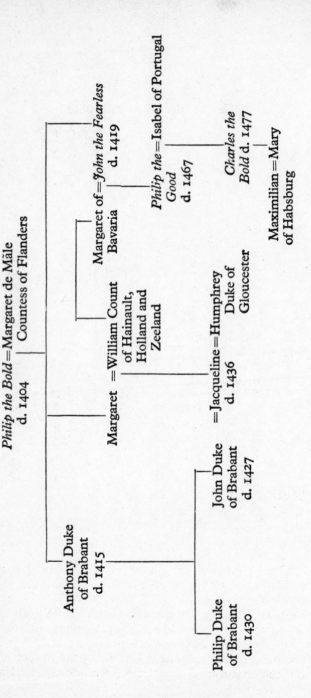

THE VALOIS DUKES OF BURGUNDY

Philip the Bold = Margaret de Male
d. 1404   Countess of Flanders

Anthony Duke
of Brabant
d. 1415

Margaret = William Count
of Hainault,
Holland and
Zeeland

Margaret of = John the Fearless
Bavaria   d. 1419

Philip Duke
of Brabant
d. 1430

John Duke
of Brabant
d. 1427

= Jacqueline = Humphrey
d. 1436   Duke of
Gloucester

Philip the = Isabel of Portugal
Good
d. 1467

Charles the
Bold d. 1477

Maximilian = Mary
of Habsburg

FURTHER READING

GENERAL

Most aspects of this period are covered by *The Cambridge Medieval History*, ed. J. B. Bury etc, vols. VII and VIII (1932, 1936), a useful work though now outdated in approach. C. W. Previté-Orton, *A History of Europe 1198–1378* (3rd ed., 1951) and W. T. Waugh, *A History of Europe 1378–1494*, (3rd ed., 1960), are both textbooks, strong in political history. A more thematic and structural approach is to be found in Denys Hay's *Europe in the Fourteenth and Fifteenth Centuries* (1966). The *Nouvelle Clio* series has volumes dealing with different aspects: J. Heers, *L'Occident aux XIVᵉ et XVᵉ siècles: aspects economiques et sociaux* (1963), P. Chaunu, *L'Expansion européenne du XIIIᵉ au XVᵉ siècle* (1969), B. Guenée, *L'Occident aux XIVᵉ et XVᵉ siècles: les états* (1971), F. Rapp, *L'Église et la vie religieuse en occident à la fin du moyen âge* (1971). There is a miscellaneous collection of essays on particular questions in *Europe in the Late Middle Ages*, ed. J. Hale, R. Highfield and B. Smalley (1965). R. C. Storey, *Chronology of the Medieval World 800–1491* (1973) is an invaluable reference book.

THE PAPACY AND THE CHURCH

There is no good general history of the Church at this period in English. A very useful French introduction by F. Rapp is mentioned in the previous section. A recent survey of the evolution of the papacy is W. Ullman's *Short History of the Papacy in the Middle Ages* (1972). For the Avignon papacy there is a good brief introduction by Y. Renouard, *The Avignon Papacy 1305–1403*, trans. D. Bethell (1970). A more detailed account of many aspects of the subject is contained in G. Mollat's *The Popes at Avignon, 1305–1378*, trans. J. Love (1963). The best general account in English of the papacy after 1378 is still the classic work by Mandell Creighton, *A History*

of the Papacy during the period of the Reformation, vols. I–II
(1882). The best modern survey, with up-to-date bibliographies,
is in A. Fliche and V. Martin, *Histoire de l'Église*, XIV: E.
Delaruelle, E-R. Labande and P. Ourliac, *L'Église au temps du
Grand Schisme et de la crise conciliare* (2 parts, Paris, 1962–4),
written from an orthodox standpoint but containing useful
introductions to many aspects of religion at that period.

The history of the papal state has recently been told by Peter
Partner, *The Lands of St Peter* (1972). The theory of papal
monarchy is dealt with by M. J. Wilks, *The Problem of Sovereignty
in the Later Middle Ages* (1964). Conciliar theory and other
aspects of the Church at this period are considered in the essays
of E. F. Jacob collected in two volumes, *Essays in the Conciliar
Epoch* (2nd ed., 1953) and *Essays in Later Medieval History*
(1968). See also A. J. Black, *Monarchy and Community: Political
Ideas in the Later Conciliar Controversy 1430–1450* (1970).
Papal finance may be approached through W. E. Lunt, *Papal
Revenues in the Later Middle Ages* (1934). There are few good
studies of individual popes in this period. J. Gill's *Eugenius IV*
(1962) is a recent one.

UNIVERSITIES AND SCHOLASTICISM

The best introduction is Gordon Leff, *Paris and Oxford Universities in the Thirteenth and Fourteenth Centuries* (1968).
There are detailed accounts of all the universities in the ancient
but still useful book by Hastings Rashdall, *The Universities
of Europe in the Middle Ages*, ed. F. M. Powicke and A. B.
Emden (1936). Scholastic thought, particularly at this period,
is a difficult subject to approach. Étienne Gilson's *A History of
Christian Philosophy in the Middle Ages* (1955) is an excellent
handbook with further references. There is a recent book on one
aspect of William of Ockham's thought: A. S. McGrade, *The
Political Thought of William of Ockham* (1974).

RELIGIOUS MOVEMENTS

There is a compendious account of the doctrines of the various
heretical movements by Gordon Leff, *Medieval Heresy* (2 vols.

1967). The stimulating study of medieval millenary movements by Norman Cohn, *The Pursuit of the Millenium* (1957) is to be recommended also. Among the studies of particular movements are: E. W. McDonnell, *Beguines and Beghards in Medieval Culture* (1954), R. E. Lerner, *The Heresy of the Free Spirit in the Later Middle Ages* (1972), J. M. Clark, *The Great German Mystics: Eckhart, Tauler and Suso* (1949), A. Hyma, *The Christian Renaissance, a History of the 'Devotio Moderna'* (2nd ed. 1965).

THE HUSSITE MOVEMENT

There is an excellent modern account down to 1422 by Howard Kaminsky, *A History of the Hussite Revolution* (1967). The political story of the 1420s is told by Frederick Heymann in *John Žižka and the Hussite Revolution* (1955) and of mid-fifteenth century Bohemia by the same historian in *George of Bohemia, King of Heretics* (1965). R. R. Betts collected his studies of Hussitism in *Essays in Czech History* (1969). The later ideology of the Movement is the subject of Peter Brock's *The Political and Social Doctrines of the Unity of the Czech Brethren in the Fifteenth and Early Sixteenth Centuries* (1957).

FRANCE

The best introduction in English is E. Perroy, *The Hundred Years War*, trans. W. B. Wells (2nd ed., 1965). Aspects of French history during this period have been interestingly surveyed by P. S. Lewis, *Later Medieval France, the Polity* (1968). For a detailed account of French political history the reader must still revert to the old but still good *Histoire de France* edited by Ernest Lavisse: vols. III, ii (1226–1328) by Ch. V. Langlois (1901); IV, i (1328–1422) by A. Coville (1902); IV, ii (1422–92) by Ch. Petit-Dutaillis (1902). There is a lack of separate accounts of the kings' reigns but R. Cazelles, *La Société politique et la crise de la royauté sous Philippe de Valois* (1958) and P. Champion, *Louis XI*, (Eng. trans. n.d.) may be mentioned.

There is a comprehensive study of institutions in the three-volume co-operative work *Histoire des Institutions françaises au Moyen Âge*, ed. F. Lot and R. Fawtier (1957–62). Other institutional studies are J. R. Strayer and C. H. Taylor, *Studies in Early French Taxation* (1939), J. B. Henneman, *Royal Taxation in Fourteenth Century France, the development of War financing 1322–1356* (1971), J. R. Mayor, *Representative Institutions in Renaissance France, 1421–1559* (1960) and Philippe Contamine, *Guerre, État et Société a la Fin du Moyen Âge, Études sur les Armées des Rois de France 1337–1494* (1972). There are valuable collections of essays on aspects of French history in the period by Kenneth Fowler, *The Hundred Years War* (1971) and P. S. Lewis, *The Recovery of France in the Fifteenth Century* (1971). The social and literary ideals of the French and Burgundian nobility are the main subject of J. H. Huizinga's famous book *The Waning of the Middle Ages* (English trans. 1924).

Two notable monographs about French rural society at this period are R. Boutruche, *La crise d'une société, Seigneurs et paysans du Bordelais pendant la Guerre de Cent Ans* (1947) and G. Fourquin, *Les Campagnes de la Région Parisienne a la Fin du Moyen Âge* (1964).

THE LOW COUNTRIES

The best general account is still that by the great Belgian historian, Henri Pirenne, *Histoire de Belgique*, vol. II (1902, 4th ed. 1947). There is a shortage of books in English. Aspects of the pre-Burgundian period are discussed by D. M. Nicholas, *Town and Countryside, social, economic, and political tensions in Fourteenth Century Flanders* (1971). For the period of the Valois dukes there is now a most useful account in the four biographies by Richard Vaughan: *Philip the Bold* (1962), *John the Fearless* (1966), *Philip the Good* (1970), *Charles the Bold* (1973). Netherlandish painting may be approached through the introduction by Margaret Whinney, *Early Flemish Painting* (1968) and the large-scale monograph by Erwin Panofsky, *Early Netherlandish Painting* (1953).

GERMANY, THE EMPIRE AND CENTRAL EUROPE

Literature in English on Germany at this period is very scanty. A brief introduction and interpretation is given by G. Barraclough in *The Origins of Modern Germany* (rev. ed. 1947). E. Bonjour, H. S. Offler and G. R. Potter, *A Short History of Switzerland* (1952) and H. W. A. Leeper, *A History of Medieval Austria* (1941) cover parts of the German-speaking world. There are two excellent analyses of the development of individual states during the fifteenth century: F. L. Carsten, *The Origins of Prussia* (1954) and H. J. Cohn, *The Government of the Rhine Palatinate in the Fifteenth Century* (1965). Carsten also surveys some other states briefly in his *Princes and Parliaments in Germany* (1959). A good introduction to German institutions at this period is provided by H. S. Offler in his essay on 'Aspects of Government in the Late Medieval Empire' in *Europe in the Later Middle Ages*. Some essays about Germany at the end of the fifteenth century have been collected by G. Strauss in *Pre-Reformation Germany* (1972). Readers of German will find a useful guide to the subject in B. Gebhardt, *Handbuch der deutschen Geschichte*, vol. I (9th ed. 1970). Chapters in *The Cambridge History of Poland to 1696*, ed. W. F. Reddaway etc. (1950) and O. Halecki, *Borderlands of Western Civilization* (1952) are useful for central and eastern Europe.

IBERIA

The best account of the political history in English is still that contained in R. B. Merriman's *The Rise of the Spanish Empire*, vols. I–II (1918). There is very little in English on fourteenth-century Spain. J. L. Shneidman, *The Rise of the Aragonese-Catalan Empire 1200–1350* (1970) is useful as far as it goes. P. E. Russell, *The English Intervention in Spain and Portugal in the time of Edward II and Richard II* (1955) deals with the period c. 1362–94. A number of insights into recent writing is given in the essays collected in R. Highfield's *Spain in the Fifteenth Century 1369–1516* (1972). For the end of the fifteenth century an introduction is provided by J. H. Elliott, *Imperial Spain*,

1469–1716 (1963). There are some important books in English on Spanish economic history: the translation of J. Vicens Vives, *An Economic History of Spain* (1969), J. Klein, *The Mesta* (1920) and E. J. Hamilton, *Money, Prices and Wages in Valencia, Aragon and Navarre, 1351–1500* (1936).

BYZANTIUM AND THE OTTOMANS

There is now a very readable general account of the later history of the Byzantine Empire in D. M. Nicol, *The Last Centuries of Byzantium 1261–1453* (1972). Various aspects are dealt with in the revised edition of *The Cambridge Medieval History*, IV, *The Byzantine Empire*, ed. J. M. Hussey (2 parts, 1966–7). A briefer consecutive account is to be found in G. Ostrogorsky, *History of the Byzantine State* (1956). There are brief treatments of two topics by Steven Runciman: *The Fall of Constantinople, 1453* (1965) and *The Last Byzantine Renaissance* (1970). A modern introduction to Ottoman history is given by Halil Inalcik in chapters in *The Cambridge History of Islam*, I, ed. P. M. Holt, A. K. S. Lambton and B. Lewis (1970). The best approach to the various Latin states established in Eastern Mediterranean is probably still through William Miller, *The Latins in the Levant* (1908, reprinted 1964). For crusading enterprises see the essay by Anthony Luttrell in *Europe in the Late Middle Ages*.

ITALY

There is no good general history of Italian politics in English. The subject must therefore be approached through the histories of the individual states. For Florence there is a readable narrative by F. Schevill, *History of Florence* (1937), in more detail G. A. Brucker, *Florentine Politics and Society, 1343–1378* (1962), C. Gutkind, *Cosimo de' Medici* (1938), N. Rubinstein, *The Government of Florence under the Medici 1434–1494* (1966), a constitutional study, and the essays collected in N. Rubinstein, *Florentine Studies* (1968). For Venice there is a general history by F. C. Lane, *Venice, a Maritime Republic* (1973), a collection of his essays, *Venice and History* (1966), and another collection edited by John Hale, *Renaissance Venice* (1973); also a brief survey by David Chambers, *The Imperial Age of Venice, 1380–1580* (1970). Other places are much less well covered. Naples may be approached through E. G. Léonard, *Les Angevins de Naples* (1954). Individual rulers are the subjects of E. L. Cox, *The Green Count of Savoy, Amadeus VI* (1967) and D. M. Bueno de Mesquita, *Giangaleazzo Visconti* (1941). Other local studies are C. M. Ady, *The Bentivoglio of Bologna,* (1937) and P. J. Jones, *The Malatesta of Rimini and the Papal State* (1974). There is an attractive and illuminating collection of essays about political and cultural subjects edited by E. F. Jacob, *Italian Renaissance Studies* (1960). Readers of Italian will find a useful general political history in the volumes by Luigi Salvatorelli, *L'Italia Comunale dal Secolo XI alla meta del secolo XIV* (1940) and Nino Valeri *L'Italia nell Eta dei Principati dal 1343 al 1516* (1949).

ITALIAN RENAISSANCE THOUGHT

The best general introduction is probably Denys Hay, *The Italian Renaissance in its Historical Background* (1961). Another, more confined to ideas and by an Italian Historian, is E. Garin, *Italian Humanism*, trans. P. Munz (1965). The period is also covered in an interesting way in two books by John Larner, *Culture and Society in Italy 1290–1420* (1971) and Peter Burke, *Culture and Society in Renaissance Italy, 1420–1540* (1972). The important theories of Hans Baron are to be found in *The Crisis of the Early Italian Renaissance* (2 vols. 1955, one vol. ed. 1966) and *From Petrarch to Leonardo Bruni* (1968). They have been criticized by J. E. Seigl in 'Civic Humanism or Ciceronian Rhetoric?', *Past and Present*, 1966. For an introduction to Italian art and architecture the reader may turn to John White, *Art and Architecture in Italy: 1250–1400* (1966), L. H. Heydenreich and W. Lotz, *Architecture in Italy 1400–1600* (1974) and the first two volumes of John Pope-Hennessy's *An Introduction to Italian Sculpture* (1955–63). On the ideas which influenced art see Michael Baxandall, *Giotto and the Orators* (1971) and *Painting and Experience in Fifteenth Century Italy* (1972), and T. Wittkower, *Architectural Principles in the Age of Humanism* (1952).

ECONOMIC AND SOCIAL HISTORY

The best approach in English is through the volumes of the
Cambridge Economic History of Europe, I, *The Agrarian Life of
the Middle Ages* (2nd ed. 1966); II, *Trade and Industry in the
Middle Ages* (1952); III, *Economic Organization and Policies
in the Middle Ages* (1963). A general account of medieval
agrarian history up to the fourteenth century will be found in
G. Duby, *Rural Economy and Country Life in the Medieval West*,
Tr. C. Postan, (1968). Among the interesting studies of Italian
commerce are Y. Renouard, *Les hommes d'affaires italiens du
moyen âge* (new ed. 1968), I. Origo, *The Merchant of Prato*
(1957) and R. de Roover, *The Rise and Decline of the Medici
Bank 1397–1494* (1963). Northern industry and commerce are
less easily approached. Some of the useful works are: P. Dollinger,
The German Hansa, tr. D. S. Ault and S. H. Steinberg (1970),
J. A. van Houtte, 'The Rise and Decline of the Market of
Bruges', *Economic History Review*, ser. 2, XIX, 1966, and H. van
de Wee, *The Growth of the Antwerp Market and the European
Economy (fourteenth to sixteenth centuries)* (1963).

There is a useful survey of *The Popular Revolutions of the
Late Middle Ages* by Michel Mollat and Philippe Wolff (1973).
The best general introduction to the early period of European
expansion is P. Chaunu, *L'Expansion européenne du XIIIᵉ au
XVᵉ siècle* (1969). For the Portuguese role see V. Magalhaes-
Godinho, *L'Economie de l'Empire Portugais au XVᵉ et XVIᵉ
siècles* (1969) and E. Prestage, *Portuguese Pioneers* (1933).

INDEX

INDEX